Hiking Trails in the Northeast

Hiking Trails in the Northeast

By Thomas A. Henley and Neesa Sweet

CONTEMPORARY SPORTS BOOKS
CHICAGO

HIKING TRAILS IN THE NORTHEAST
© Thomas A. Henley and Neesa Sweet 1976
International Standard Book Number 0-915498-18-9
Library of Congress Catalog Card Number: 75-41637
Printed in U.S.A.

Published by arrangement with
Greatlakes Living Press

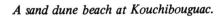

A sand dune beach at Kouchibouguac.

Photo Credits

Photo on page 27 by Richard T. Nelson
Photos on pages 141, 149 and 153 by Laraine R. Henley
All other photos by Thomas A. Henley

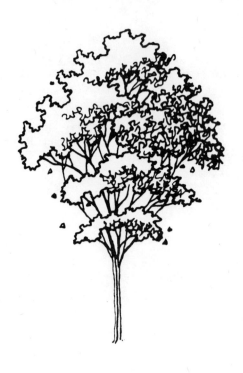

1

Welcome to the Northeast

The mountains of the northeast have been blessed and cursed, sometimes in the same breath, viewed either as lousy little lumps coated with carnivorous scrub or rippled velvet spattered with quicksilver and veined with golden brooks.

Backpackers' opinions of themselves range from "berserk masochist" to "seekers of the divine rapport with nature." Yet, common to all, is the realization of the power held over them by the forces of nature. Each devotee to the art of suffering for pleasure on the quiet paths and rugged trails forges a bond between body, mind, and nature that in time becomes the finest thing the hiker knows.

It's too much to ask that any hiker really define his feelings toward the "sport" of backpacking. He'll probably lie through his teeth and jabber on about how he loves it.

Love isn't an adequate word, obviously, to describe an activity that includes exposure to bugs, hunger, exhaustion, and pain. But the sheer determination demanded from anyone exposed to nature's assaults is part of the sport's appeal.

Two centuries ago the forests were feared, the animals fought, and beauty was defined by the lack, not the presence, of trees. Those old enemies that put temper into the souls of frontiersmen, settlers, and early farmers, are now what we seek in order to put some temper and perspective into our own lives.

Two hundred years ago, the new settler stood on a stream bank and faced a wall of forest, seeing years of grueling labor standing between him and a farm with pasture and crops. He squandered trees with fire, used them as fodder for cattle, and made his pin money only if he was lucky enough to be able to sell any logs at all. The bear, wolverine, wolf, lynx, mountain lion, and other predators were his enemies, to be killed or avoided. Little of what he destroyed was really used. He had very little idea, in fact, that he was destroying anything, since the forest was everywhere and tillable land was at a premium.

Now, though, when we go out in the forest, that "endless twilight beneath the solid cover of branches" stretching from the Appalachians to the Mississippi is gone. None of the predators will really threaten.

1

There is none of the battle with the land the settlers knew.

Yet we've begun fighting a battle all our own—one with two fronts. The first one—to develop a bond between ourselves and natural forces— is fought by slogging through the rain, toiling up the mountains that were just "in the way" to the settlers, and enduring the minor hardships of exposing the modest defenses of the human body to the attack of nature.

Our second front in the modern battle is not out in the hills; it's in the political realm. It is a fight for the very survival of the plants, the animals, the land itself, and finally, for our own chance to come into direct contact with that land and all it means. Battles for this or that hunk of land, length of trail, or area of timber are part of the steady diet of depressing daily news in the past few years. What may have faded from sight is why what we do have is still here.

Backpackers must pay sincere homage to that sacred cow of the depression years, the Civilian Conservation Corps. The effect of the CCC was gigantic, not just on those who found better lives through the CCC program, but on us too.

In the 1930's there were hundreds of thousands of raped acres lying around—naked, smoldering ruins where forests and "useless" land had been. Into the mountains and wastes of the northeast went bands of trail-marking, shelter-building, tree-planting CCC boys. In the few years the program lasted they created most of the trails and parks that we have today. What has been done in the U.S. toward trail building since then has been five parts nature reclaiming its own, one part political effort and three parts commercial profit incentive. And one part pure luck where a trail or park has sprung up out of spontaneous use. Little is left to show the original intent of the many private donors who gave land for parks that were supposed to remain forever wild.

One way of understanding the impact CCC effort had on U.S. parks and trails is to visit Canada, where there are no major trail systems. In New Brunswick and Nova Scotia, for example, the clock is a gentle century behind. Giant lumbering operations still have something to work on, and parks until recent decades were few, small, and anything but a setting for backpacking. Then the Canadian government entered the park battle with a solid program aimed at preserving tracts of land all over the Canadian countryside. Each would be a distinctive type of terrain or ecological structure. Each would be developed or not according to the prospect and impact of use, economic demands of the locality, and so on. As a result, there have been parks established all across Canada and, through them, the largest development of formal trails and recreation areas ever produced in this huge region of unspoiled or reclaimable land.

As any old-timer in the U.S. knows, the trails have been getting harder to reach in spite of the fact that we can get to them quicker. This is due, in part, to the rapid expansion of controls and regulations imposed on parks and the overuse of many areas. New highways, population booms, and massive commercialization of the backpacking industry have funneled new users, more demanding users, into a limited number of trails, parks, and acres.

Even preservation of the trails that the CCC did construct has been patchy. New Hampshire's Department of Resources and Economic Development claims that CCC trails in state lands were not maintained because of a lack of interest in hiking and a lack of maintenance funds. In New York, there is a conflict, since some feel the CCC didn't build any trails, but at any rate there is little available record of what was done. Overlooked by most states is the fact that many forest roads built by the CCC gradually became trails.

Unfortunately, little credit is given CCC projects for what they established. Over their nine years of effort all the major wilderness areas of the northeast were subjected to some wilderness project or other—whether insect control, tree plantings, fire control, or (in Maine) a massive recovery operation from a hurricane that blew down an estimated 90 million board feet of timber, of which about 80 per cent was salvaged for use and to reduce fire hazard.

All such operations left woods roads and trails, bridges, some shelters, and campsites that gradually became part of the backpackers' realm or else faded back into the brush. Still, it is CCC work that founded the trails systems of the Adirondacks, White, and Green mountains.

Canada, without this base effort to work with, has no major trails systems. Its trails are being formed by the lumbering operations whose roads will be trails after regrowth of the lumbered areas. Hiking in the two provinces included in this book will very often be on lumber roads and your hiking could well help establish the hiking trails of the next generation.

Not that the CCC had no problems. The federal authorities required assurance by the state that new facilities could be adequately maintained by the state after the termination of the CCC program. In New York, for example, most CCC work was reconstruction, not construction.

The New York State Department of Environmental Conservation has indicated that the effect of the CCC was probably to start the pursuit of outdoor recreation in New York as well as in other states. Many of the CCC facilities in New York still remain and have been maintained and updated.

In Rhode Island, the CCC constructed nearly all of the forest roads in the state. These areas, as well as the waterholes and fire towers then built, are still in use.

The Connecticut Department of Environmental Protection, by contrast, says that "for all practical purposes, there was no direct effect (by the CCC) on the trail situation." In Connecticut, the CCC concentrated on construction of access roads rather than trails.

In New Hampshire, the CCC was responsible for the construction of many miles of trail in state parks and national forests. They were built with steps in steep areas and include water bars and bridges. Most of the trails on state lands, however, have fallen into disrepair.

Even where such disrepair has occurred, however, trail books can help renew use of fading routes, or establish new ones by simply not being quite so stodgy about defining wilderness, or getting rabid about "pure" experience. Having a route follow an old forest road rarely detracts from the hike, and in many cases, will provide an experience with an area that would otherwise be overlooked, possibly lost. To concentrate on the limited number of trails in formal use will only contribute to over-use of these trails, and a general degeneration of the wilderness experience.

Though little of the U.S. routes reclaimed by forest will be included here, much of the Canadian information is based on routes that, without interest and use, could fade and be lost. All the battles to preserve and protect the woods needn't be in the political and legal offices. If you find an old woods road or come across a potential route, get in touch with an outdoor club or conservation organization and try to get the route established again. Where a state, province, or national government might think only in terms of millions of development dollars, you might be able to cause spontaneous development of a trail with a postage stamp and some jaw wagging. The U.S. Bureau of Outdoor Recreation suggests that persons interested in stimulating development of trails near where they live contact local trail clubs, scouts, or their state park or forestry department or contact the Secretary, Department of the Interior, Washington, D.C., 20240. Attention: Bureau of Outdoor Recreation.

There are a few major trail development hopes around. In the U.S. there is the National Trails system, an effort to re-establish routes of historic interest. Of these, only the Appalachian and Pacific Crest, about 4,400 miles worth, are in operation as National Trails. In the northeast, there are the Long Trail, Vermont's spur to the Appalachian, and the proposed North Country Trail from the Appalachians in mid-Vermont approximately 3,200 miles through New York, Pennsylvania, Ohio, Michigan, Wisconsin and Minnesota to the Lewis and Clark Trail in North Dakota.

In Canada, the Maliset Trail Club hopes to run a trail out to connect with the Appalachian from Fundy National Park and on to connect with the Acadian Trail that will come from the outer tip of Cape Breton to the New Brunswick border. In time this will allow a single continuous hike from Cape Breton to Georgia.

While all of this effort is still in formative stages, 65 miles of the Acadian trail is marked, and the Maliset Trail Club is still working on rights of way for the first leg of its route near Woodstock, New Brunswick. Most trail use is, and will continue to be, on those spaghetti trails lacing through the forest that have no intention of crossing countries and no great historic import—just a lot of nice miles for backpackers to savor.

Our trail descriptions won't just be of the "three trees, 60 feet past Wiffle Brook, mark junction of a main trail with blue side trail" type. We'll be trying to provide an idea of the kind of place the trail is in and some helpful information on using it and finding it. The reason you would want to hike it is to find out what's there, so find out on the spot, not in a book.

Some routes will be suggestions leaving finding out just where the heck you are in doubt—like it was for us. Some will be like the Salmon River of New Brunswick. Well folks, the trail *was* there; we didn't find it; maybe you can. And of course there has to be a little of the bush-wack-orienteering type thing; North Mountain of Cape Breton has lots of Jeep roads, and plenty of bush to bust overlooking the sea with occasional views of Newfoundland through the twigs. By going out and picking your own route it's possible to leave something for the next generation—a new trail. More likely, you'll get some of the experience sought by all backpackers, experience with wilderness. And, by absorbing the effects of that experience, help to insure that the insane desire for pleasant suffering will be passed on by example to those who might not otherwise follow on your trails.

Have a good hike.

Trail Use Impact and Ethics

So now it even costs to be free in the woods. The campsites are all full. There's no fire wood left and no place where you're allowed to build one anyway. Too many people, too much trash, and a wave of rigmarole to go through getting in, staying in, and getting out.

The trails feature muddy bypasses bypassing muddy bypasses.

Sorry, no campsites open until six weeks after next year, but you can have two days then, at site 637. Arrive at 10 a.m., leave prior to 9 a.m. on departure date, and please pay in advance.

There is no question that there is a tinge of the unpleasant creeping into the backpackers' world. And no lack of unpleasant comment strewn around as a result. Still, the direction that future policy and attitude takes depends on us, on our ethics, tolerance, and sincerity about preserving wilderness.

States, provinces, and U.S. national organizations have discovered that there are economic advantages in backpackers' devotion to the woods. A whole new sub-culture of travel has sprung up in roadside campsites that replace the use of hotel-motel lodging en route, and nobody has objected to the idea of charging fees on the newly proposed "National Recreation Trails." Most people today expect cost to be tacked on to everything. Very little commercial conversion of free space ever faces real resistance.

Sweat, taxes, and devotion to wilderness are not enough. In a not very distant future, backpackers may end up paying for parking, campsite, fire permit, park entry, and per-mile of trail hoofed.

Part of this trend is due to lack of information on alternate choices of backpacking country, or just strong attachment to the "old stomping grounds." Another factor is that whenever a commercial facility is established, advertised, and just "there," people descend on it begging to pay. They expect to be taken care of, provided direction, showers, campsites, and good roads. People massed up in such places try hard to get what they pay for, make the most of their time, and minimize their uncomfortable direct contacts with nature. But there is no ethical excuse for pay-as-you-go wilderness. Paying will do less for preserving the wilderness than plain old devotion. Building that devotion is difficult between

7

budget checks and rule compliance. But with the devotion, and with
some solid experience of having been chewed up, dragged out, and sent
home happy by raw direct contact with nature the need for rules
declines.

To avoid the proliferation of use fees, however, we must be careful
to leave each mile of wilderness as pristine as we found it. Be it irresponsible kids or a sour pack of Boy Scouts, bad conduct is just that
and is not something any backpacker can afford to ignore. If you see
someone littering, please let them know, tactfully, that they're damaging
something you respect.

If there were a magic formula for making good woodspeople it would
have long since been on the market for $3.98 a bottle. In lieu of that,
the best route to good woodsmanship I've been able to see in 20-odd
years of roaming the woods is to let nature take hold. This means
getting away from the protections, letting time, distance, rain, hunger,
and cold, and all the rest, help form values, judgments, and knowledge.

Nature does a fine job on a person if that person exposes himself
sensibly and long enough. It takes several days to get over the culture
shock of getting into the woods, even for experienced backpackers. Feet
have to "grow eyes" and stop stumbling over roots and rocks; eyes and
nose adjust to smoke; the body builds immunity to insect bite, and a
host of other adaptations set in. It is only after this period of culture
shock that we begin to experience the joy of real solitude and beauty.
In the adaptive period, people in groups turn to the familiar things for
comfort: transistor radios, frisbees, and quarreling. On the bank of a
pond with the loons calling and sunset putting on its show it's hard to
see why so many minds are insulated from experiencing the surroundings, but they are.

Trips with enough days to permit adaptation and interest in the area
tend to produce the classic "lean, brown, ragged hiker pleasant to share
time with round the campfire."

Trip days themselves undergo a metamorphosis. From struggles and
aggravations are born the comparative values that make latter jaunts of a
"few hours walk" up a steep mountain less strenuous. Fire smoke that
drove people into the darkness on the first night becomes something
that keeps the bugs off. Time turns from hours, minutes, and meal
periods into morning wet, evening sun, afternoon heat, late morning
perfection, night quiet.

The first blister hurts like hell; the first mountain slope causes steam
engine gasps; the first bear puts the blood into high gear. The twentieth
blister is just annoying, the fifth mountain shrinks down to human size,
and the fourth bear becomes a friend and partner in the night and the
food supply.

There are many ways of modifying wilderness use to minimize impact, even in high-use areas.

Start, of course, with the oft-repeated and steadily ignored "carry it in, carry it out" maxim. Leave nothing behind but footprints and don't be too messy about that. In roaming the northeast we saw some areas where this simple rule has taken hold and other areas where it didn't. Packers have no choice but to impose the principle on themselves and to try passing it on to those who ignore it.

Choice of a trip location can help too. Merely avoid going to the high-use areas. There is a surprising pull toward the "old stomping grounds" even when they are jammed. Get to know another area, in depth, and it will often do as well if not better.

Industrial backpacking gear has also tended to crowd us out of our own camps. I've seen fluorescent orange tents that caused a stomach twinge and eye pain from just looking in the door. Pick gear color for its comfortable effect on the eye and camp, not for high visibility. A reversible jacket or garish windbreaker for visibility on the trail in hunting season is fine.

A camp of subdued color, however, is much less distracting and makes popular camping areas seem less crowded. Light green absorbs no more heat than fluorescent orange, and dark green leaves a tent almost invisible a few yards from camp. Wildlife also tend to associate the reds and oranges with danger, and with man. Less obtrusive colors may permit much better contact with wildlife.

This effect on the animals, and the fact that Army clothing is so rugged and available, has resulted in my "going green" for years. Tent, pack, clothes, and even hat, socks, and tee shirts are all green. It's much less alarming to wildlife encountered on the trail or around camp. It's also far less "crowding" on the trail. Quite often groups have passed by within a few feet while I was sitting by the trail on a rest break without even seeing me. Wearing green is a way of trying to belong in the woods.

Much of the adverse impact users have on an area is created when they get lost and cause all kinds of havoc. Lost is a state of mind; it is also a result of sloppy navigation. The ability to pay attention is one of the first lessons one learns on a trail.

If you do get lost, on a gray day in the North Maine Woods flat country for instance, where there are no prominent landmarks to guide you, don't panic. Normally though there is up, down, and a river, trail or road reachable for orientation or rescue without a great deal of privation. Serious trouble arises from illness, injury, exposure, and mental unbalance. Usually the last one. If lost, cope. Not with the titanic struggle for survival, but with the mind and its tricks. With some experience most people can say "so what?" and carry on. With some calm thought even beginners can survive.

According to a newspaper article (November 14, 1975) 20 people died while on a vacation trip near the Black Sea. Under the assault of a sudden storm, 51 individuals, including two instructors, panicked, scattered, and preyed upon each other. One group was reported to have built a fire and been forced away from it by a stronger group. Individuals abandoned packs, supplies, and warm clothing in the insanity of a group failing to cope with what should have been little more than an interesting bout of discomfort.

Outside force cannot be blamed for such incidents. Nature itself rarely kills. But groups and individuals can destroy themselves quickly and efficiently.

A cardinal rule of contact with nature is to know your own limits. Each error compounds itself, beginning with preparations before the trip. Untested equipment, overestimation of abilities, food supplies vulnerable to animals and elements, and complete failure to consider the "ifs" ahead of time cause a lot of useless grief. If there is no time to work on basic gear, no knowledge of weather conditions to be expected, and no working plans that take into account the if's of injury, accident, flood, or suddenly being alone and poorly equipped for a safe return, then there should be no time for a serious hiking trip into the wilderness either.

When we say "experienced hikers" might find a place enjoyable, it means the area is such that the intruder had better have his kit and brains organized, tested, and proven. These trails, such as the cliff tops along the northern coast of Cape Breton, are not for children to go play on. They are for people involved in open meeting with the dangers and demands of nature with nobody else around to take the pressure off if the going gets sticky. In time, the rugged experiences which we all go through will become a valued part of backpacking trips.

On the trail expect good and bad. The bad will happen on occasion and might as well be expected. When it does, accept it and begin solving the problem then, not after something more happens and the odds get worse. When lost, keep the blood pressure low by staying calm. If it doesn't sort out, make a calm decision as to the best way to get yourself out and stick to that decision. No halfhearted guessing games that change tactics every hour will help, unless you happen to benefit from pure luck. Climb to a lookout, even if it means spending an uncomfortable night out. Follow water downstream. There's almost always a road or a trail somewhere below. Know in advance where the boundary roads or major trails are. If need be, aim for a road that you know runs directly across a steady direction. If it does turn into several days' hike to get somewhere, then quit early in the evenings, find shelter or make it, and take time to find food. Use known plants, or take the time to catch animals, fish, frogs, worms, grubs, whatever. Eventually it'll taste just fine raw. Failure to maintain a certain intake of food and to use shelter during the first day or so will determine a great deal of your chance to survive without falling prey to exposure and illness.

If injured, care for the injury as well as possible and then make a calm plan of survival, stick to it, and keep on thinking.

Make sure you've told somebody — family, hiking club, forest rangers or local police — where you're going and how long you plan to stay.

One more point on the subject of good sense. When suddenly confronted with a bear, mountain lion, bobcat or whatever, instead of running, putting up a noble fight with a water pistol or waking the banshees with useless noise, how about just saying a mild mannered hello to the critter? Once, on a bushy trail, I got between a she bear and her cub by accident. Momma and I had quite a conversation. But between her woofing cuss-out and my stammering explanation of the offense, we settled the matter without any one-sided battle. They went off convinced they'd met a coward, who also went off convinced he was a coward, but an unharmed coward.

Injury caused by animals without rash action on the part of human beings is almost unheard of. Any animal that acts strangely should be suspected of rabies and avoided at all costs. There is never any excuse for assaulting an animal. In fact, I once vacated a tent rather than argue with a big garter snake that was annoyed, shedding, and happy with my sleeping bag.

On a related matter, trite as it sounds, people have forgotten that firewood is not inexhaustible. In many of the northeastern states there is precious little firewood left.

Large campgrounds look like the battles of the Civil War, with despondent early risers huffing a smudgy fire to life and twig scavengers tripping over tent lines in the early morning light. For what? A fellow I met in the Adirondacks had a rather drastic test of a "usable" camp fire: "If you can't straddle it, you can't cook on it." He was right and proved it with fine vittles. Camp fires out of control are a gastric calamity, a clean-up nightmare, and an easy way to shave or get a hair cut. The sparks are hard on nylon and the light prevents the eyeballs from adapting to the night so that trips to the latrine can be fine fun with a branch in the nose, an unintentional dip in the stream, or a long hunt just to find the outhouse or cat hole. Do yourself and the environment a favor and cook with a portable backpackers' stove. If you must have a fire keep it low and fuel it slowly. It will serve all the camper's needs except one; it does not push back the fearsome dark.

Up in Lake Colden, one of the highest use areas of the northeast, our party of four once spent three days cooking on firewood totally overlooked by the campers next door who were off in the distance scrounging wood. We just used some of the chips, twigs, and leavings around the lean-to. There was plenty for several 8-inch diameter cooking fires and we ate fine bread "baked" in a Teflon frypan with cover. One very useful item for conserving fire, plus cutting the junk toted along, is to get an old welded-seam army canteen and set it next to the *small* fire. It heats about as fast as any pot set on top and uses what would otherwise be completely wasted heat. Next day it still serves for lugging water on the trail.

For light, candles and carbide lamps work fine. The carbide light is best and any extended trip into the woods where it's possible to be faced with a night return to camp should have one. It isn't the lightest thing in the world, but is a fine light source to hike by, lights an entire camp well, even provides tent heat, and will keep coffee water hot long after the campfire is out. With a carbide light in the kit you can start a fire any place, any season.

With positive attitudes and congenial conduct, without condoning irresponsible acts by others, even high-use areas can be brought back to a state of peace. Our own forethought and respect for the forces of wilderness will enrich everyone's experience in the woods.

There is no measuring the effect of kindness, calm, and experience in coping when applied to a wilderness region. We know its effect in camps. A woodsman is one who helps produce warmth, richness, and a reward that surpasses every form of pain, danger, hard work, and strains on the mind that the forces of nature can produce. Be at peace with yourself, with others, and with the land. Have a good hike.

Nova Scotia

Nova Scotia is a quiet province of Canada, almost an island in the Atlantic, 350 miles long and never more than 70 miles between coasts. Hiking varies from rolling hills and lake-dotted wilderness to rugged mountains with steep, deep ravines coated with a scrub it would take the vernacular of six languages to compliment properly. Trails range from rocky cliffside paths to beaches strung along 4,600 miles of coast. Lumbering has left thousands of miles of old lanes in a tangled mess of directions fit to test the best of follow-your-nose hoofers.

Getting there is half the fun. From anywhere in the northeast U.S. a day gets you to Portland or Bar Harbor in Maine with auto ferry service from there to Yarmouth at Nova Scotia's extreme western tip. Bar Harbor is closer, a six-hour run, and gets you there in mid-afternoon which leaves time to poke around and get settled.

There is little, if any, difference between the cost of the ferry ($11.00 per adult, $27.50 per automobile in summer) and driving a-round to the land link in New Brunswick, and there is no casino or duty-free shop in most vacation vehicles.

Air connections may be made to Halifax, Sydney, and Yarmouth.

Customs in Canada are usually no problem. One carton of cigarettes per person and limits on booze are the only things that tend to snag people. No money changing is required, and U.S. dollars are accepted throughout most of the province, though it would be wise to change at a bank to get the benefit of any exchange rate in your favor. (Note: If you use credit cards, you won't get the exchange rate on your card purchases — a matter of two to six percent in your favor.)

Camping accommodations along the road are plentiful. The federal and provincial governments, as well as private individuals, have developed and expanded campgrounds and trailer parks in all sections of the province.

Nova Scotia is also a great place to have a bicycle. The low hills encourage bike tours along both coasts. With frequent towns and villages and ample campsites, a bike tour is one of the best ways to really see the province.

A note for photographers: Nova Scotia will soak up film fast. There

Near Kejimkujik National Park, Nova Scotia.

is a land/sea/fisherman theme that can easily become addictive. But film prices are high, and camera shops are rare in the fishing villages. Be prepared to function throughout the trip on what you packed up at home. While all other supplies for travel and backpacking are quite easy to find, film, if you can find it, will not be gentle on your wallet. And to repeat: you'll use more film than you think. Count on a lot of roadside shooting, plus the camping and scenic stuff.

The coastal waters are generally around 46 degrees, keeping the winters milder than might be expected and the summers cooler. Although it seems as if the region should have a more arctic environment it actually has seasons very similar to those of upper New York, Vermont, Connecticut and southern Maine, with the inland and Cape Breton areas getting their spring about two to three weeks later than the coast, and fall arriving correspondingly early.

Late May and June is full spring in the western and coastal areas, with quite a bit of fog common to the western coast. In the Scottish highland type farm country around Yarmouth, are carpets of lupine blossoms, and in the Annapolis Valley of the French Coast, the orchards are in bloom.

Winters in Halifax have a mean temperature of 31 degrees, summer 72 degrees; June and October run about 65 degrees. Add a few, lose a few, for coast or inland, Cape Breton or Yarmouth. The key point is that the range is fairly mild, but not all that warm, and nights tend to be a bit below what might be expected.

Red oak and pine dominate the rolling hills of the province, except for Cape Breton which favors balsam fir. Swamps, bogs, and low ground produce black spruce. Other vegetation is similar to New England. You will find an exceptional number of pitcher plants in the highlands of Cape Breton. In the southwest shore bogs the bake-apple (cloud berry) ripens in August and in many areas you can find extensive cranberry bogs.

In general, the best times for hiking in Nova Scotia are Spring and Autumn, when many places blocked by the undergrowth of summer are accessible. (It's a good idea, by the way, to remember that the countryside is always clear along the route of overhead power lines.)

A note of caution, though, about autumn hiking: take care in the wooded areas, except for game sanctuaries, during the hunting season, normally October 15th to November 30th lest you end up as someone's prize catch.

Nova Scotia is notable for its moose and bald eagles. Salmon run many of the rivers. Even caribou reindeer have been reintroduced in an experimental project in Cape Breton. The black bear is a common prowler, that tends to be more numerous and wilder than its counterparts elsewhere.

A number of species now rare or lost to the U.S. northeast are still around in Nova Scotia, and many sea birds are seen on its coasts. If you like birds, drop a line to the Editor, Nova Scotia Bird Society, Nova Scotia Museum, 1747 Summer Street, Halifax.

White tail deer were imported in 1894 and are now well established. (Hunters account for 46,000 in a year as compared to about 1,000 moose per year.)

One critter that is lacking is the common old woodchuck, which makes for fewer ankle busting holes along fence rows.

There are no poisonous snakes in Cape Breton (unable to establish for certain that there are none in the rest of the province, but it is unlikely that there are).

Naturally there are black flies and mosquitos. More important, especially in the western areas, there are wood ticks. Ticks are an unpleasant addition to the bug world and people who come from a tick-free area should pay close attention to detecting and removing the monsters. Don't pull them out. Gasoline or stove fuel will help them ease their hold, and the old cigarette butt or match in a steady hand usually convinces them that they have buried their head in the wrong hide. Pulling breaks off the head under the skin and it can cause a bad sore. Use persuasion. And prevention. A good trick is to stuff pants cuffs into sock tops, or tie them down with the boot laces. This helps stop ticks and reduces invasion by black flies to nil. Elastic sleeve cuffs and tighter types of shirt collar also help. Shake out clothing outside your tent in the evening, and comb your hair before bedding down, or they will have had a good dinner on you by morning. Being picky about shaking out clothes, tents, bedding, hair, etc. will go a long way toward reducing the number of scars left by ticks; though tick-picking each other in the evening is a friendly sort of pastime, it can be done without.

Some say you should wear yellow to reduce the number of blood-sucking bugs that zero in on you. This type of advice is seen most often in Canada. Possibly it's suggested in order to make it easier to spot lost city-folk. It certainly doesn't discourage mosquitos. With a bug battle that is never far from surrender, insanity, or anemia facing the backpacker, yellow is not the best battle gear available. Sometime you might try laying out cloths of various hues a good distance apart and checking to see which are most attractive to the critters. New England drill noses seem very partial to yellow, much less so to blues and greens.

In hunting season however, flaming orange has its place ... bugs or no.

Lastly, Nova Scotia is the haunt of whales and seals. They are frequently seen off shore, and often on shore. The sight of a whale spouting or broaching adds a special excitement to coastal hikes, and seals are a friendly sort of wayfarer to have a bark or two with. Late June to October whales play around the northern Cape Breton coast, easy and spectacular to see from the shore cliffs. Local fishermen grouse a lot

The Atlantic Coast of Nova Scotia.

about what happens to their nets, but the whales still come close inshore without causing any great amount of problem.

If it were not for the fact that seals are still slaughtered during their migration, their presence could be added to the list of reasons for hoofing the edges of the Cape Breton Highlands, but two companies still "harvest" about 30,000 seals each per year and this is not one of the attractive aspects of the region.

At some place along the coast of the province you will be able to find every phase of lobstering. From the great preparation of the fleets for sailing, to the baulking up for off-season painting and storage. Careful controls limit the number of traps per lobsterman, and the odd habits of this weird crustacean have made it the most significant focus of activity and economics of the coast. Food in the villages along the road is something worth exploring. Many dishes are still prepared in the ethnic tradition ... including English trifle, sigh. Smatterings of Scottish, French, British, and New England dishes may ruin your diet and shorten your wind but they'll give you a delicious insight to the cooking of a century ago.

People of the sea, farm, and mine tend to appreciate their food. Be prepared to discover fine, strange, and superb things to appreciate too.

WESTERN NOVA SCOTIA, YARMOUTH TO HALIFAX

Yarmouth is the southernmost tip of Nova Scotia. Its Historical Society Museum contains a stone, certified by runologists, etched with letters that supposedly read "Leif Erikson, 1000 AD."

There is an eight-mile trail north of here, running along the rugged Bay of Fundy coastline between Comeau Cove and Cape St. Mary. The cliffs are high and many alcoves and rock formations can be explored without the aid of ropes.

From Yarmouth, it is just over 200 miles to the capital of Halifax by either the North or South coast routes.

Generally, the pattern of development in all of Nova Scotia has resulted in towns and villages strung out along the coast with a rapid decline in population as you go inland. In western Nova Scotia there is no road through the middle area (east and west) and only three going north and south. (Everyone tends to refer to the long line of the province as east and west and crossways as north and south, even though the true lines of those directions are tilted off this axis.) This leaves a gigantic area of hills (up to 600-odd feet), lakes, and lumbering areas with very sparse population ringed by the narrow strip of coastal development. In many areas, the timber country joins with coastal marshes and beach with only one main highway and smaller seaside roads to break it up.

The North Coast is known locally as the French Coast and has the customs, language, and architecture of the French Acadians. It is so French that a working knowledge of the language would be a great help in begging directions and in overcoming the rather hesitant cordiality you may encounter.

In 1755, during the Seven Years War, the Acadians refused to swear allegiance to the British king. At least 6,500 people were deported to places like the West Indies and Louisiana. The Acadians were permitted to return when the war had ended (one group of 900 walked from Boston), but the British and New Englanders had occupied their lands. So they settled in separate Acadian areas, many on Cape Breton, without diffusing through the province. It is possible to believe that many Acadians never forgot 1755.

The north coast has a great many beaches of sand and cobble, but it is generally fairly straight and rocky with low cliffs lining the Bay of Fundy, St. Mary's Bay and Minas Basin. As many trails lie along the coast and walking the shores for impromptu jaunts is irresistible, take a word of warning about a phenomenon that dominates *any* coast, shore or bay on the Bay of Fundy.

Twice a day 3,600 billion cubic feet of water move up a 145-mile trough that narrows at the end to compress the moving water into the world's highest tides. Don't fool around with the tides! They range from 11 feet at Yarmouth to 54 feet at Minas Head at the tip of the bay.

Rivers joining the Bay of Fundy in the relatively flat areas are subject to the same phenomenon in the form of a tidal bore that is, in effect, just the same as a flash flood. In many places a wall of water 18 inches high charges upstream while the river level itself changes 10, 20, even 30 feet. It happens quickly, so take note of the tide times and don't hike river beds without first checking to see if they are subject to the tidal bore. A high banked, reddish mud channel is good enough warning to stay out!

Joggins is a little town on the shore south of Amherst. To get there, take the Joggins Road south of Canadian Route 104 just east of Amherst. Joggins means "place where wide shoals warm the tide as it comes in." A shore walk lets you hunt fossils, and the bay water pulls so far out from shore you can't see the difference between mud bottom and water. You can walk along the beaches from about five hours after the bore goes by to the next time it appears, but during high tides, the water goes right up to the base of the fossil cliffs. The tides here range in height from 33 to 44 feet. The cliffs themselves tower 75 feet in places.

Walking along the cliffs with the water maybe a mile away can be deceptive. It comes in fast. Always give yourself enough time to get out of the way — or be prepared to climb the cliffs. Along the outer shores, the current of the tide going through the bay is quite visible and rather strong.

With this in mind, though, there are three different places to get to at Joggins. One is a road leading to the beach from the Bayview Municipal Campsite; one is at Lower Cove, where the highway is so close to the beach you can walk toward Joggins and see the fossil cliffs, and the third is at the wharf. This is the one to be careful of. At low tide, the fishing boats will be trapped on the gravel bars; at high tide, the water will be near the top of the wharf. Don't get trapped with the high water.

After seeing a few big ships sitting on the mud with no water even reasonably near, the idea sinks home.

One unique place to view the tidal bore is the Lower Maccan Tidal Bore Picnic Area on the Lower Maccan Road, four miles from the Maccan River Bridge, off route 242. Maccan is just a few miles northeast of Joggins.

Here the bore, coming in from Fundy by way of Minudie, splits into two bores, one going left into the River Hebert, the other on into the Maccan. The bore travels about six mph, and varies from about 18 inches high at high tides, to six-eight inches high at medium tides. At low tides, the water changes its direction of flow. Due to the way the Hebert and Maccan are positioned, the bore can be seen three times in two hours: Once, at the picnic area; an hour and a half later, at the River Hebert Bridge, and a half hour after that at the Maccan River

Camping at the Auter Bald Camp in Nova Scotia.

Bridge. The River Hebert bore reaches 12 inches at high tides, the Maccan, 12 to 16.

For the Micmac Indians, the original Nova Scotians, the great tides of Fundy were the work of the god Glooscap, who, with the aid of thunder, lightning, tide and Indian Summer ruled from the top of Blomidon Mountain (the Cape Split area).

Geographically, the north coast of Nova Scotia consists of a ridge (Digby Neck) which runs east and west along the Bay of Fundy from the basalt columns of Brier Island to Cape Split. South, inland from the ridge is a trough of low fertile land with some large areas of meadows formed by dikes. This trough is known as the Annapolis Valley. South of the valley is a broad strip of woodlands and lakes.

Digby Neck provides a barrier between the chilly waters of the bay and weather moving in from the mainland, and gives the Annapolis Valley a distinctly mild climate famous for its early June blossoms and Apple Blossom Festival.

Cape Split, 11 miles, is a good place for an outing. There are several sections of good, rugged trail. Remember here to avoid the logging trails since they don't go anywhere, and to keep to the high point of hardwood ridge. One trail starts on the end of the road past Scots Bay on the west side of Cape Blomidon. The trail is an extension of the dirt road which ends at a house past the village. To reach Cape Split keep bearing to the right. From the Cape you can view an island housing thousands of birds.

Out on the eastern edge of the Valley, on a jut in Minas Basin, is Grand Pre, one of the old French settlements involved in the disputes of the 1755 period and the site of Longfellow's famous poem "Evangeline."

From **Grand Pre**, follow the unpaved road to the Gaspereau River crossing for a light, wooded trail. From the river, follow either bank south to Hell's Gate fish ladder. Keeping to the south for a quarter mile, drop down to the old river bed. The seven mile trail starts on the north side, and leads to an old dam. (If you cross the dam and follow the power lines to the power station, the station's occupants might tell you a good different route for the return trip.)

The other route from Yarmouth to Halifax is along the South shore on the "lighthouse route." There is a fast modern highway drilling directly through to Halifax, but the twisty shore route is worth the extra time.

This is the domain of the lobsterman, tuna fisherman, coves, bays and harbors, the Atlantic surf, and just as promised in the travel literature, lighthouses. There are cobble beaches and small villages — an uncluttered landscape facing anywhere but to the sea.

Peggy's Cove, about thirty miles southeast of Halifax, is a fishing community with everything your camera is looking for — pounding surf, granite rocks, weather-worn fishing shacks, clear blue water, and, occasionally, stormy skies. A twelve-mile hike through a wooded area, including several lakes, stretches from the Prospect Road near Goodwood to the Peggy's Cove Road at Glen Margaret. The only problem with Peggy's is that thousands of cameras are drawn here every year. So don't miss it but wander on down the shore.

Other good hikes in this region include:

Duncan's Cove to Ketch Harbor, 3.5 miles. The starting point is at the end of the road that goes down to the Cove. Here there are old batteries, a watch tower, good campsites and an abundant supply of firewood. The distance depends on how closely you follow the shoreline.

Pennant. 8 miles, round trip. The trail starts just past a no-exit sign near the end of Route 349 at Pennant. There is a very large boulder about 400 yards from the start on the west side of the trail. Just to go back on our own advice, this is an old logging road leading north through barren lake land. The first several miles are wet in the spring.

Crystal Crescent Beach and Coote's Cove, 3.25 miles, starts 1.3 miles past Sambro on route 349. The sea is always in view as the trail winds over rocks and barren land. There is a good beach and campsite, but no drinking water.

Glen Margaret to Fourteen Mile House, 9 miles. This trail starts at Glen Margaret just north of the Hosier River, and provides a pleasant hike along the river and overland to Hubley's Big Lake. In the spring, the flowers are in bloom. There is water and campsites.

Glen Margaret to Dover, 6 miles. The trail starts on the east side of Route 333 at Glen Margaret. It is wet, so bring boots. At one point the trail may appear to be lost, but look on the west side of the meadow.

Basically there are hundreds of miles of beach walking to do, with relics of ship wrecks, washed up lobster traps and buoys, and wild sea scapes that help turn a hike into a reversion to childhood. Just pick a jut of land, bounce out to the end of the road, and have a fine sea side hike. Outlining all the possible routes would take a big book and wouldn't help a bit. Just have a ball finding your own walks. And don't miss the chance of hiking a stretch during heavy weather. In fact, during the spring fogs or autumn storms, it's far superior to sloshing along what we think of as normal hiking trails, since the flavor and the wildness are so distinct and powerful.

Hiking between the south coast villages while the lobster boats dance among their floats just off shore requires little if any knowledge of the terrain except for avoiding bad marshes. The sea provides all the directional aid needed. Just don't wear your expensive hiking boots. Between cobbles, sand, salt, and assorted seaweed muck, good boots will retire or expire in short order. The leather-canvas jungle combat boots available from most Army-Navy and many department stores seem to work well if treated with mink oil and cleaned frequently. Otherwise, rot out a few pair of high top sneakers.

With some obvious exceptions visible on a highway map the idea of just up and picking a shore to hike holds for the entire length of the south shore clear to the extreme eastern tip of the Cape Breton Island. Which might explain why the descendants of British and New England stock, plus the Scotsmen in Cape Breton give you a funny look when you ask about hiking trails in the area. Marked trails are rare, and then confined pretty much to the parks and formal enclaves. Local people just bust bush or follow old logging or coach roads, and tend to figure you are balmy for just walking down the beach.

There is so much walking available that trails and, worse, marked trails, are redundant and useless. It's so bad that the only trails you'll hear about are the Cabot Trail, Sunrise Trail, Glooscap Trail and such. All of which are highways the Tourist Bureau calls trails just to confuse the backpacker when he first arrives.

Even at the tourist centers, let alone when talking to local people at the general store, inquire about places to see, lookouts, and scenic spots, not trails. Quite often you'll get no response to "trails," or a few recommendations to take a tour trip to Oak Island (Mahone Bay) for a treasure hunt walk. Captain Kidd, it seems, did bury three chests there (150 feet deep and 50 feet below water level), but the shaft has been lost and it would be easier to find gold coins by sifting beach sand.

CENTRAL REGION: HALIFAX TO AMHERST AND NEW BRUNSWICK

While the coastal pattern of fishing villages remains the same here as to the west, there is more of a mixed agricultural and industrial character to the inland portions. To the north are coal mines (much of the industry is past tense due to "bumps" that cost a great many lives). The Chignecto Game Sanctuary in the northwest and the Liscomb Game Sanctuary east of Halifax, occupy the least settled areas. These are not parks; they are merely map designations used in conjunction with hunting rules designed to strengthen the population of moose and other troubled species. There are usually no "offices" at the location, and little to encourage backpackers to enter.

Central Nova Scotia contains most of the cosmopolitan life of the province, except for the Sydney complex on the east side of Cape Breton Island. All the red tape centers, museums, and universities tend to be found in Halifax/Dartmouth. The Youth Hostel headquarters, federal and provincial bureaus of tourism, "Natural Resources," and Forestry, can be hunted down here by just stopping at one of the Tourist Bureau offices and asking.

Steeltown Centennial Park in Trenton is a 500-acre park located off Route 104 at New Glasgow. Here you can find eight miles of hiking in a deep, rustic woodland complete with shady trees, animals, and birds.

Nova Scotia coast and church.

And, strangely enough, one of the most delightful walks in this region may be taken near a city. Victoria Park, in the Truro District, has miles of wooded paths complete with waterfalls and streams.

Porter's Lake to Goff's, 9 miles. Just south of the Halifax International Airport, there is a dirt road following the west bank of Porter's Lake. A very flat trail with several side paths extends from the old bridge at the end of the road.

Wentworth Youth Hostel, 40 miles. Turn left into the Valley Road from the Trans Canada Highway at Wentworth. Turn left after one mile. The hostel is ½ mile up on the right. Trails usually used for cross-country skiing wind over the hills and valleys of the area and offer some good views.

CAPE BRETON ISLAND

Cape Breton has but one access by land — across the Canso Causeway at Port Hastings. The three major roads on the island converge there: Route 4 (the Cabot Trail), running south of the large inland lake, Bras d'Or, and on to Sydney; Route 105, crossing the center of the island on the north side of the lake; and Route 19, winding along the north sea coast.

From Port Hastings to Sydney, via the south side of the Bras d'Or, is about 90 miles. From the causeway to Cape North (the northernmost point of the main highway) is about 130 miles via either Route 105 or the north shore route.

The Cabot Trail route, a scenic coastline highway circling the island, offers several points at which spectacular hiking can be found. Just get out of the car and walk.

One spot that should not be missed is the Alexander Graham Bell Museum at Baddeck Bay on the Bras d'Or. Bell spent summers here from 1886 until his death in 1922. Although his name is now synonymous with the invention of the telephone, Bell was a man of far-reaching genius, and the museum exhibits show his experiments with flight, energy conservation, and genetics, as well as his work with the deaf.

A topographic map would show that Cape Breton Highlands National Park, on the north end of the island, rises at several points to more than 1,700 feet. This is an area of deep ravines and ragged scrub cover; the home of moose, bear, and other wildlife, and the site of a lot of spongy ground both on and at the bottom of the hills. The entire northern half of the island is quite wild, relatively rugged, and beautiful. Few areas of the world have quite the same feeling of a century kindly turned back: Wild hills and, always, a close touch with the power of the sea. You'll find the cliffs get bigger here, and up along Bay Saint Lawrence they are almost continuous.

Cape Breton Highlands National Park, like Kejimkujik National Park on Nova Scotia proper, follows the Canadian policy of reserving unique samples of each different type of topography and ecological composition to be found in Canada. Kejimkujik is a low lake region of rolling forests; Cape Breton holds the bigger hills and wilder country, with moose, bear, and other wildlife. A visit to each park is well worth while just to see the contrast between the natural and physical make-up of the land.

On the topo maps, it is possible to get the idea that the cliffs in the region might be good for rock climbing. Although many are high enough for a good climb, the main challenge of these cliffs lies in avoiding them: We saw none that was stable enough for climbing. They are mostly broken-up sandstone or shale, and altogether too crumbly for a foothold. In fact, some were shaky enough to warrant some delicate footwork just to find a good spot to shoot a picture, though the clifftop walks themselves are among the finest and most memorable routes in the northeast.

One more note on Cape Breton: In addition to our suggestions, be prepared to pick a route on your own. Markings are rare, but *don't* think you'll just go zipping off through the bush. The ground is snow-covered well into June and remains boggy after that, and with spruce scrub, rock, and most everything else that's nasty in generous servings — not to mention the steep ravines — the going gets sticky. (Any veteran of busting bush and cursing the cripple brush of the Adirondack off-trail mountains will know what we mean.) Aside from wear and tear to clothing and hide, this terrain is rough on one's time-and-distance judgment. Pick routes on old log roads and such trails as there are, even if they double your distance. After a while, the quiet life and rhythm of the tides on Nova Scotia get to a person, and buzzing around slows to a more comfortable pace. Relax, be safe, and savor what's offered.

Cape Breton's Western Shores
Mabou Highlands This is a lovely area between Mabou and Inverness, with views of ocean, hills, and valleys as you hike along narrow cart tracks.

Margaree Valley The hills above the Margaree River have many winding trails offering seclusion and superb views.

Central Region
Baddeck The Uisge Bhan Falls Walking Trail is about 10 miles north of Baddeck which is just off Route 105. Travel about three miles west on Red Bridge Road, then east on Forks Road about four miles to a sign directing you to the trail.

Whycocomagh The provincial campsite here is the start of a trail leading to the top of Salt Mountain and a breathtaking view of the Bras d'Or.

Hunter's Mountain A sign saying "MacMillan Mountain" leads to a dirt road on the right about a mile northeast of the junction of Route 5 and the Cabot Trail. Two miles down this dirt road is a path leading to a bluff with an extraordinary view of the Baddeck River Valley.

South
Isle Madame An excellent hiking trail on this island leads from Sampson's Cove to Gros Nez.

Note: The waterways of Cape Breton offer the canoeist a wide selection of surroundings and wildlife. Although most are relatively short, each offers a distinct personality that makes canoeing in this area well worthwhile. For a good description of routes, access, supply sources, and campsites, see the Cape Breton Development Corporation's booklet "Canoe Cape Breton."

The Acadian Trail
The Acadian Trail, most of it still a proposed route, is being estab-

End of a typical dirt trail in Nova Scotia.

lished largely through the efforts of the Canadian Youth Hostel Association. The route runs from the tip of Cape Breton down the west coast and into New Brunswick. It will connect eventually with the Appalachian Trail. To date, about 65 miles on Cape Breton, from Petit Etang (near Cheticamp) to Mabou Harbor, have been completed. Competent hikers can follow the route without a great deal of trouble, but it is not for anyone in poor condition or unprepared for a real workout.

Trail Sections

Meat Cove to Cape St. Lawrence and Lowland Cove, 10 miles. This section of the trail is not yet marked and should only be attempted by experienced hikers. Made up of old gravel and logging roads, the trail offers some spectacular views.

Petit Etang to Grand Etang, 13 miles. Access to the trail is via a small back road in Petit Etang (ask someone). A hike through wildlife-filled woods and over a flat shore good for camping.

Margaree Harbour to Inverness, 18 miles. The trail, along the banks and cliffs of the shore, becomes very difficult when the tide is in. The beaches at both ends make the trip worth it, though. Carry a canteen.

Beinn Bhiorach Trail – Sight Point to Mabou Harbour, 10 miles. The trail begins at Sight Point Road at the south end of the town of Inverness. Cross the small bridge leading to Putney Camp, and continue on a few hundred feet to a grassy area. The trail, marked by blue tin cans, is on the right. It follows a steep bank along the shore (be careful here) before entering a meadowed area. There are two routes from here to the Mabou Harbour mouth. One is an old dirt road; the other, which we recommend, goes over the mountain for some comprehensive views of the countryside.

Cape North to Pollett Cove, 12 miles. The trail starts at the bridge over Gray Glen Brook near Cape North. This is definitely not for the novice. There is no real trail here, so be sure you have a compass and map. Also, be prepared to climb above 1,500 feet. There is a good campsite at Pollett Cove.

Pollett Cove to Red River, 5 miles. This is a rugged, interesting area. The path follows the edge of the coast; it is quite hilly but has an ample supply of water. There is camping at Pollett Cove.

NATIONAL PARKS OF NOVA SCOTIA

Both Kejimkujik and Cape Breton Highlands are Canadian National Parks, devoted to preserving distinct types of ecological or topographic areas. Facilities are extensive, trails marked or self-guiding, use fees in effect.

Most Canadian National Parks have been established with careful selection of sites and well-planned development, and are backed by rather good funding. They have a polished flavor, show little sign of wear or overuse, and sport most of the conveniences of a commercial camping park for travel trailers.

Although other areas of the province are more suited to backpackers, with little or no development or controls, the national parks "take care" of the visitor. This might make them preferable for the family group on a tight schedule.

Cape Breton Highlands National Park

Route 19, along the northwest coast, circles around the park and connects with main highway 105. (Taking 105 north to Route 395 is a little faster.)

The park includes 367 square miles, circled by the 185-mile-long Cabot Trail. The area is inhabited by people of Scottish descent. Mostly northern conifer, plentiful bogs, steep gullies, moose, caribou, with large burned-over areas on both the coasts. It is extensively developed with trails. (See other Cape Breton trails outside the park.) Views from above the seacoast are excellent; inland is bushy, wild, often bleak. Seven campgrounds are open from late May to mid-October, with backpacker camping on the trail by arrangement with the park wardens only.

The highlands are wild country. Lynx, bobcat, beaver, martin, and the rest of the mammals associated with true wilderness live here. Nests of the bald eagle occasionally can be spotted. Terrain ranges from cliffside or rocky seashore to an interior reminiscent of arctic muskeg. In addition to beach walks, impromptu hikes can be taken via stream beds, some of the old logging roads, and through the burn areas. Crosscountry travel in the bush and bog is rugged. Only experts should try it, and then only if prepared. Talk with the wardens first and check out the nature of the ground ahead.

Cheticamp, the west shore entry to park and campgrounds, has several trails to warm up on, including one of about 5 miles that runs above the road and leads out on a circuit with an overlook at Jerome Brook. Others run up the Cheticamp River. New trails may be opened here as well as in several other places in the park in the near future; inquire at the entrance and get a topo map to mark them on.

Cap Rouge, 2-mile circuit. Three-tenths mile past Jerome Brook, this trail follows the phone line where it leaves the road. Trail climbs briskly up Cap Rouge and provides a little scenery and wind testing.

Jumping Brook Trail, 7 miles. The road follows the coast at first, then turns up and inland. Watch for trail sign on the left. This trail goes down the shoulder of French Mountain to the seaside cliffs and across to rejoin the road several miles farther on. Condition of this trail varies, but it is considered one of the "official" park trails.

Fishing Cove Trail, 4 miles. Watch for trail on left about one mile after Jumping Brook. This trail is a classic for the area, dropping 1,000 feet into a rocky cove, then back up again. Follows Fishing Cove River for 3 miles and returns from the cove to the road.

South Mountain to Lobster Lake Trail, 4 miles. Another "official" trail, this takes the hiker past the lakes of the northeast corner of the park. It starts at the end of South Mountain Road, midway between Neils Harbour and Cape North.

Another east-side trail leads from the end of the road at Mark Ann Brook up to Lake of Islands, eight miles in. Check at the Neils Harbour warden station for directions; we passed this up during a bout of gloomy rain. We're told that this is a good trail for sampling semi-arctic muskeg and has a good lookout about two miles in.

Rain or no, our best "trail" was found around Green Cove and Black Point on the seacoast. For a mixture of boulders and gravel beach, hike the coast from Rocky Bay campground all the way up to Neils Harbour, about 9 miles. The trail may run right next to the road, but it's good coast, wild, rocky, with that good, clean, Atlantic wind. (Be prepared for some rock hopping and beachcombing!)

There are also trails around the Ingonish entrance to the park, a short

one out to Middle Head, and a couple inland. Check there for directions, new trails, and camping.

Kejimkujik National Park (Ked-jim-koo-jick, or "Kedge.")

The park is about 120 miles via north coast from Yarmouth, 50 miles
from Digby and the Saint John Ferry, and 130 miles via the south coast
from Halifax.

It includes 140 square miles of mixed northern hardwood and conifer
forest amid the low hills of lake country. Overnight camping is allowed
on hiking and canoe routes. Open year-round, although campground
(250 units in 1975) is open only mid-May through September. Canoes
rented.

To get the bad things about Kedge out of the way first: Look out
for poison ivy, and get geared up for ticks. This is a gentle, lakeland
sprawl of glacial boulders and mixed forest. Naturally, you can expect
the normal wetland bugs of summer.

The eastern part is flattest, with slightly more roll in the west, where
there is more granite.

Indian petroglyphs, pottery shards, and arrowheads can be found
around the lakes. Micmacs wintered in the inland lake country. There
are also many stories of lost gold mines, supposedly within the park
boundaries.

Mills Falls/Slapfoot Trails, 7 miles. From park headquarters area to
Jeremy Bay campground, following the quiet bends of the Mersey River
to the shores of Kejimkujik Lake. This is a quiet walk to warm up on
and get acquainted with the region. And a place to start wondering why
the Micmacs called the lake "Kejimkujik," which means "place that
swells."

As there is a great deal of canoeing designed into the layout of the
park, we won't describe the portage trails here. Hiking trails, damp at
times but no portage required, nearly circle the entire park on its outer
border. Overnight camping is required for the circuit; permits are available at the camp office.

Big Dam/Frozen Ocean Trail, 6.5 miles. From parking lot at eastern
tip of Big Dam Lake to Frozen Ocean warden's cabin. Begins on the
north side of park perimeter route. This trail is popular for canoe trips,
with campsites on the northeast side of Big Dam Lake and at Frozen
Ocean.

Campsites are all open. The only shelter we saw, on the south end of
Frozen Ocean, was for the use of canoeists. Check with the park before
your trip and ask if new shelters or trails have been developed.

Frozen Ocean – Peskawa Lake, 15 miles. Eight miles from Frozen
Ocean the trail splits, east to the West River campsites (3.5 miles), south
to Peskawa Lake (7 miles). By the time you get to the lake, you'll have
seen a lot of the boggy lake borders that have helped plentiful frogs,
salamanders, and turtles survive a slightly more northern climate than

what they are usually found in. Of special interest for the naturalist would be sighting either the ribbon snake or Blandings turtle, which are unique to the region. There are great amounts of blueberries in season, huckleberry, leather leaf, wild iris, etc. Spring, before the leaves close over the canopy, is a time to see lady slipper, trillium, starflower, and many other early blossoms.

Peskawa Lake — Mersey River, 11 miles. On the east end of Kedge Lake, the circuit joins with roads coming in from Grafton Lake and the park entrance.

Kejimkujik Circuit, 33 miles. No serious hills, though boggy spots can become difficult during heavy rain. The trail, mostly soft, is new from Big Dam to Peskawa Lake. Campsites are well scattered over the entire length.

View north over Pleasant Bay.

New Brunswick

New Brunswick is a 28,000-square-mile forest bordered by the Gulf of Saint Lawrence, the Bay of Fundy, Maine, and Quebec. It is relatively sparse in population: 625,000 people, with nearly all settlements to be found along coasts or rivers — particularly the Saint John River.

The province is a contrast of recent development overlying the historical water-route settlement. Naturally, the principal industry is lumber (pulp and paper), with fishing and tourism competing for second place.

Hikers visiting the area should assume at least two things: Travel campsites are only along the principal tourist routes, and sheer aggression is needed to find trails outside the parks. In spite of the province's reputation as a center for guided moose hunting and salmon fishing, the interior has virtually no formal trails established. Several efforts, discussed later, have begun to make significant additions to the backpackers' type of development, but real enjoyment of the region at present requires following determined nostrils out into uncharted grounds.

For planning your own trails — in addition to those suggested in this chapter — there is a publication that cannot be advocated more strongly than by saying: Don't go without it! This is the "Atlas of New Brunswick," a booklet of maps with a three mile-to-the-inch scale available from the Department of Natural Resources, Lands Branch, Room 575, Centennial Building, Fredericton, New Brunswick. During the summer of 1975 the book was $3.24.

It is a compilation of all roads, the majority being old lumber roads, in the province. Though there are few formal trails, and though it may require a heroic vehicle to get around some of the usable roads, the atlas will provide about three centuries' worth of exploring potential, especially in the mountain areas of northwest and north central New Brunswick.

One small example may help to explain the character of the land and the state of its development: Before the development of the new Mt. Carleton Park in the heart of the north central mountains could be completed, the only road in the area had to be improved and extended about 15 miles, from Nictau to the 2,600-foot mountain.

Giant lumbering operations have left, but others are forming, and hundreds of miles of their logging routes are usually open to hikers. But it pays to ask. At least one big land holding is *not* open (on the road from Grand Falls to Campbellton), owing to a bit of sweat over things not related to backpackers in any way. Where the signs say to stay out, do so.

There may also be some limits to access resulting from salmon-fishing concessions; check as you go. Rarely will there be any real resistance — these are nice people, rugged and friendly — but they may be unaccustomed to the nutty objectives of backpackers.

We had considerable fun trying to find trails in New Brunswick. Our request seemed to mystify many of the people and amuse others; usually we were referred to Fundy National Park. (Truth is, after the first few days of fruitless inquiry, we pulled to a dusty halt somewhere east of Woodstock, got out, plunged 50 feet into the brush, and came back snickering over having managed to "get on the trail" at last.) Still, with the atlas on hand, there are endless hikes possible, some in game refuges (check locally), some in lumber holdings, and the rest, in general, anywhere you turn.

Travel to New Brunswick is quite easy. Interstate 95 cuts through the wilderness of Maine and nearly all the way to Woodstock, providing access to the central St. John River area. Following Route 1 up through Maine to St. Leonard provides access to the northern areas as well as the Gaspe Peninsula of Quebec and the Trans-Canada Highway. On the south end, the principal border crossing is at Calais. You should inquire what hours the customs posts are open — on both sides — or your trip may be delayed overnight, especially at the smaller posts. (See Customs and Border section of chapter on Nova Scotia.)

When you enter the province, stop at a Tourist Bureau office. Officials there will tell you how and where to obtain Woods Use Permits from the Forestry Service. These are free but required for any sort of camping.

In addition, the Tourist Bureau is very well organized and distributed over the province, and the parks are part of the same operation. Therefore it's a good place to go when in doubt about anything, and it's just as well to get acquainted as soon as possible.

One nice aspect of traveling through New Brunswick is the chance to exercise the tongue and imagination with a variety of Micmac Indian and French place names. Some lilt, like Miramichi, others get tough, such as the Becuguimec Stream, and some are just plain defiant: Mistigougeche, Kouchibouguac, Magaguadavic.

Another fact about New Brunswick that becomes quickly apparent is the strong segmentation of interests converging on the woodlands. There are, of course, the lumber companies, which tend to get along with

Along the St. Johns River in the heart of New Brunswick.

recreational users much better than might be expected. There are the National Parks, oriented toward preserving areas, while at the same time provincial governments are trying to develop certain areas for their economic and tourist value. Involved with both of these are the guides and hunting and fishing people, but again, with surprisingly little friction. In fact, when Mt. Carleton was being planned, the guides of New Brunswick urged that the park be closed to hunters to help keep moose, deer, and other game animals in a stabilized population.

There are some points of conflict, though. It is possible that Fundy Park will be expanded to the southwest, including a large tract of regrown wilderness reputed to be the last area inhabited by the eastern panther. This region currently has a lumbering operation in full swing. How extensive the lumbering will be after it is taken over, or even if Fundy Park will actually expand, is uncertain, but the elements of park versus industry are there.

New Brunswick feels like a newer, rougher country than, say, Vermont. The ferries, for example, are still part of the highways; no charge.

In some areas you are likely to encounter use of natural resources at a pace that seems spendthrift. On the whole, though, such wounds won't lessen an experience with the wilds of New Brunswick.

The terrain of this maritime province, Canada's eighth largest, varies from rolling farmland with rivers, lakes, deep green valleys, and blossoming fruit orchards to mile after mile of hemlock, spruce, and fir forest. Covering an area about the size of Scotland in southeastern Canada, it contains 512 square miles of inland water and offers about 750 miles of coast.

The climate is more extreme than in Nova Scotia, with temperatures ranging from 95 degrees to -25 degrees at various places and times of the year. Although New Brunswick is as far south as southern Quebec, it is colder since it is far from the warming influence of the Great Lakes. Annual snowfall, especially along the northern coast, may reach 120 inches, while inland there is a "moderate" 60-inch fall. (But nature, of course, is never consistent. Although the 1974 snowfall in Fundy reached 60 inches, there was no snow in 1973 and in 1972 it measured a mere three feet.) June, July, and August are the vacation months, with cool evenings and warm, lazy days. September and October are pleasant, but frost may be apparent.

The Appalachian Ridge divides the province conveniently – in the west the forests rise to meet the mountains; in the east the fertile, red-colored soil forms low hills. In the north and east the land slopes to the low, sandy coast of the Gulf of St. Lawrence, while in the south the Bay of Fundy is bordered by a high, rocky ridge.

New Brunswick is a wildlife paradise. You might meet a moose, black bear, deer, beaver, marten, skunk, otter, mink, rabbit or squirrel; these are just the common species. The Fundy Coast is also on the path of the northeasterly warbler migration, so expect to see these birds there in season.

At Kouch, an avifaunal survey was done in 1974. Over 225 species of birds were classified as to habitat, frequency of sighting, whether or not the species is endangered and whether or not breeding takes place in the area. A checklist, available from the national parks, lets you mark the birds you happen to meet. There are no pictures, though – identification is up to you. Similar lists for birds and mammals are distributed at Fundy, although no similarly detailed surveys have been done there.

Do fill out these checklists and return them to the parks. Not only will you learn something; you'll help the professional bird and animal counters keep up to date.

Of course, the birds are never far from the trees. Fundy contains some fine big red pine forest, with areas of black spruce, red spruce, balsam fir, yellow birch, and sugar maple. Smaller plants here include pitcherplants in the bogs and lady's slippers which appear from the middle to the end of June.

TRAILS ON THE FUNDY COAST

The weather and the scenery here are dominated by the tides of Fundy. These dramatic rises and falls, along with the work the water does on the land edges, makes for rugged, unique shoreline formations. Fog from the chilly waters is common, persistent, and aggravating unless you can get used to periods of dripping trees and a nose well-shined by the drifting mist. For people who enjoy a cottony wrapped dawn along the sea, though, this is the perfect region.

The structures of man and sea combine to practical and esthetic effect along this coast. In places, there are nets on poles set into the tide's shallow bottom. Between high and low tide, the fish are caught in the nets, and at low tide, the fishermen take a truck or wagon out, on "dry" mud flats to gather the catch. In some places a small boat is used.

Lobstering leaves a lot of barrels, floats, traps, and line littering the beaches to help make beachcombing fun. Old sailing day harbors, lumber loading piers, and other signs of mining, commerce, and strife from a century ago are also common finds.

Sections of the coast are completely wild, a refuge for salmon fishermen and moose hunters as well as hikers. These areas are filled with old lumbering roads, some passable with rugged vehicles, and some grown over with vegetation to the point that even hikers might not be able to follow them easily. Since fogs and scrambled routes can make navigation a serious chore, it would be advisable to pack along a good compass and make full use of current local information.

The Fundy Coast Walking Trail, about 25 miles. Take Route 111 from St. John to West Quaco. Take the road to St. Martins and follow it northeast, keeping to the coast. Its condition will gradually degenerate until you're hopping along an old lumber road with wooden culverts. About the time you want to quit, the road will go down a steep hill with an old sawmill on the right and then will go a short way up the Salmon River to a swing bridge and a ford.

(Note: A dirt track continues on the other side of the ford and cuts up through the hill to connect with a major lumbering road that, followed east, comes out almost in sight of the south gate of Fundy National Park. Four-wheel drive is recommended. And be sure to have the gears in four-wheel mode before trying to cross the river.)

If you can't locate the trail, check out the old dam and logging operation ruins along the mouth of the river.

We have to mention that small problem of finding the trail.- Quite honestly, we didn't. But we'll give the description as given to us, with a few extra words to help you appreciate the area in general.

To eliminate one tricky bit of confusion right off: This area is the southwest end of the Fundy Walking Trail, not to be confused with the formal, marked, Fundy Hiking Trail from Moncton to Fundy National Park. The Fundy Walking Trail runs from Salmon River Ford to connect

Hopewell Rocks in New Brunswick, tide in (left) and tide out (right).

with Fundy National Park trails at Goose River.

According to an elderly salmon fisherman we met at the river, a party of people on horseback did cross the trail in 1972 or 1973. They made it in three days of rugged going. Our investigations around the specific area where the trail should start, and while roaming around the Fundy region in general, have led us to feel that the trail suffers from several basic problems.

First, in November 1974 high winds did extensive damage to New Brunswick. They left extensive blowdown, washouts, and slides around the Salmon and other river gorges, just the sort of damage to camouflage trails effectively.

Secondly, the coastal area the trail penetrates is not gentle. The hills, though not extremely high, are steep, and the streams almost always lie at the bottom of deep cuts. Much of the area is a heavy gravel-type glacial till, making the steep banks less than a joy under a pack (or even without a pack).

Lastly, the trail sees little use since it is in a remote place, is longer than casual hikers like, and is not easily set up for transportation from start to finish. It's a long roundabout drive from one end of the trail to the other.

However, from what we saw of the area, it seems like one in which experienced cross-country backpackers could delight.

The scenery is lovely and the region is the heart of the reputed last roaming grounds of the eastern panther.

From the north shore of the Big Salmon River the "trail" climbs up to the height of ground and then straggles back toward the steep-sided hills and cliffs bordering the Bay of Fundy. After crossing the deep Long Beach Brook and following the shore, the trail drops down onto Seely Beach to bypass Seely Brook at mile 4. This is a potential campsite.

Climbing inland from Seely Beach the trail goes over the hills, then drops down to the outlet of the Little Salmon River where there is a good campsite (used in the past by bear hunters) and an old dirt road running inland to connect with the tangle of logging roads that in turn connect with new logging roads and the road to Fundy National Park. This is not a good way of getting out of there, but a remotely possible one. About 9 miles from the start.

After following the high ground and touching the shore once it's another four miles or more to Martin Head lighthouse. A four-wheel drive road goes north here to connect with the logging road from Fundy. Just follow it up about eight or nine miles, hang a right on the first (only) big new dirt road, and it will bring you out near the gate of Fundy National Park after 10 or so miles. Coming in this way is *fairly* easy. From Fundy headed west turn at the first dirt road (big) after leaving the park. Following it straight through eight to ten miles (our odometer wasn't functioning well) you'll cross a large concrete culvert and see a dirt track leading off to the left. It drops down and crosses a stream, then leads to Martin Head. Our van did not manage to make it, though. It required a crowbar on the tie rod after a few exposed rocks. The trail itself follows this road north nearly three miles before cutting off east and gradually working back to the coast, zigging over the hills and ending with a connection to the trails of Fundy National Park after crossing the Goose River, about 10 miles from Martin Head.

This is one of the trails we would very much like to go back and try again. It could make a nice segment for a continuous trail system from Cape Breton to the Appalachian Trail in Baxter Park, Maine; it's also in some nice wild rugged country with plenty of bear and other wildlife and a fascinating coast line.

To repeat: Do not try this trail without full and serious preparation. It is only for persons prepared to cope with foul weather, worse foot conditions, and less than no navigational aid.

Two local fisheries wardens gave us some pleasant advice. "Forget it," they said. They hadn't heard of a trail in the area. But hikers have. Someday we'd love to find out just what the situation really is in that long wild hunk of coast.

FUNDY NATIONAL PARK

To get there, take Route 1 north from St. John to Route 114 north of Sussex. (Very well marked at every point). Turn right on 114 to the park. It is about 80 miles from St. John.

Fundy National Park is a well-established, though fairly new park which preserves a unique area of the Fundy coast. The park is polished, with fine lawns, flower beds, self-guiding trails, good roads, campsites, even an excellent golf course, a swimming pool, tennis, and bowling greens. But while "polished" was the only word we could come up with to describe the "general" tenor of the park, and while it is fine for families, it is just as fine for backpackers and hikers ready to do something a bit more rugged. The park contains some 50 miles of formal trails.

Within its 80 square miles are several Fundy bays, coastal hills, bogs, and several rivers. Motels, supplies, and miscellaneous requirements are available in Alma, just outside the north gate. There is a motel in the park, as well as camping.

Mornings tend to be cool and foggy. Sometimes the cool water of the bay combines with weather coming over the highland interior of the park to produce a mist cover that hangs for long periods.

Large areas of the park are relatively inaccessible, except on foot. There are seldom formal trails but stream beds make fine natural routes. Cutting across country off-trail is tough. Again, the typical deep, steep, rocky-dirt banks of each stream prevail. Often, even a small stream that can be jumped will have 50 to 100 feet of bank and will be several hundred feet deep. Allow extra time and breath to estimates when the map shows such streams. Flash floods or quick changes of water level can seriously influence these streams. Keep this in mind if rain threatens.

Also, as with any area on the Bay of Fundy, beware of getting cut off by the tide when hiking along the shore. It becomes habit to watch the tide after being in New Brunswick awhile, but if you're a newcomer, remember the tide comes up fast and can be a problem.

Park naturalists, many of whom are college students, conduct numerous lectures and hikes. They can also usually advise backpackers about current conditions.

FORMAL TRAILS:

Dickson Falls, ¾ mile. It begins near Point Wolfe Road about 1.5 miles west of park headquarters. This is a highly used but very pretty walk looping its way through the woods, past the 27-foot Dickson Falls and along Dickson Brook.

Kinnie Brook Nature Trail, a one-mile loop. It begins 2.2 miles northwest of park headquarters on the east side of highway 14. This is 11.5 miles southeast of the northern park entrance. Opposite the picnic area, a roadside sign indicates the trail. It leads across two open fields, passes through a typical Acadian forest, passes a bubbling brook and skirts the edge of Kinnie Brook valley. Although this is another short popular trail, a more strenuous offshoot leads down into the valley of Kinnie Brook.

Caribou Plain, 2.5-mile loop. It begins on highway 114 five miles northwest of park headquarters. The trail passes through the plateau forest and raised peat bogs of the Caledonia Highlands, past a beaver pond and a raised peat bog.

Big Dam Trail, 5.5 miles round trip. To reach the trailhead from Alma, follow Route 14 along Cleveland Brook northeast about two miles. The first turn on the left is Forty Five road. Follow this for about 4.5 miles until you reach a covered bridge. The trail is just beyond to the left. The trail rises twice before dropping to waterfall where the Broad River runs into the Upper Salmon.

Laverty Trail, 5 miles. It begins off Old Shepody Road about one mile east of Haley Brook. The trail may be followed five miles to where it crosses Route 14, or, after three miles, the trail along the Upper Fault Brook may be taken and followed another three miles to the Upper Salmon River. At this point you are less than a mile north of the rapids.

Tracey Lake Trail, 3 miles. It begins off Route 14 by Bennet Lake Dam and follows Bennet, Tracey, and Bruin Lakes to Old Shepody Road.

THE FUNDY HIKING TRAIL

This privately developed trail, some 40 miles long, runs from Riverview near Moncton south to Fundy National Park. Although the park doesn't make any fuss over it, it is the longest marked trail system we found anywhere in the province. Developed by Dr. J. Arthur Dobson and a number of volunteer workers, it is located on privately owned and leased Crown woodland. For registration information contact the Trail Shop, 343 A, St. George St., Moncton (845-8011).

The trail's northern terminus is about three miles from downtown Moncton, opposite Pine Glen. The southern terminus is on the New Ireland-Elgin Road about 2.8 miles from the northeast corner of Fundy National Park. Except where it crosses back roads, this is a wilderness trail with no stores or towns. Water is widely available and safe, although Mill Creek consists mostly of bog drainage. Except during a very dry season, you shouldn't need to carry water.

There are two Appalachian type shelters about six and 22 miles along the route from the north end. Otherwise camping is near water sources.

The trail is well marked — the main trail with white paint slashes, the side trails with green. Most springs are marked; some, which are off the trail, have a green side trail leading to them. Mile trees every one-half mile show the mileage from Moncton. The trail is divided into segments for description here by the points where it crosses the road. This should let you plan day trips or store supplies if you are less than a purist. Signs with mileage and points of particular interest are mounted at each road crossing.

(We did not gather information on the first four miles along the bank of Mill Creek and the last two miles from Blackwood Lake to the New Ireland Road.)

TRAIL SECTIONS:

Pine Glen-Tower Road, 9.3 miles. To get there, take Route 112 from Moncton across the Petitcodiac River to Riverview Heights. Between two service stations is the Pine Glen Road which should be followed to Mill Creek (about 1.9 miles). Cross the old sawdust area on the south side of the creek to the right of the highway. A small sign with the trail crest is located in a large pine tree. The trail passes underneath, follows Mill Creek to its head and on to the railroad and Tower Road. There is a hut at about six miles.

Sand Hill Side Trail, .08 miles. The trail begins beyond a highway curve sign on the right 6.3 miles toward Dawson Settlement coming from Mill Creek, goes from Sand Hill to meet with the main trail at Mill Creek Meadows (6.4 miles along main trail).

Tower Road — MacFarlane Bridge, 1.3 miles. Take Pine Glen Road to Dawson Corner and turn right on Tower Road. 0.8 miles from the corner, the trail crosses the road. The trail follows Levi Road before crossing the bridge.

MacFarlane Bridge – Berrytown, 5.4 miles. To reach this trailhead, continue straight through from the Pine Glen Road toward Osborne Corner from Dawson Corner. MacFarlane is the first covered bridge you will see. Most of this section of the trail is through open hardwood area. You will cross a pleasant brook halfway along the route.

Berryton-Prosser Ridge, 4.6 miles. From Dawson Corner take the Tower Road toward Turtle Creek and follow the detour to Turtle Creek Road. Turn left and drive 3.8 miles to the Berryton highway bridge. If you're coming from Moncton, take Route 112 across the Petitcodiac River to Turtle Creek Road, and drive 8.9 miles to Berryton. The trail follows Berryton Brook before rising to the ridge between this brook and Prosser.

Prosser Ridge – Kent Road, 6.1 miles. Drive two miles from Berryton up Turtle Creek Valley. Turn right at the Rosevale Prosser Brook Road and climb about two miles to the hilltop where the trail is evident. The trail climbs up Prosser Valley, down Upham Brook and over to Hayward Pinnacle.

Hayward Pinnacle Trail, 1.3 miles. This is a side trail starting from Hayward Road. To reach Hayward, drive west 3.5 miles from Prosser Ridge. The trail is 0.6 miles up the road. After passing the Pinnacle, the trail eventually runs into the Main Trail.

Kent Road – Teahan's Corner, 6.6 miles. Go on to Prosser Brook from Parkindale and follow the road to the Meadow for 3¼ miles. The Sherman Road, on your left, is a woods road, but usually passable. Follow this three miles to the trail. The trail uses the Kent Road for 1.3 miles before proceeding across country to Blackwood Lake and the New Ireland-Elgin Road.

New Ireland, (Trail terminal). Access is via the Forty Five, Old Shepody, or New Ireland Road. Drive to Teahan's Corner at the northeast corner of Fundy National Park. Proceed north on the New Ireland-Elgin Road for 2.8 miles to where the trail begins at an abandoned farm on the right side of the road.

THE ISLES OF FUNDY

There are three Fundy Isles: Deer, Campobello and Grand Manan Islands. They are located off Eastport, Maine and the southern tip of New Brunswick.

There are interesting walks on Campobello (where Franklin D. Roosevelt spent summers as a child) and on Deer Island, offering seashore and hill, fishing villages, and historic sites.

By ferry from Black Harbor near St. George on Route 1 between Calais and St. John, it is an interesting short trip out to the largest of the Fundy Isles, Grand Manan. Famous for its scenic appeal to painters and photographers, the isle also has some fine, rugged coast, hills, and hiking potential. Part of the reason for the rugged rocks of the shore is that the west side is composed of the same bedrock as the continental land mass, but the east side is volcanic — and probably almost six billion years younger than the surrounding mass. Grand Manan was the only Fundy island to suffer the effects of this undersea volcano, and geologists from all over the world have come here to study this phenomenon.

John James Audubon, too, enjoyed the island. He found hundreds of bird species to paint here back in 1831, including puffins, the bald eagle, the arctic tern, and other rare birds. Many of these species are still around. They enjoy sharing the primary industry of these shores: fishing. Ask the herring fishermen if you can accompany them on their boats. The people of this island are renowned for their friendliness, and maybe if we stay nice, they will too.

The trails of the North Head of the Island are particularly lovely and exciting. An interesting rock formation called the "Hole in the Wall" can be reached by a short walk beginning on the grounds of the Marathon Hotel.

Ferry service in the summer consists of three runs a day except for Sunday when there is only one.

Having discussed the Fundy area, we've covered the bulk of New Brunswick trails. Other parks are being developed, but the speed of that development depends on those eternal uncertainties — funding and weather. Much of what we describe here will be *indended* development at press time, but not necessarily a true picture of what is actually on the ground at the moment. If you're planning a trip, write to the park or the Tourist Bureau for current information.

KOUCHIBOUGUAC PARK Couch-a-bo-quack (Kouch for short)

Kouch is a new park, established in 1969, that takes in a large hunk (93 square miles) of seashore, dunes, rivers, and marsh on the northeast shore of New Brunswick. It is on a border between northern and southern forest types and includes 14 different ecological communities. Trails range from sand beach to winding riverside logging roads, to foot trails, to marsh boardwalks. It's new, rough, and highly diversified.

The salt marshes at Kouch are one of the best representations of this kind of environment in a national park. Marsh plants are a great source of food for many kinds of marine life since they are the most efficient converters of the sun's energy into organic matter.

Following Canadian National Park system policy, a river wharf remains in active use by the local fishing fleet even though it is inside the park boundary. Also in accordance with park policy, roads have been closed to motor vehicles in some sections and turned into trails. (A beaver helped do that on one road!) It may take a few years, but this will be a very interesting park. In many ways, it is already.

To get there take Route 11, 26 miles south from Chatham; or follow

Routes 115 and 11 about 60 miles north from Moncton.

SUGAR LOAF PARK

Based on the 1,000-foot-high Sugar Loaf Mountain, a massive park is being planned for the area just outside Campbellton.

Currently under construction, it will be a polished park that will include all the usual facilities.

The walk up Sugar Loaf, about a mile's worth of puffing, is easy to find once you're in the vicinity; but be prepared for a lot of effort.

MOUNT CARLETON PARK

The highest point in New Brunswick, 2,600-foot Mt. Carleton in the north central highlands, is the focal point for a giant park being developed for multi-dimensional recreational use. Plans are for a 70-square-mile park in this landscape area of mountains, valleys, rivers, and lakes.

This, too, is to be a "resource park"; that is, "the harvesting of natural resources will be allowed under controlled supervision and is intended to demonstrate the continuing use of renewable resources." Therefore the forest has been mapped according to its logging potential and is expected to stay in use.

The area is rich in wildlife — 100 species of birds and 30 mammal species have been sighted.

Government officials in Fredericton had no information about possible formal opening dates. They did say that "primitive" camping and some trail was open, in spite of construction. (They seem to feel that racking out in a tent is some kind of hardship.)

Since interviews and letters failed to get any strong idea of what will be in use next year, a query to the Tourist Bureau is the best way to get information.

5

Northeastern Miscellany

Most of the land in the east was under private ownership before hiking trail systems were even thought of. And, although state and federal park agencies have been able to return a good deal of land to the public for recreational use, many miles of the longer trail systems remain in private hands. This is particularly true of the systems maintained by non-government private organizations, such as the Appalachian Mountain Club or the Connecticut Forest and Park Association.

Continued availability of these systems depends on the good will of these owners and this is in large part dependent on what you, the hikers, do on the trails. Don't ruin it for everyone. Be aware of the regulations governing any particular section of trail. If the owner doesn't want you to hunt, fish or camp, don't hunt, fish or camp. Don't carry firearms. Do carry your own water or obtain it at public places. Stay on the trail. And, above all, be courteous and friendly; clean; and respectful of animals, buildings, and property fixtures.

—   —   —   —

Northeastern mountain peaks are often rocky places of sparse vegetation. Some have smooth, polished looking summits. Much of their character is a result of the huge glaciers that covered the Green, White, and Katahdin ranges during the Ice Ages.

If you look at the different sides of a mountain, you'll be better able to see the glacial action. The north and west slopes, which were hit first by the ice, are worn smooth. The ice took the topsoil and loose rock and left smooth peaks, such as Mount Monadnock, behind. Or, the ice may have melted, leaving the residue to form the kind of rock and soil deposits called terminal moraines, which may be found on Mounts Washington and Katahdin.

In either case, after polishing the northern and western slopes, the ice proceeded to tear apart those of the south and the east. Huge sections of these slopes were ripped away and deposited as rocks, boulders, and drift in the valleys below. The Agassiz Basin in the White Mountains is the result of such a collection. But the ripping left etched peaks and rock formations such as Katahdin's Knife Edge, or the rock sculptures of the Franconia and Crawford Notch areas.

Waterfalls in the northeast are also the result of glacial work. Unlike the southern waterfalls, which were frequently caused by water wearing down softer layers of rock, northeastern waterfalls were formed as the glaciers simultaneously wore down the peaks and deposited the debris in the rivers and creeks. The rocky refuse compacted as water went over it, establishing new water routes that dropped over the steplike ledges. The falls became longer and faster as the debris piles grew.

Much of the results of this glacial sculpturing was accounted for by the Indians in the story of Taweskare and Tsentsa, the powerful twins who shaped the earth. Tsentsa, the embodiment of good, would work to create fertile plains and valleys. Whenever he rested, his brother, the evil Taweskare, changed the landscape. He made the mountains barren and created the chasms and swamps. In the latest legends, he went west to sculpt the Rockies.

One problem that must be stressed, particularly to visitors from outside the northeastern area, is that of the gypsy moth. This killer of oak and harmer of other hardwood trees has been a serious problem in the area since the late 1800's when it was brought over from Europe by mistake. In time, it could cripple or destroy as much as 100 million acres of oak-based forest land.

While there are problems in getting conservation, state, and environmental groups to agree on a program against this menace, one thing they all agree on is don't spread it any farther. The current quarantine area includes southern Maine, New Hampshire, Vermont, most of New York, southwestern Quebec, Massachusetts, Rhode Island, Connecticut, New Jersey, and most of Pennsylvania.

If you are out in these areas during May, June, or early July, you might be out during the fairly short egg-laying period of the gypsy moth. Just inspecting your camp gear, vehicles, and clothing can help contain the critters. One egg mass, a fuzzy, tan lump about an inch wide, can contain up to 900 eggs, and every one of these can hatch a black worm with orange and blue spots capable of consuming a square foot of leaf per night. Campers who take an egg mass or two home on a tent, camper trailer, or car body, can establish a new center of gypsy moth infestation in their own backyard.

We've had the moths lay eggs on backpacks and clothing. Check thoroughly and burn any tan egg masses, including those on the undersides of tree trunks and limbs you might see around campsites or on the trail. But don't kill larvae unless they can be positively identified. Among the nasty larvae of the gypsy moth, spruce bud worm, and tent caterpillers, are the larvae of luna moths, monarch butterflies, polyphemous moths, Cecropia and other beautiful creatures, some of which are rare and all of which are threatened by the same programs aimed at the evil worms.

It would not be a bad idea to check with your local conservationists to see what can be done to suppress gypsy moths in your area. Being faced with a forest stripped naked of all greenery in July is grim. When you crush gypsy moths, they leave a nice green smear, but that's about the only thing green they will leave. So be careful, check your belongings, and help keep this menace contained.

6

Maine

Rocky coast, panoramic beaches, a wilderness of forests, islands, jagged peninsulas and mountains. All this is Maine, taking up as much room on a map as the rest of New England combined and offering hikers the biggest and most ecologically varied samples of unspoiled land still left on the East Coast.

Boreal forest stretches across the upper half of the state, its topography punctuated by mountains up to 4,000 feet in elevation and hundreds of clear, glacial lakes. Baxter State Park and the Allagash Wilderness Waterway preserve large parcels of the North Maine Woods for exclusive recreational use, while privately owned timber lands are accessible to backpackers who pay a nominal use fee to tour cross country or camp beside streams or old logging trails.

Mount Katahdin, northern end of the Appalachian Trail, is also in this region. It is said to be the first place in the United States to catch the sun's rays each morning.

The state's rocky coastline and the islands offshore were formed during the Ice Ages when peaks along the coast were pushed down. Coastal Maine in its natural state can best be explored by hikers on the island near Bangor that has been designated Acadia National Park.

Jesuit missionaries traversed Maine in the 17th century on their way to convert the Abnakis Indian tribe to Christianity. Benedict Arnold, another early hiker, walked through on his way to meet General Montgomery at Quebec. Jefferson Davis visited the Lead Mountain area around Baddington somewhat later with a surveying party.

Early settlers' homes and forts dating from French and Indian War days are still intact in villages along trail routes. And the state recently acquired, for preservation, an ancient oyster shell heap on the banks of the Damariscotta River that bears evidence of human activity long before Europeans arrived.

The climate in Maine is colder than many places in the same latitude because it is accessible to Arctic wind currents. Summers are brief with few actually hot days. Nights are always cool enough to light a fire, especially on the coast. Winter is accompanied by heavy snowfall and bitter winds.

A visitor at Camden Hills Campground in Maine.

Caribou and moose are said to have once ranged as far south as southern New Hampshire and Vermont. Moose are still seen in Maine, but infrequently, along isolated stretches near the Canadian border. The spruce-fir forests are also meccas for warblers and such exotic northern bird species as the white winged crossbill, while the lakes are home to the loon, whose wild call symbolizes the spirit of north woods wilderness probably better than any other sound or sight.

The gregarious gray jay is known to local hunters because of its fearlessness in stealing camp food. If you're lost, oldtimers say, follow a gray jay and it may lead you to camp.

Many of the wildflowers are those known throughout eastern United States, but boreal plants more common in Canada extend south to the North Maine Woods. Pipsissewa, pyrola, and dozens of ladyslipper varieties can be found there. So can the small, pink-blossomed twinflower which Linnaeus chose, out of all those he classified, to name after himself.

Thirteen of the 25 state parks in Maine list hiking trails, and 14 have designated campsites. Of these, Baxter is the only one which accepts reservations. Fees and regulations vary, so check with the Bureau of Parks and Recreation in Augusta before finalizing your plans.

The Maine Forest Service, in cooperation with private landowners, has developed an additional 121 campsites throughout the state. These

Site of Thoreau's sojourn at Walden.

are either free or $1.00 per party per night. If you plan to build a fire, remember to secure a permit in advance from the State Bureau of Forestry or from rangers in the local district.

Hikers and campers are allowed into a remote 2.5 million acres of commercial forest spanning most of northwestern Maine, but developed trails are few. Most of those that exist serve the fire towers. Logging roads may be followed, but don't rely on maps to tell you which one you're on. New ones are constantly being cut as timber crops mature. The most accurate, up-to-date maps of the region available, other than U.S. Geological Survey maps, are published by Prentiss and Carlisle, 107 Court Street, Bangor, Maine 04401.

"Backpacking in the North Maine Woods is not for the novice," wrote Hugh H. Penney, secretary for an organization of the region's landowners, in a letter to us. He added, however, that experienced outdoorspeople would find it "a great place to get away from it all."

Tollgates and checkpoints, pinpointed on most road maps, surround the area and provide access as well as a record of people using it at any one time.

This country is Thoreau's Maine Woods. It encompasses all of Aroostook county, encloses the Allagash Waterway, and adjoins Baxter State Park. It has many separate owners, but most of it has never been formally divided.

Ancestors of the current proprietors bought acreage in 1820, when Maine separated from Massachusetts and the state needed operating capital. Since it had to be sold a township at a time and purchased unseen, people joined together to buy property as a group and thus spread out the risk.

The resulting "shares" of land were passed down from generation to generation. Heirs of those original owners today still divide timber profits from any section based on what percentage of the entire region they own.

There is a $2.00 entrance fee and a $2.00 camping fee per person per night, payable at the checkpoints. There are ten of these: at Oxbow, Six Mile, Fish Lake, Allagash, Dickey, Estcourt, St. Pamphile, Daaquaam, Telos, and Second Musquaciik.

For more information on the North Maine Woods, write Box 1113, Bangor, Maine 04401.

MOUNT DESERT ISLAND (Acadia National Park)

To get there, head southeast from Bangor on U.S. Alternate Route 1 to Ellsworth. Continue southeast on Maine Route 3, across a bridge onto the island. Route 3 circles the island's north half and provides access to trails and campsites.

This heart-shaped island, about 18 miles long and 13 miles wide, includes Somes Sound, often called the only true fjord in North America, and Acadia National Park, which some have called the most beauti-

Female polyphemous moth, native to the Northeast.

ful of the national parks. There are more than 17 peaks on the island, carved here, as throughout Maine, by glacial action. They were reduced to bare granite by the ice sheets, lakebeds were hollowed out between them, and rocky debris was deposited at the feet of the polished peaks.

To get an overview of the park, follow Maine Route 3 (Ocean Drive) around the park loop. At Anemone Cave, where the water has tunneled 85 feet into the granite cliffs, pools shine amidst the algae, kelp, anemone and rockweed. From the island's highest point, Cadillac Mountain, on a good day, you can see all the way to Mount Katahdin.

Trails on the island are well maintained and marked and provide an excursion for all types of hikers: from mountain climbing enthusiasts who prefer plenty of exercise to those who want non-strenuous seaside strolls. In addition to trails, there is a system of dirt roads called carriage roads on which motor traffic is not allowed. These are marked where they cross the highway.

Among seaside walks maintained by the National Park Service are the Great Head Circuit, about 3½ miles along the cliffs above the sea; Ocean

Drive, 1.8 miles over rock ledges paralleling the State Route 3 to Otter Cliffs; and Hunters Beach, a ¼-mile walk along the surf.

Somes Sound divides Mount Desert Island in two. **Cadillac Mountain**, at 1,530 feet the highest island peak, is on the northern segment, just east of the town of Bar Harbor. It is accessible by car and cog railroad as well as by foot. Trails include the **South Ridge Trail**, a 3½-mile path beginning 50 yards west of the Black Woods Campground on the north side of Maine Route 3. It culminates at the parking lot on the mountain top. The steepest trail up Cadillac is the **West Face Trail**, 2.3 miles, starting at the north end of Bubble Pond and passing through woods and over ledges to the South Ridge Trail and the summit. The **North Ridge Trail**, 1.8 miles, has few trees and therefore offers good views. It starts ½ mile east of Jordan Pond Road on Kebo Mountain Road.

Sargent Mountain is another untimbered peak rising to 1,373 feet above sea level with a pond at its base. The **Giant Slide Trail**, 4.6 miles, is the longest route up, starting at St. James Church, ¼ mile north of Sargent Drive on Maine 198. It takes its name from the huge boulders it passes shortly after meeting Sargent Brook. An alternate route, **Sargent Mountain North Ridge Trail**, 1.2 miles, leaves the Giant Slide Trail after 1.8 miles and completes the journey to the peak over open ledges.

The **Hadlock Brook Trail** and the **Maple Spring Trail** are two parallel trails to the Sargent summit from the west. Both start from the Norumbega Mountain parking area. They run together for 0.4 miles and split. Both are wooded and steep and reach the top in two miles.

Penobscot Mountain (1,194 feet) is only a mile from Sargent, accessible by road from the east side of Sargent Pond. The **Penobscot Mountain Trail**, four miles, intersects both peaks. It is reached by a 0.1 mile path going west from the Jordan Pond House. The trail follows gently sloping granite ledges to Penobscot's top where it merges with the Sargent Pond Trail and eventually the **Sargent Mountain South Ridge** trails to the summit of Sargent.

A more exciting route traversing both peaks is the **Jordan Cliffs Trail**, 2.9 miles, leaving the Penobscot Mountain Trail 0.4 miles west of the Jordan Pond House near an intersection with a carriage road. This trail connects to the Sargent Pond Trail via a section of ladders and handrails that offers some incredible panoramic views of the Pemetic and Bubbles mountains and Jordan Pond.

Champlain Mountain (1,058 feet) is the easternmost mountain on the island with a sharp eastern face. The **Precipice Trail**, 0.8 miles, climbs this face from the Precipice Trail parking area on Ocean Drive at the base of the mountain. It climbs over slopes, along ledges, and in some places, completely vertical ascents over ladders. An easier route up the same peak is the **Champlain Mountain Trail**, 4.1 miles, starting at the south end of The Bowl, a mountain pond. There are some excellent views of Frenchman's Bay and the Schoodic Peninsula on this trail, which reaches the summit and descends to the Bear Brook Picnic Area.

Southwest of Somes Sound is **Acadia Mountain**, from which the park gets its name. It rises from Man O'War Brook flowing into Somes Sound, which once provided a deep water anchorage for sailing frigates looking to renew their water supply. The **Acadia Mountain Trail**, four miles, starting on the Robinson Road fireroad 0.1 miles east of Maine 102, has several good views, including those of the Sound on the summit, before descending steeply to Man O'War Brook and back to Robinson Road to circle back to the beginning.

Flying Mountain (284 feet) has the lowest elevation of all the peaks on Mount Desert Island, but one providing one of the best views without a lot of work. The **Flying Mountain Trail**, 1.8 miles, starts at the east end of the parking lot at the Fernald Cove end of the Valley Cove road, climbs 0.3 miles to the top of Flying Mountain before coming down through a spruce wood and meeting the Acadia Mountain Trail at Man O'War Brook.

Western Mountain has two peaks, Bernard (1,071 feet) and Mansell (949 feet). Although views are not the high point of trails up these summits, they do provide some nice wooded hiking. The **Great Pond Trail**, 2.9 miles, begins at the pumping station on the edge of Great (or Long) Pond, follows the pond, travels through a birch forest, and follows Great Brook to meet the Western Trail. The **Western Trail**, 4.2 miles, which has no views, climbs the mountain from the north. The trail starts from the east branch of the Great Pond truck road about 0.1 mile below the Pine Hill turnaround. The **South Face Trail**, 3.6 miles, begins at the reservoir (Mill Field) on the Western Mountain truck road and follows an old ski trail for a bit, offers spectacular views of the Island and Blue Hill Bay, and ends at Little Notch.

Beech Mountain (839 feet) is just west of the Beech Cliff-Canada Cliff area. These rocky cliffs provide a good vantage point from which to view Echo Lake. They are swiftly reached by the **Canada Cliff Trail** via ladders and switchbacks and the **Canada Ridge Trail**. The **Beech Mountain Trail**, 0.6 miles, takes a little longer but requires less effort. It follows a fire road from the west side of the Beech Cliff parking area and climbs gently to the summit.

Other areas in Maine are more easily definable in terms of counties rather than land regions. Therefore, the remaining Maine trails will be delineated in that manner.

AROOSTOOK COUNTY

Aroostook County covers the north and northeastern sections of the state, including much of the North Maine Woods and part of the Allagash Wilderness Waterway within its borders. The mountains here are widely scattered and the highest peak, Peaked Mountain (2,260 feet) has no trails on its slopes.

Mars Hill (1,660 feet) is one of the better known peaks of the region.

From its summit, there are some excellent views since it is a monadnock rising from an almost level area of potato fields and woods. There is a 1.6-mile rough surface road which may be used as a trail to the top.

To reach the trail, drive north ½ mile on U.S. 1A from Mars Hill Village (a town located on U.S. 1 some 28 miles north of Interstate 95's eastern terminus at Houlton). Turn right on a road marked "Ski Area," follow it for 0.6 miles, turn right again and then left at the first crossing, where the trail starts at the edge of a field.

Round Mountain Trail, 7¼ miles. Drive 22 miles on the American Realty Road west from Ashland (a town on Maine Route 11 directly west of Presque Isle). The trail begins on the lefthand (south) side of the road, skirts Round Mountain Lake and partially circles the mountain base before climbing to the firetower on the mountain top (2,147 feet).

Horseshoe Mountain Trail, 1½ miles. Drive west 41 miles from Ashland on the American Realty Road. (If you reach Upper McNally Pond Campsite, you've gone 2.5 miles too far). Turn south on side road at this point one mile to the trailhead (at a point where the road turns left). A side trail, reached after 3/8 mile, goes to Horseshoe Pond while the main continues 1-1/8 miles to the top (elevation 2,052 feet). The climb is strenuous, but views from the top make it worthwhile.

Priestly Mountain Trail, two miles. Drive west from Ashland 67 miles, past the Allagash River, and turn south on Churchill Dam Road 7½ miles. The trail begins on the west side of the road and climbs to the firetower on the summit (1,900 feet).

PISCATAQUIS COUNTY

Piscataquis County, covering a large area in the center of Maine, contains Baxter Park and the mountain area to the west and southwest of it. The **Boarstone Mountain** area, near Monson (on Maine Routes 6 and 15) offers not only the mountain itself (1,947 feet), but **Little Wilson Falls**, a 57-foot cataract in the slate canyon of Little Wilson Stream. Boarstone has good views, two peaks, and three ponds. There are two good trails.

Moore's Pond Trail, 4.8 miles. It starts at the Elliottsville Road, 0.1 miles past the Canadian Pacific tracks, passing through a gate and following a private road. This route over the top of Boarstone Mountain goes through private property but is open to hikers and covers the mountain's two summits. The three Moore's Ponds, Sunrise, Midday, and Sunset, are on the southwest slope. The trail passes them before ascending the two peaks.

Little Wilson Falls is reached via a section of the Appalachian Trail, 2.4 miles. The trail is a not-too-visible dirt road crossing Elliotsville Road at Big Wilson Bridge. Turn left on the trail and follow it to the Little Wilson Forest Service campsite. From there, follow the white blazed trail 1.3 miles to a blue blazed trail. Turn left on this trail and

Bird on commemorative plaque along Ocean Drive
on the east side of Acadia National Park, Maine.

follow it to the falls.

High Cut Hill Trail, 0.9 miles. Access is by Maine Route 15 to West Charleston. From there turn west 3.2 miles to a dirt road marked "Fire Tower." The trail starts 4/5 mile down this road at the second pasture gate, passes through a pasture before climbing the High Cut Hill Mountain (955 feet) and offering a panoramic view of the surrounding country.

Mount Kineo Trails, one to two miles. Mt. Kineo is accessible from the town of Rockwood, on Maine Routes 6 and 15, some 29 miles east of Jackman where Route 6 joins U.S. 201. Moosehead Lake forms part of the western boundary of Piscataquis County.

Climbing Mount Kineo (1,806 feet) above Moosehead Lake starts with a boat trip from Rockwood, provided during the summer months for a small fee by the Mount Kineo Hotel. There are three trails to the summit, which towers 800 feet above the lake. The Chain Trail, steepest of the three, leaves from the 12th hole of the hotel's golf course. The Bridle and Indian Trails both leave from the hotel and pass together under Kineo flint cliffs before splitting. The Bridle Trail, easiest to climb, follows the base of the mountain awhile before starting up. The Indian Trail, most scenic, follows the cliff tops.

Squaw Mountain Trail, 6¼ miles. Access to the trail is off the Scott Paper Company road ½ mile west of Maine 15. The Scott Road is just north of the bridge over Squaw Brook, 5¼ miles north of Greenville.

Squaw Mountain (3,196 feet) is southwest of Moosehead Lake and provides some spectacular views. The trail is fairly difficult in places, rising almost vertically with rocks forming places to step. (The peak also may be reached via ski lift).

Gulf Hagas Trails near White Cap Mountain. Take Maine 11 5½ miles north from Brownville Junction. Here signs on a gravel road will direct you to the Katahdin Iron Works, where the caretaker will collect a nominal fee for use of the area. Trails begin at the iron works.

The west branch of the Pleasant River has cut a narrow canyon through slate walls in this area, forcing the river into a collection of waterfalls, rapids, pools and chutes as it drops almost 250 feet over four miles. Although the canyon is on land owned by two paper companies, the area has been declared a Natural Landmark and the companies have agreed to leave the land intact. The trail system of the area is quite good, allowing not only an overview of the area, but side trips to waterfalls and scenic spots. Since it is quite complex, however, involving the intersections of several trails including the Appalachian, we don't recommend trying it without USGS maps for First Roach Pond, Sebec and Sebec Lake quadrangles.

The trails may be reached from the Iron Works, but it is worthwhile to stop and take a look first. Containing a beehive charcoal burner as well as a blast furnace, the Iron Works are now a State Historical

Memorial.

BAXTER STATE PARK (The Mt. Katahdin Area)

Katahdin, the first place in the U.S. to feel the sun's rays each morning, is considered by many to be the most magnificent mountain in the east. Actually, it is not one mountain, but four peaks, arranged around a Great Basin: **Hamlin** (4,751 feet) in the north, **Pamola** (4,902 feet) in the east, **South Peak** (5,240 feet) in the south and **Baxter** (5,267 feet), the northern terminus of the Appalachian Trail, in the west. The mountains are not really high — they only appear so because of the levelness of the surrounding territory — but they are rugged, so rugged that parts of the area have barely been explored.

Located eighty miles north of Bangor, near Millinocket, the Katahdin area, although enclosed by Baxter State Park, is difficult to reach. From the north, enter via Patten, Maine, on the Grand Lake and South Branch roads. From the south, the 16.2-mile dirt road from Millinocket leads to the Roaring Brook campground on the east side. From the west, the approach is via the Greenville-Millinocket road from Greenville, Maine.

The park is intersected by 140 miles of trail over 46 peaks and ridges. There are nine campgrounds, including two, Russell Pond and Chimney Pond, that are only accessible by trail. Reservations, necessary to prevent crowding, are required for both the campgrounds and the wilderness campsites. Fees in 1975 were $1.00 per person per night for tent space, with a minimum $2.00 stay. Reservations are available from the Reservation Clerk, Baxter Park, Millinocket, Maine 04462.

There are no supply stores in the park, so come prepared. Millinocket and Greenville have stores, but, as with all commercial establishments near tourist attractions, it would be wise to check the prices.

The park itself covers more than 200,000 acres of mountains, woodlands, ponds and streams, most of it bought and donated over a period of 30 years by former Maine Governor Percival Baxter — that's why the highest peak was named in his honor. Although the area has been a park since 1933, it reached its present size in 1962, as a result of his final gift.

Particularly exciting trails in Baxter include the **Knife Edge Trail**, a 1.1-mile walk from Pamola to Baxter along the edge of the Great Basin. At times this trail is only a few feet wide, with drops on either side of 1,500 feet. This is not recommended for everybody.

The **Abol Trail**, 3.78 miles from Millinocket-Greenville Road, 23½ miles northwest of Millinocket, is a short route to the summit used by Thoreau in 1846.

Hiking in Katahdin is rugged. Even the Indians thought so. They were in awe of the mountain and their legends range from making it the home of the Great Spirit to the meeting place of the Council of the Gods. One angry council member, Pamola, lived on Pamola Peak. Even today, he is considered by some to be responsible for storms in the region when he becomes displeased with people venturing onto his peak.

The Katahdin area trails are extensively documented, both textually and by map. In addition to the park publications and the Appalachian Mountain Club Guide, the Maine Appalachian Trail Club in Kents Hill, Maine, publishes an extensive guide entitled "Katahdin Section of Guide to the Appalachian Trail in Maine." The book is available from the club, so we will not duplicate its descriptions. (Write Appalachian Trail Conference, P.O. Box 236, Harpers Ferry, W. Va. 25425).

The Maine Department of Commerce and Industry in Augusta publishes a list of the 34 main trails and their lengths. These range from .43 miles to more than 22 miles with as much variation in type of trail experience required as in length.

OXFORD COUNTY

Oxford County in southwestern Maine may be divided into the Grafton Notch area and the Mahoosuc Mountain Range, and the Oxford Hills area which juts into Franklin County.

Grafton Notch State Park is accessible from Maine Route 26 about 15 miles east of the New Hampshire state line.

This 3,132-acre park is a relatively new hiking center with new areas still being opened up. Several parking areas provide access also for short scenic walks.

One of these areas, **Step Falls** on Wight Brook, is a 200-foot series of cascades off the slope of Baldpate Mountain. The ½ mile trail starts at the south end of the notch, ½ mile from the eastern part of the Pools.

Screw Auger Falls, farther north, has a large pothole called the "Jail" just west and above it, which may be reached by entering the woods 100 yards below the first highway bridge above the Falls. Travel about 170 yards east, turn south to the brook, and take the brook upstream to the falls. The "Jail" is on the right bank of this falls.

Old Speck (4,180 feet) provides some of the finest hiking in the state of Maine. In addition to the section of the Appalachian Trail known as the Old Speck Trail, there are numerous other interesting paths to and around this summit.

The **Old Speck Link Trail**, 2.5 miles, and the **East Spur Trail**, one mile, are both offshoots and alternatives to Old Speck. Both may be reached via Maine 26, about 2.6 miles northwest of Screw Auger Falls on the west side, at a place where there is a small waterway and the ground is level. They are marked and follow the Old Speck Trail before turning right.

The blue blazed Old Speck Link Trail is a fairly steep ascent to an open meadow at the top with some spectacular views. The East Spur Trail, also blue blazed, turns left from the Old Speck, and provides good variety and some nice views. This trail becomes difficult when it is icy or wet.

The "Eyebrow" is the name of the cliff forming the summit at the north end of the Notch. The **Eyebrow Trail**, 3.1 miles, together with the **Cascade Brook Trail**, 1.6 miles, form a loop offering some spectacular overviews of the surrounding mountains. Both start from a gravel pit, 1/8 mile north of the start of the Old Speck Trail on Maine 26. Both follow west for 200 yards and then the Eyebrow Trail goes straight and the Cascade Brook Trail forks to the left. The Eyebrow Trail is marked with orange blazes, and provides some spectacular woodland as well as outstanding outlooks. It is recommended that the Cascade Brook Trail be taken up and the Eyebrow Trail down to enjoy the best views. In dry weather, take water with you, particularly on the Eyebrow Trail.

The recently completed **Skyline Trail**, 3.5 miles, is perhaps the best route for backpackers from Grafton Notch to Old Speck. The views are excellent as the trail follows along the ridges, and the grades are never particularly steep. The only disadvantage is that there is no water. Access is from the west side of Maine 26, about 180 yards north of the Appalachian Trail. When you see an orange marker, walk west and climb the ledges to where the orange markers continue. This trail can also be started at the start of the Eyebrow Trail.

Baldpate Mountain (3,812 feet) is east of Grafton Notch and has two summits, the East and the West Peaks. The **Table Rock Trail**, 2.8 miles, is a magnificent climb over switchbacks, ledges, hardwood forest, and a large system of slab caves. There is a prominent ledge on the top which affords views of Old Speck, the Notch, the Eyebrow, and the surrounding area. Caution should be taken so as not to fall into the caves, which are deep, or to be cut on the sharp rock edges of the ledges. The trail begins on the east opposite the start of the Old Speck Trail off Maine 26.

The **Mahoosuc Mountain Range** runs southwest to northeast in southwestern Maine along the New Hampshire border and Maine's part of the White Mountain National Forest. The Mahoosuc Trail, running nearly 300 miles and largely following the Appalachian Trail from Gorham, N. H. to Old Speck, covers most of the range. Several short spur trails may be reached via the **Success Pond Road**, which is reached by turning right (north) on Hutchins Street in Berlin, N. H., from the east side of the Androscoggin River at the Berlin Mills Bridge. Follow Hutchins for 0.4 miles, turn left, pass through a mill yard, and find the road about 200 yards off the edge of the woods.

The **Goose Eye Trail**, three miles, is an Appalachian Mountain Club Trail heading east from a point 8.4 miles from the beginning of Success Pond Road in Berlin, and intersecting the Mahoosuc Trail. It varies from old logging road to a fairly steep ledge requiring caution on the summit. The **Carlo Col Trail**, 2.57 miles, follows along with the Goose Eye for a while before ascending separately to the Mahoosuc Trail. This trail crosses the main brook several times, but the Carlo Col Shelter, on the trail, is the last water for several miles, if you are continuing on in the mountains.

The **Notch Trail** to Mahoosuc Notch, 2.8 miles, begins at a clearing 11.3 miles along the Success Pond Road. It eventually leads to the Mahoosuc Trail at a place where the cliffs, boulders, and rock formations are extraordinary.

Green Mountain, (3,300 feet) a very attractive summit, is the highest and westernmost member of the **Bear Mountain** range, which is southeast of the Mahoosucs. Unfortunately, neither it nor its sister **Robinson Peak**, (2,800 feet) have marked trails, but they can be bushwacked to the top.

They and **Sunday River Whitecap** (3,376 feet), **Locke Mountain** (1,880 feet) and **Puzzle Mountain** (3,133 feet) offer several different types of trailless opportunity, ranging from fairly easy going on Locke or old logging roads on Puzzle, to the more difficult Sunday River Whitecap which is advised only for serious climbers. Views from all of these peaks are excellent.

To climb **Bear Mountain** (1,207 feet), for which the range was named, start (with permission from the owner) in a field reached in the following manner: Turn west on Maine 219 from Maine 4 at North Turner. After 0.4 miles, turn right, cross Bear Pond, turn left and follow the gravel road along the north shore of the pond for 2.3 miles. The trail, 2.8 miles, is the road that extends past the farm buildings.

The view from the firetower atop **Mount Zircon** (2,240 feet) near Milton is outstanding. The trail, 2.7 miles, leaves a dirt road that heads south from the highway (U.S. 2) between Abbotts Mill and Rumford. The road comes in west of a bottling plant; drive south two miles where the trail begins on its east side. Water is obtainable at the beginning of the trail, which is open to the summit although steep.

Blueberry Mountain (1,820 feet) offers a top with several open spaces for good views, particularly from the southwest. The **White Cairn Trail**, 2.5 miles, leaves from Shell Pond Road, at a point 1.1 miles west on that road from junction with Route 113, continuing just less than a quarter of a mile beyond a gate. The trail follows old logging roads before climbing to the ridge atop Blueberry. A circuit may be made with this trail and the **Stone House Trail**, 1.5 miles, which starts almost half a mile to the left beyond the gate and meets the White Cairn Trail at the top. A side trail off the Stone House leads to a pretty cascade at Rattlesnake Pool.

FRANKLIN COUNTY (also including parts of north Oxford county)

This area includes many of Maine's highest mountains, but since it has been heavily developed for skiiers, hiking opportunities are few.

The firetower atop **West Kennebago Mountain** (3,705 feet) offers

On the ferry leaving Bar Harbor, Maine, going to Nova Scotia.

outstanding views from this isolated peak. The top is reached via a firewarden's trail, two miles, off a Brown Company tote road. From Maine 16, turn north 4.9 miles west of the place where Maine Routes 4 and 16 meet the Old Cupsuptic Tote Road. After two miles, bear right at a fork, then bear right again at another fork three miles later. The trail is marked on the left with Maine Forest Service signs. The trail climbs steeply through a ravine for 1¼ miles until you reach a warden's cabin. Water is available between the trailhead and the cabin, but not between the cabin and the firetower at the summit.

Saddleback Mountain (4,116 feet) and its companion peak, **The Horn** (4,023 feet), in the Saddleback Ski Area offer many kinds of experiences for the hiker. The views from the exposed summits are outstanding. The Caves offer hours of exploration, and Piazza Rock is an interesting boulder formation. The ski area is in Franklin County north of Maine Route 4 and south of Maine Route 16. **Saddleback Trail**, 2.5 miles, is reached from the lodge at the Saddleback Ski Area. Leave your car here. The trail begins at the right of the longest chair lift, and follows the route of the lift to a point where the trail splits. The east route (turn left) is a gradual ascent that leads to the firetower at the summit. The other route is longer and ends about ¾ mile from the tower. Both intersect the Appalachian Trail. High winds on the open areas of the mountain make caution advisable.

Benedict Arnold's route to Canada is visible from the trail to the top of **Snow Mountain**, 5.3 miles (3,948 feet). To reach the trail, travel 14.3 miles north on Maine Route 27 from Maine Routes 16 and 27 in Stratton. Turn left (west) on a dirt road, follow it three miles to a fork, then follow the right road as far as it is passable, about four miles. The trail begins at the warden's cabin at Snow Mountain Pond.

The Bigelow Range, running southwest to northeast south of Stratton, offers some of the finest hiking opportunities in Maine. It is a 17-mile range highlighted by the twin "horns" **North Horn** (3,810 feet) and **South Horn** (3,831 feet), and the twin "cones" **Avery Peak** (4,088 feet) and **West Peak** (4,150 feet). East of Avery Peak is the **Little Bigelow Mountain** (3,040 feet) and farther west is **Cranberry Peak** (3,213 feet). The views of the surrounding rugged territory, including Flagstaff Lake, are superb, particularly from Avery, and the area offers not only excellent ridgecrest trail walking but several ponds and other interesting features.

The **Bigelow Range Trail**, connecting to the Appalachian Trail, may be followed for the full length of the range, 11.98 miles (to Appalachian Trail), 22.10 miles (to Avery Peak). It starts on Maine 27, one-half mile southeast of Stratton and about 100 yards northwest of the Eustis-Coplin town line. Take the dirt road east from the highway by automobile as far as possible. The trail starts in about one-half mile through a clearing. It follows a lumber road, travels along the first ledges, and is blue blazed to "The Cave" (a large outcropping of rock). The trail then follows the north edge of the ridge with good views through wooded areas to Cranberry Peak. At times, the trail might be hard to follow here. After you descend, the trail turns right, then left, then right, then left and begins to climb. At 6.4 miles, there is a view of the Horns Pond, and the Horns rock formation itself is about 17 yards to the right. In another quarter mile the Bigelow Trail ends at the Appalachian Trail which continues over the Horns to Avery Peak.

The shortest route to Bigelow's main peaks is the **Firewarden's Trail**, 8.4 miles. The trail can be reached from a dirt road running east from Maine 27 about 3.2 miles west of the Sugarloaf Ski Area access road. The Appalachian Trail access is also here. For the Firewarden's Trail, turn right (east) 1/8 mile north of the second fork on the access road. The trail is very steep for one-half mile, becomes easier, and then steep again. Although it is the shortest route, the Firewarden's Trail is not as scenic as the Appalachian Trail or the Bigelow Range Trail.

7

New Hampshire

Covered bridges and the White Mountains characterize New Hampshire. The bridges are a reminder of a bygone day; the Mountains — named for the snow that blankets them from December to the middle of April — are the here and now. Originally, they were a barrier to the early settlers who crowded along the coast and only gradually moved back through the passes. Today, the mountains, along with the hundreds of lakes, ponds, rivers, and waterfalls throughout the state, make New Hampshire a center of recreational activity in all seasons.

New Hampshire's 9,304 square miles may be divided into six geographical areas. In the Northern Hill Region, rolling grasslands mesh into wild forests. Farther south are the White Mountains. The Connecticut Valley, bordering Vermont, provides some of the best farmland in the state, while the Hill and Lake region, forming a semi-circle along the Connecticut Valley and the area south of the White Mountains, combines forested hills with hundreds of bodies of inland water. The Merrimack Valley is rolling irregular land, but the soil is deep and fertile.

The White Mountains boast most of the higher mountains in New England with 46 peaks towering over 4,000 feet. Mount Washington at 6,288 feet is the highest point in the northeastern U. S. Most of the major peaks are laced with well-marked hiking routes. The state has the most far-reaching trail system in the east, and the trails, added to the possibilities for hiking down logging roads, fire lanes, and back country roads make New Hampshire a good place to be if you want to hike.

White Mountain National Forest covers almost 725,000 acres, 46,000 in Maine and the rest in New Hampshire. Included within the forest are the Great Gulf Wilderness, 5,552 acres of land set aside to "be preserved for use and enjoyment by future generations"; the Presidential Range — Dry River Wilderness, comprising 20,380 acres, and nine scenic areas which are designated to preserve places that are particularly beautiful or unique. These are Bibbs Brook, Snyder Brook, Sawyer Ponds, Greeley Ponds, Nancy Brook, Pinkham Notch, Lafayette Brook, Lincoln Woods, and Rocky Gorge.

Permits are required for wilderness usage in the National Forest. The

Presidential Range — Dry River Wilderness year-round entry permit covers both day and night use in the area at all times of the year. A separate permit is required for each entry and is obtainable in person at the AMC Pinkham Notch Camp, any of the AMC huts, or at the New Hampshire State Parks at Mount Washington and Crawford Notch. Permits may be obtained in person or by mail from the Forest Service District Ranger Offices at Bethlehem, Gorham, Plymouth, or Conway or from the Forest Supervisor, White Mountain National Forest, P.O. Box 638, Laconia, NH. 03246.

Great Gulf Wilderness day use permits are needed to enter or pass through the Great Gulf area. A separate permit is required for each entry here also. Overnight use permits for this area are issued between June 1 and October 31. The total number of permits issued is limited to 60 and the maximum stay is four nights. Permits must be picked up by noon on the day of use. They cannot be picked up more than seven days in advance, although reservations may be made 30 days in advance.

The day use permits may be obtained from the same places that provide permits for the Presidential Range — Dry River area, while overnight permits must be obtained from the Androscoggin Ranger District Office, Gorham, NH 03581 or at the Dolly Copp Campground.

Presidential Range — Dry River permits allow camping and fires below timberline if the campsite is 200 feet from the trail or at a designated site. No camping or fires are allowed above timberline. Great Gulf overnight permit holders may camp anywhere except within a quarter mile of another camp, within 12 feet of a stream, within a quarter mile of Spaulding Lake, or within 200 feet of a trail (except at designated sites). Fires are limited to overnight permit holders from June 1 through October 31. From November 1 through May 1, day users are allowed to build fires.

One unique feature in the White Mountains is the hut system operated by the Appalachian Mountain Club. These are a series of nine huts located about a day's hike from each other on the mountain trails. The huts provide bunkrooms and meals and can save you the weight of food, sleeping gear, and tent in your pack. The company is good, too. For information on seasonal operations and to make reservations (necessary — the food has to be packed up) contact Reservations Secretary, AMC Pinkham Notch Camp, Gorham, N. H., 03581, 603-466-3994.

Camping at unsupervised state forest areas in New Hampshire is generally allowed wherever it is not specifically prohibited, subject to rules similar to those in the National Forest. At supervised parks, regulations are posted.

State parks in New Hampshire do not generally have extensive hiking trails except for those that are part of larger trail systems in the National Forest or those that are privately maintained.

Off-trail camping on state park land is not permitted. There are about

12 public campsites reasonably close to hiking trails, however. Where other regulations apply, they are posted.

The weather in the White Mountains can be treacherous. This cannot be stressed enough. Change comes suddenly in the alpine peaks above timberline. And sunny, warm, 80 degree weather at the bottom can mean 20 degrees, freezing rain, and 40 mph winds at the top.

Snow has fallen every month of the year in these mountains. Mount Washington not only has one of the lowest annual temperatures in the country outside of Alaska, but the weather observatory at the top has measured the highest wind velocity ever recorded in the world — 231 mph for one minute. The average annual wind velocity is 39 mph on this mountain (it's higher in January), and wind gusts above 100 mph every few days are not unknown.

The first thing to do is to be prepared. Wool clothing, raingear, extra emergency clothing, food, a compass, and matches are a must. Second, don't panic. When every footstep is hitting ice, and freezing rain is blocking out the landmarks, the most important thing you need is a clear head. Don't be afraid to turn back if you're having problems. The storms will lessen as you descend and your life is more important than finishing the climb. Many lives have been lost in every month of the year in these mountains, and there is no need to become another tragic statistic.

Most of the trails we discuss will be in the White Mountains, traveling, loosely, from west to east. First, however, two other mountains bear mentioning.

MOUNT MONADNOCK AREA

The first is **Mount Monadnock** (3,165 feet) in Jaffrey, about 10 miles north of the Massachusetts line. A monadnock is a mountain standing alone. The open views this provides, plus the fact that, compared to the White Mountains, a hike up Monadnock is relatively easy, have combined to make it the "most climbed mountain in America." This alone is enough reason for us not to describe it in detail here, but the *Monadnock Guide*, published by the Society for the Preservation of New Hampshire Forests, 5 South State Street, Concord, New Hampshire, does. This book not only describes the trails on the mountain, it deals extensively with the history and natural history of the area and the plant and animal life of the mountain region.

MOUNT CARDIGAN AREA

Mount Cardigan (3,121 feet) in Orange and Alexandria, is another relatively easy climb. The easiest route up is the **West Ridge Trail**, 1.3 miles. It is reached from Canaan by taking the highway to Orange, (it begins east of the intersection of U.S. 4 and Canaan Street), crossing Orange Brook, keeping right onto Grafton Road when the road forks the first time, then bearing left and turning right to Hoyt Hill. In 1/8 mile is the State Reservation entrance, from which a road leads one-half mile up past some cabins to a parking area and the start of the trail. The trail is marked on the ledges by white blazes and cairns. It intersects several other trails on the way up and passes one shelter, the Hermitage. The trail goes to the firetower.

The **Hurricane Gap Trail**, 0.9 miles, commemorates the hurricane of September 21, 1938. It starts at the Hermitage on the West Ridge Trail, crossed the col, and merges with the Clark Trail.

The **Clark Trail**, 3.5 miles, marked in green, starts at a point 0.6 miles before the Cardigan Lodge and 0.8 miles past the red school house on the road to the Lodge. From Alexandria, take the road going northwest 4.5 miles. One mile past Knudson is the Lodge. The trail starts off this road. From its starting point on a ridge, the trail is first a side road, but gradually ascends into the State Reservation, goes through open woods, enters the Cathedral Forest, crosses several other trails, passes a brook flowing from a spring which is the last water for more than half a mile, and finally, reaches the firetower at the summit.

The **Skyland Trail**, 4.4 miles, marked in pink, crosses five of the six mountains extending south and southeast from Cardigan. It travels from the bridge about 0.3 miles from the start of the West Ridge Trail, to Alexandria Four Corners; (about 4.5 miles west of Alexandria) and crosses Rimrock (2,900 feet), Mount Gilman (2,620 feet), Crane Mountain (2,400 feet), Grafton Knob (2,300 feet), and Church Mountain (2,280 feet).

THE WHITE MOUNTAINS

Mount Moosilauke (4,810 feet), in the southwestern area, is not too hard to climb and has one of the best views. It should not be approached lightly, though. Although it is not too high, a large area is above timberline. In the winter, it is possible to be blown off the rocky, craggy peak. The Dartmouth Outing Club used to maintain a cabin with cooking and sleeping gear near the top, but these were removed due to overuse and the cabin is now for emergency use only. There is no camping allowed in the area. (Take Route 112 about five miles northwest past Kinsman Notch to Noxon Road, which ends at Tunnel Brook. Noxon Road is 1/3 mile southeast of Route 116.)

The **Tunnel Brook Trail**, 6.5 miles, runs from Noxon Road at Tunnel Brook to the North and South Road, following Tunnel Brook for most of the way.

The **Benton Trail**, 3.5 miles (past Tunnel Brook Trail), which used to be a bridle path, leaves Tunnel Brook 1.4 miles south of Noxon Road. The trail comes up through the South Wall of Little Tunnel Ravine. It then climbs fairly gradually through evergreen forest, crosses a flat, crosses the treeline 0.3 miles below the top, and finally, reaches the top.

The **Carriage Road**, five miles (a former actual road), starts at Moosi-lauke Inn 2 miles from NH 118, at a place called Breezy Point. To reach Moosilauke Inn, go northeast from Warren on Route 118, take the first turn to the right after the Glencliff cutoff two miles to Breezy Point. The trail ascends to the south ridge, and continues to ascend in easy grades. At 1.6 miles, the trail to the abandoned Ravine Lodge turns right. This is followed by a series of switchbacks and junctions with other trails, including, at about 4.1 miles, a 0.1-mile trail climbing to the top of Moosilauke South (4,560 feet). (The next section, leading to North and South peaks, is a cairn-marked, exposed, ridgewalk. It should not be tried in bad weather.) There are some good views from a point midway between the North and South Peaks, and the ruins of a small house at the top.

The **Gorge Brook Trail**, 2.7 miles, connects the abandoned Ravine Lodge with the summit. (Ravine Lodge reached off the Carriage Road Trail above.) It is very lovely in places. The trail first follows Gorge Brook, then climbs fairly steeply through some fir and other trees, then ascends to the east ridge for some views of the Pleiades Slides and the surrounding peaks. The views continue past timberline and to the cairn-marked route to the top. One advantage of this trail, besides its scenic beauty, is that there is plenty of water along the way.

The **Snapper Ski Trail**, 1.1 miles, follows the Gorge Brook Trail for 0.2 miles, then ascends fairly steeply for a junction with the Carriage Road and the top. The Snapper Ski Trail starts at Ravine Lodge, climbs, then turns right into Carriage Road. It is a not-too-difficult climb up Moosilauke's south peak.

The **Franconia Range** includes Mount Lafayette (5,249 feet), Mount Lincoln (5,108 feet), Little Haystack (4,513 feet), Mount Liberty (4,460 feet) and Flume (4,327 feet). This range offers some good views, but can be dangerous, as described below.

The **Greenleaf Trail**, 3.25 miles, leads to the summit of Mount Lafayette. It is reached at the north end of Profile Clearing, on the east side of US 3 as you go north through Franconia Notch. It ascends via switchbacks and zigzags past some nice views and rock formations. As it rises more steeply caution should be observed as loose stones become slippery when the weather is wet. At 2.07 miles, a reservoir is passed, and, at 2.15 miles, the Greenleaf Hut is reached. This hut can house 46 people, is open from the middle of June to the middle of September, and overlooks Eagle Lake. It is 7.75 miles from the Galehead Hut, (the Garfield Ridge Trail leads to Galehead from Greenleaf) which is the next nearest hut. From the hut, the trail first dips, then ascends gradually to the summit.

The **Falling Waters Trail**, 2.8 miles, starts across from the Lafayette Forest Service Campground on the east side of US 3, and climbs Little Haystack. The trail passes four waterfalls — Walker Cascade at 0.3 mile,

Stairs Falls at 0.9 miles, Swiftwater Falls at one mile, and Cloudland Falls at 1.4 miles. (There are two additional falls at Cloudland's head.) The trail ascends via switchbacks and then graded sections before Cloudland Falls, comes out for a view, continues to climb, passes under Shining Rock Cliff, enters forestland and passes the timberline about 500 feet from the summit.

The **Franconia Ridge Trail**, five miles, connects the Greenleaf and Falling Waters Trails, and goes on to Mount Liberty and Mount Flume. (Mount Lincoln is halfway between Mount Lafayette — the end of the Greenleaf Trail — and Little Haystack — the end of the Falling Waters Trail.) The ridge between Lincoln and Little Haystack can be treacherous. It is a knife edge with a sheer drop on each side, and, in wet or windy weather it is very dangerous. In addition, the rock cairns above timberline on this trail are frequently hard to follow in bad weather as they are not particularly prominent. From Little Haystack the trail descends into the woods, which are followed to Mount Liberty. The Liberty Spring Shelter may be reached by following a fork to the right before reaching the mountain, for a quarter mile. There is water at this shelter. The trail climbs Liberty, descends slightly, and then climbs Flume. The trail ends .09 miles past the summit of Flume at the Flume Slide Trail.

The **Flume Slide Trail**, 3.45 miles, is reached from a point 150 feet above the head of the Flume, which is a well-known narrow gorge in the Franconia Notch area. Go through the Flume entrance at the south corner of the Flume Store (At the Flume 1/3 of the way north through Franconia Notch.) At this point you will be on the wide, gravel Wildwood Trail. Take this 500 feet, turn right on the Boulder Trail, and continue .07 miles to where both the Flume Slide and Liberty Spring Trails begin. The Flume Trail is on the right. The trail follows logging roads to the slide. Caution is urged on the slide due to the poor footing which becomes even worse in wet weather. The trail is marked in white on the slide. Near the top, the trail enters woods, continues to climb and emerges at the Franconia Ridge Trail. The only water that can be counted on in this trail is below the slide. Allow extra time either climbing or descending the Flume Slide Trail, since the footing is so poor.

The **Liberty Spring Trail**, 3.45 miles, beginning at the point described above, climbs to the Franconia Ridge Trail just north of Mount Liberty. The Ridge Trail leads to the summit. Liberty Spring Shelter, and water (mentioned above) are on this trail.

Various combinations of hikes can be arranged along Franconia Ridge. Since the best part of the trail is between Lafayette and Liberty, a good one-day trip might involve going up the Liberty Springs Trail and down the Greenleaf. If you have more time, plan on staying at the Greenleaf Hut, go up the Greenleaf Trail, and continue over the ridge to the Flume.

Mount Garfield (4,488 feet) is north of Lafayette. The **Garfield Trail**, 5 miles, starts at the end of a road reached by turning south off Route 3 about 20 yards west of the Gale River Bridge, and driving 0.8 miles. The trail first follows a logging road, then a tractor road. As the trail heads south, it ascends more and more steeply, reaching a section of switchbacks after about 2.2 miles. Shortly after the switchbacks, a junction with the Garfield Pond cutoff on the right is reached at 4.5 miles. This may be taken to the Garfield Pond Shelter. The trail continues, joins the Garfield Ridge Trail and reaches the summit.

The **Garfield Ridge Trail**, 6.53 miles, connects Lafayette to South Twin, joining, for a time, the Garfield Trail. From Lafayette, the trail follows the ridge, descends, climbs toward Mount Garfield, passes the Garfield Pond cutoff (to Garfield Shelter—.09 miles) at three miles, climbs Mount Garfield and reaches the Galehead Hut. The Galehead Hut is located on the ridge between Mount Garfield and the Twin Mountains.

The **Pemigewasset Wilderness Area** is a loosely defined area east of Franconia Ridge. Main automobile access is via the Kancamagus Highway (NH 112) which cuts right through the mountains. There are no huts in this area, but there are six shelters. The main hiking access is via the Wilderness Trail.

The **Wilderness Trail**, 8.7 miles. The trail starts at the junction of the Kancamagus Highway and the East Branch of the Pemigewasset River, at a point just west of the bridge over the river, about 4.7 miles from Lincoln.

The trail follows an old railroad bed. At 2.7 miles from the starting point, a side trail leads to the Franconia Brook Shelter; and, from there, another path leads to the spectacular Franconia Falls. There is another shelter at five miles and several junctions with other trails. The trail ends at Stillwater Junction where it meets the **Carrigain Notch Trail** leading either northwest to **Desolation Shelter** in another one-half mile, or southeast out on the Sawyer River Road.

The **Black Pond Trail**, .83 miles, is a short offshoot of the Wilderness Trail. It leaves it to the left at 2.4 miles, follows a logging trail for a time, then follows the Black Pond outlet to Black Pond itself.

The **Franconia Brook Trail**, 7.2 miles, is a link between Garfield Ridge and the Wilderness Trail. It leads from a point 1.2 miles east of Mount Garfield and 1.3 miles west of the intersection of the Garfield Ridge and Gale River Trails, to a point on the Wilderness Trail 50 yards east of the Franconia Brook bridge. Following logging roads and the railroad grade, the trail at 2.2 miles passes the No. 13 Falls waterfall and the 13 Falls Shelter, and comes within 80 yards (turn right) of the Camp 9 Brook Shelter after 6.9 miles.

The **Bondcliff Trail**, six miles, starts 100 feet west of Black Brook

crossing on the Wilderness Trail, at the Camp 16 clearing, and travels to
two of the summits of the Twin Range: Mount Bond (4,714 feet) and
Mount Guyot (4,589 feet). The trail goes along logging roads and old
stream beds, crosses Black Brook eight times, travels up two switchbacks, over Bondcliff ridge, to the Summit of Mount Bond, down into
the col and up Mount Guyot. The last place you can be sure to find
water on this trail is at the sixth crossing of Black Brook. On the ridges,
if visibility is poor, remember to keep to the east. A quarter mile side
trail leads from the col to Guyot Shelter, which is one of the best places
to watch the sun rise.

Mount Carrigain (4,680 feet) in known for its views. The trail to the
summit begins 2.05 miles from Route 302 on the Sawyer River Road.

After about 1-1/3 miles the trail joins a logging road, which should
be followed straight. After about three miles, the trail rises steeply and
turns into zigzags ascending Signal Ridge. The trail enters forestland on
the ridge, ascends again and comes out among the trees on the mountain. There is a steel tower on the summit. Water is available at 3.1 and
3.5 miles and at an abandoned fire warden's cabin on the ridge.

Mount Chocorua (3,475 feet) is a cone-shaped rocky mountain south
of the Kancamagus Highway (N.H. 112) and southeast of the Pemigewasset Wilderness. It is quite lovely, with a pool at its feet, and is not
too difficult to climb. It has several trails.

The Piper Trail, 4.1 miles, is an ascent from the east. Access is on
N.H. Route 16 at the Piper Trail Cabins and Restaurant. The trail does
not begin to really climb for almost two miles. At 3.05 miles, Camp
Penacook Shelter is reached. The trail then rises to the ledges which are
marked with yellow paint, and to the summit.

The Brook Trail, 4.2 miles, an approach from Wonalancet, offers
some beautiful scenery. Go to Fowler's Mill road between Route 113 A
and Chocorua Lake. The Paugus Mill road runs north of that road and in
2/3 mile, the Liberty Trail, 4.5 miles, turns right and the Brook Trail,
300 yards later, branches left. It follows wood roads through fine forestland, ascends gradually, then reaches the steep Farlow Ridge ledge. The
trail is marked with yellow paint and cairns on the ledge. Before the
summit is reached, it is joined by the Liberty and Piper Trails. (There
used to be a toll on the Liberty Trail — the Brook Trail was constructed
as an alternative.) The Jim Liberty Cabin with stove and beds is 3.97
miles from the trailhead.

The Presidential Peaks, the most interesting range in the White Mountains, are a series of eight peaks, all reaching above timberline. They
stretch northwest from Crawford Notch. Several of them are named for
former presidents. They include Mount Washington (6,288 feet), the
highest mountain in the northeast, at the head of the ridge, followed
by Mount Clay (5,532 feet), Mount Jefferson (5,715 feet), Mount
Adams (5,798 feet), which has two minor peaks: John Quincy Adams

(5,470 feet) and Sam Adams (5,585 feet), Mount Madison (5,363 feet) and Pine Mountain (2,404 feet). Just slightly lower than the Smokies, the Presidentials, particularly Mount Washington, offer much more rugged hiking.

There are public campgrounds accessible to these peaks at Dolly Copp Campground and at Gorham. There is parking at Randolph East, Lowe's Store, Appalachia, the Dolly Copp Campground, Pinkham Notch Camp, the Glen House Site and Marshfield. There are also places to leave cars at some of the high points on the highways.

Probably the best way to see the Presidentials is via the **Gulfside Trail**, between the Madison Hut and Mount Washington's summit. With the exception of Mount Washington, it does not touch any peaks, but it does go through all the major cols.

The **Madison Hut** is open from the middle of June to the middle of September and sleeps 76 people. It is reached via the **Valley Way Trail**, 3.47 miles, which starts at the parking space at Appalachia. This is the most direct route to the hut and the best in bad weather. Unfortunately, although the trail used to be nicely graded, much of it has washed away and might be rocky. After the first two miles, the trail becomes fairly steep.

The Gulfside Trail is marked so as to be followable in bad weather. There are large stone cairns with a yellow stone on top of each, which can be seen even through snow or fog, showing the way. And snow and fog should be expected on this trail. If you are caught in bad weather, try to make it to a shelter or hut. If this is impossible, just go down into one of the ravines. Exposure has proven fatal many times along these paths and you are much safer off trail in a ravine than on the ledge. It is not advisable to be hiking here without a topo map and compass.

The first section of the Gulfside Trail, 2.25 miles, runs from the col between Mounts Madison and Adams and ends at Edmands Col (4,930 feet) between Adams and Jefferson. There is shelter here for emergencies only. Camping is not permitted.

From Edmands, 3.8 miles, the trail enters a steep climb over rocky terrain, and passes a good view at Dingmaul Rock. There is a loop trail to Mount Jefferson passed shortly thereafter that will only add about 0.4 miles to your total. This section of the trail ends at the Clay-Jefferson col.

From this col, the rough **Mount Clay Loop** splits from the Gulfside Trail to make its ascent up Mount Clay. Its views are much better, although it adds about 20 minutes to your trip and has no water. The trails reunite behind Mount Clay in the Clay-Washington col. About .12 miles further on, the Westside Path leads to the **Crawford Path** and the Lakes-of-the-Clouds Hut in the Washington-Monroe col. This hut is also open from mid-June to mid-September and can house up to 90 guests.

Clay-Washington col: 4.9 miles. Lakes-of-the-Clouds hut: 6.77 miles.

From the Clay-Washington col, the trail ascends Mount Washington, reaching the summit in 6.25 miles.

A good two-night trip can be planned by utilizing both the Madison and Lakes-of-the-Clouds Huts. The Lakes-of-the-Clouds may also be reached from the Marshfield Cog Railway station via the **Ammonoosuc Ravine Trail**. This trail offers magnificent views and fairly safe weather due to being below scrub line to within about 100 yards of the hut. The trail ascends first gradually, then quite steeply with views of two waterfalls coming together in a gorge. (You have to climb out to a ledge to really see this. Be careful, but the view is worth it.) After emerging from the scrub close to the hut, the trail follows a line of cairns right to the hut. 2.46 miles.

There are three ways up Mount Washington: one is by automobile on the toll road, one is via the cog railway, and the third is on foot. It is a good thing to remember that the railway and the road form a basically east-west line across the mountain. If you really think you're lost at any point, make your way north or south in as direct a manner as possible, and eventually, you should reach one of these routes.

The **Tuckerman Ravine Trail** follows a glacial path up Mount Washington and is the shortest path from the east. It starts at Pinkham Notch Camp on the west side; and, at first follows the Fire Trail or tractor road. After 3/8 miles, there is an excellent view of the Crystal Cascade. After this, the trail ascends first via two long switchbacks, then by just a steep grade. At 2.4 miles, the Herman Lake Camping Shelters are reached. The Herman Lake Shelters, four of which are around the Lake and six of which are nearby, can sleep about 10 people each. There is also a "cook shack" with coin operated stoves and the possibility of firewood. There is a $1.00 fee for use of the shelters and a 50c fee for open camping in the area.

After passing Hermit Lake, the trail begins to rise, and after 3.1 miles reaches the Snow Arch on the left. This arch does not always form although at times snow remains here until late summer. If the arch has formed, do not go near it or attempt to cross over or under it. At least one person has died in the attempt, and huge pieces of snow weighing tons are apt to break off at any time. If the snow completely covers the trail, take a detour over the Lion Head Trail (go back to 2.3 miles and turn left). Also be careful if you are climbing the headwall not to let loose any rocks as these may cause danger to others.

The trail turns left, goes under a cliff and begins to climb up a grassy ledge. At 3.6 miles Tuckerman Junction is reached. The Tuckerman Crossover leads southwest to the Crawford path near the Lakes-of-the-Clouds Hut and other paths lead to other trails. The trail turns right and climbs the rocks to the auto road on the mountain's top. This last section is marked by cairns and painted rocks. 4.1 miles.

The **Carter-Moriah Range** is east of the Presidentials. The **Carter-Moriah Trail** connects its two namesake peaks, Mount Carter (4,843 feet) and Mount Moriah (4,047 feet). It is reached by traveling east on US 2 from Gorham, until the road ends and the trail begins on the left. The trail follows a path, then logging roads, then climbs gently to a ledge with a view of Mount Madison, and continues on to climb Mount Surprise. From here the trail covers wooded ledges until the summit of Moriah, open, and with panoramic views, is reached. The trail descends, then ascends toward the **Imp Shelter cutoff** which may be taken right a short distance to the **Imp Shelter** (3,500 feet). One mile. The trail continues southwest, making the steep climb to reach North Carter at 7.8 miles. The trail goes south across the ridge from here, passing some good views of Wild River Valley, crossing some boggy depressions that may be wet, and reaching Middle Carter, then South Carter, and descending 500 feet to Zeta Pass. The trail then climbs 700 steep feet to Mount Hight which has some expansive views, and descends, steeply, to the Carter Notch Hut. This hut is open from the middle of June to the middle of September and holds 40 guests. 13.9 miles.   ı

The **Great Gulf** is a glacial valley loosely surrounded by the Presidential Peaks and the line of the Carter-Moriah trail. Leaving your car at the Dolly Copp Campground (just off Route 16), it is a good place to hike into for day trips up to the various Presidential Peaks. The **Great Gulf Trail** extends 7.76 miles through the Gulf, connecting Route 16 at Glen House to the summit of Mount Washington. It provides starting points for other Gulf trails and passes two of the three Gulf Shelters.

The **Six Husbands Trail** connects a point 4.42 miles from Glen House on the Great Gulf Trail to the summit of Mount Jefferson. It was named for the husbands of a Pocasset Queen, Weetamoo, who also has a waterfall named in her honor. The trail descends, crosses the West Branch and climbs the southwest bank of the stream from Jefferson Ravine. This stream is the last sure water. The trail follows the stream a bit, turns west, passes some boulders, and climbs two ladders. It passes a cave which is full of snow in August, and passes under a ledge to climb two more ladders. From here there is a good view, and the trail follows the ridge crest to come out on the North Knee of Jefferson where the ascent becomes easier. At this point, the trail is marked by cairns. It becomes steeper as the Jefferson cone is climbed and a mound of snow is passed, continuing west past the Gulfside Trail to the summit. 2.2 miles.

The **Adams Slide Trail** connects Mount Adams to the Six Husbands Trail. Its 2,308 foot climb over 1.25 miles is probably the White Mountains' steepest ascent. It starts at a point in the ravine between Mounts Adams and Jefferson, on the southwest bank of the brook coming from Jefferson Ravine. The trail climbs the slide to first turn east into the forest and then emerge on the barren south ridge of Mount

Adams. The cairn-marked trail climbs the ridge to the summit. Caution is urged on the slide, especially if coming down. 1.26 miles.

The **Sphinx Trail** is important for anyone planning to climb Mount Clay or the south side of Mount Jefferson, since it is an escape route in case of storms. It leaves the Gulfside Trail north of the Clay-Jefferson Col and descends to the Great Gulf Trail ¾ mile above the numbers 1 and 2 Great Gulf Shelters. One mile (descent 1,400 feet).

The **Mahoosuc Range** runs east of the main White Mountain Range through the Maine-New Hampshire border. These mountains are lower than most of the other ranges, nonetheless they provide some worthwhile hiking experiences. The **Mahoosuc Trail**, 27.24 miles, is a path along the entire length of the range, beginning at Gorham and reaching to Old Speck (see Maine), with many side trails into the range. The trail itself makes a nice three-day trip, although car shuttling involves a fairly lengthy ride.

The **Mahoosuc Notch Trail**, 2.75 miles, leads to very interesting cliffs and boulder formations. It starts at a clearing at the beginning of Success Pond Road, follows a logging road at first, and then a trail through the woods which climbs to a beaver pond. Where the trail meets the Mahoosuc Trail, the valley suddenly changes to one of incredible chamber formations. To fully enjoy the Notch, its high cliffs, and formations, pass through it and travel along the Mahoosuc Trail for a bit.

Although most state parks in New Hampshire do not have extensive hiking trail networks, they are not totally without opportunity. **Bear Brook State Park**, for example, in Allentown off Route 28, is the largest state park and has about 30 miles of hiking trails as well as camping facilities.

Mount Sunapee State Park, in Newbury, off Vermont Route 103, has year-round facilities for downhill skiing and other winter sports. In addition to several hiking trails, including one beginning at the 2,700-foot summit and ending at Lake Solitude, there are several miles of cross-country skiing trails that are used for hiking, too. Among these are the **Base Area Loop**, a 1¼-mile trail beginning near the base of the Elliot T-Bar. The trail passes through a grove of pine trees, crosses to the Northeast Chairlift, runs next to the parking lot, travels through a mixed forest, then a softwood forest, passes a sewage lagoon and returns to the beginning. It is marked in orange.

The **South Province Ridge Trail**, one mile, marked in yellow, begins just below the top of the Province Chairlift. The trail follows the crest, turns into a hemlock grove, follows a logging road, crosses Province Slope, and ends at the highway entrance near the No. 2 parking lot.

The **North Province Ridge Trail**, 1.12 miles, marked in red, begins at the point where the South Province Trail and the Base Area Loop both end. It rises gradually through pine and spruce forest, with a view of the trail network and ski lift system. It ends near the Province Chairlift and may be combined into a loop with the South Province Ridge Trail.

Vermont

Vermont is the Green Mountain State; *Les Verts Monts* the early French explorers called her peaks. Nestled between New York's Adirondacks to the west, the White Mountains of New Hampshire to the east, and Massachusetts' Berkshires to the south, Vermont's summits offer the hiker great variety in walking opportunities.

Vermont covers an area of 9,609 square miles. The Green Mountains split the state down the middle from north to south. The Hogback Range north of Bristol and the Granite Mountain ranges near Barre are considered a part of the Green Mountain group. The Taconic Mountains extend into the southwestern corner of the state, and the White Mountains of New Hampshire reach into Vermont in the northeast.

Other sections of the state include the Champlain Valley along Lake Champlain, the Connecticut River Valley, and the Vermont Valley in the west which includes several river beds.

New England atmosphere surrounds you in Vermont, but with a difference. Industrial development has not left a heavy mark on the state. People are much more bound to agriculture and logging than to factory schedules and the hustle of city life. This has been true throughout the history of the state. As settlers moved into the Green Mountains, the first crop they were able to harvest was timber from the rolling hills. The first sawmill was established in 1739.

The fertile valleys were farmed first, and plots of cleared land spread out from the small villages. These steady New England farmers never yielded to the pressures of the industrial revolution, maintaining the way of life they had established with hardnosed determination.

At times they needed all of that determination. Revolutionary War heroes Ethan and Ira Allen not only fought off the British, they and their Green Mountain Boys had to ward off New York and the Continental Congress as well when competing land claims forced them to form their own republic in 1777.

Vermont's weather is typical of New England. Extremes of temperature are likely, and the weather can change at a moment's notice. Summers are usually short. Hot days are rare, and in the mountains, things tend to cool after sundown. Winters are cold and long with heavy

83

snowfall, particularly in the mountains.

At one time, pumas roamed the Green Mountains, but the last recorded killing of this animal was in 1881. However, sightings have been reported on several occasions since then.

There are over 700 miles of hiking trails in Vermont, ranging from short walks in the valleys to major backpacking routes. Two hundred and fifty miles of trails are located in state and national forests, although most of these are constructed and maintained by private groups.

Most of the high mountains in the southern half of the state are within the boundaries of the Green Mountain National Forest, which was formed in 1932. The Forest is divided into two large parcels, one north, and the other, south, of Rutland. Many of the trails in the forest were built by the CCC.

Two north-south routes provide road access to the Green Mountains. U.S. 7 skirts the western boundary of the Green Mountain National Forest, while Vermont Route 100 follows the eastern boundary. Parking facilities — lots and clear pull-off areas — are provided at or near trailheads, especially in the National Forest.

The Vermont Agency of Environmental Conservation maintains 41 parks throughout the state, with 29 of them having hiking or nature trails. There are 36 state campgrounds with 2,100 sites ranging from facilities for trailers to primitive campsites. Only two state forests — Groton and Coolidge — have backpacking campsites accessible only on foot. Since camping is prohibited on state land other than in campsites most state lands can be used only for day hikes.

A three-day primitive camping permit costing $1.00 is required to camp in Groton and Coolidge. Other campsite fees vary, depending on the type and location of the site. Most campgrounds are open from the Friday before Memorial Day until October 12. However, these dates may be subject to change due to weather or other circumstances. Campsites are usually offered on a first-come, first-served basis. Reservations may be made by writing the Department of Forests and Parks in Montpelier before May 1 and at the specific park after that date.

The major trail in Vermont is the famed Long Trail stretching from North Troy near the Canadian border to Blackinton, Mass. The trail traverses the higher summits of the middle ridge of the Green Mountains.

Conceived in 1910 by James Taylor and the newly formed Green Mountain Club, the trail was completed in 1931. The main trail is 262 miles long, but 98 side trails add 174 miles, creating a system of 436 miles of trails. The main trail is blazed with white markers while the access routes are blazed in blue. There are 71 shelters — an average of one every four miles — with bunks for six to eight people. The Green Mountain Club maintains most of the trail and 49 of the shelters. The

Forest Service, the Middlebury Mountain Club, and others maintain the rest.

The Long Trail has been described in detail in the GMC guide book, "The Long Trail—A Footpath in the Wilderness," available from the Green Mountain Club, Inc., P. O. Box 94, Rutland, Vt. 05701. Since this book is readily available, we will describe only the particularly noteworthy areas and those sections which are used in conjunction with other routes.

All of the trails we describe in Vermont are in the Green Mountains. Loosely, they are described from south to north.

Mount Equinox Trail, three miles round trip. Head north on U.S. 7 from Manchester, Vt. Take Seminary Road (the first left) around the Burr and Burton Seminary. Then take the first right into a driveway leading behind the school. Leave your car in the parking area. Go up to the athletic field and cross it to the far left corner. The trail is unsigned but well traveled, with blue blazes apparent as you enter the woods.

At 3,816 feet, Mt. Equinox is the highest peak in Vermont not on or connecting to the Long Trail. In the 19th century, many trails covered its slopes, linking settlers' homesteads. But as the settlers returned to the easier life of the lowlands, the unattended trails grew over and became not readily passable. Only the Burr and Burton Trail leading to the summit is easy to follow.

Gradually meandering upward from the athletic field, you will begin to follow an old road that will straighten out. Soon, a yellow-blazed path goes off toward the left. Staying on the blue-blazed road, you will encounter a fork at approximately 0.4 miles. Bear left and cross an intersecting road at 0.6 miles. At 0.7 miles, bear left at a fork and right at the next fork. This is the last decision that you will have to make for a while, the trail being quite obvious from here. It is also your last rest, since the trail continues persistently upward to the two-mile mark.

"No Trespassing" signs are soon encountered, but these do not pertain to individuals without firearms. At 2.5 miles, a red-blazed trail intersects; pass it, following the yellow blazes. Very soon bear right onto the trail to the summit. At 2.6 miles, the Lookout Rock Trail exits right. Go left across open rock, to the top.

Those of us who had expected to encounter civilization only as part of the view will be disappointed to find the summit rather developed. The Equinox Skyline Inn and accompanying road to it are situated nearby. Various radio towers also share the advantage of this high overlook. However, the view is beautiful. Massachusetts, New Hampshire, and New York are readily visible. With excellent eyesight (and/or binoculars) Mount Royal near Montreal is faintly visible to the north.

A loop on your return trip to Lookout Rock offers a good view of the Vermont Valley and Equinox Pond. Follow the Lookout Rock Trail from the summit for 0.4 miles to Lookout Rock. This is a fairly simple walk. On the way, you will encounter a small memorial erected in honor of Mr. Barbo, the dog of a former owner of Mt. Equinox, Dr. J. G. Davidson.

Your descent continues via yellow blazes to the Burr and Burton Trail junction (unsigned). Turn left onto it and go back the way you came up.

Lye Brook Wilderness Trail, 15.4 miles round trip via North Bourn Pond Shelter. Lye Brook is one of the two designated wilderness areas in Vermont. It contains 14,300 acres of woodland. As a wilderness, it is closed to motor vehicles. There are no developed facilities of any kind except for the shelters on the section of the Long Trail that passes through the area.

A free permit must be obtained before entering the area. The permit is primarily used as an information gathering device for management and planning purposes. It may be obtained from the U.S. Forest Service, Catamount National Bank Building, Manchester Center, Vt. 05255.

Take Vermont Route 11 east from Manchester Center. After one-half mile, turn right onto Richville Road. Follow this for 1.4 miles to the intersection of Lye Brook Road. Go left on Lye Brook Road for 0.2 miles and park on the side of the road.

The blue-blazed Lye Brook Trail starts on a dirt road on your left. Soon Lye Brook will appear on the right side of the trail. The road will begin to swing widely to the right. Follow blue blazes at all intersections. The trail follows the left side of the Lye Brook Hollow, tending gradually upward for the next 3.5 miles. Several small streams will be crossed. In wet seasons, the sound of rushing water will accompany you most of the way.

After the 3.5 miles, the trail tends to become almost flat. At 6.2 miles, the trail skirts to the left of a swamp and if much rain has fallen recently, the going can get rather muddy. Keep faith, because the South Bourn shelter, home for the night, is an easy two miles away.

The Lye Brook Trail intersects the Long Trail at the South Bourn shelter. There is pure drinking water here from a mountain spring. This structure and the North Bourn Pond shelter are located on Bourn Pond, a rather large body of clear water. The shelters are supplied with a caretaker from the Green Mountain Club in the summer season and a modest fee is charged for camping.

To walk to the North Bourn Pond Shelter, follow the Long Trail north around the shore of the pond for 0.4 miles. From the shore of the pond near here, one can get an excellent view of Stratton Mountain. Camping the night at either shelter is quite pleasant, but keep in mind that drinking water is conveniently available at the South Bourn Shelter.

Lye Brook Trail to Waterfalls, 4.6 miles round trip. This is a side trail off the main Lye Brook Trail. It can be either an addition to the Lye Brook Trail backpacking trip or a scenic day's excursion in itself. Remember that even when you enter the Lye Brook Wilderness for a day hike, you need a free permit from the USFS.

Follow the Lye Brook Trail from the road for two miles. Here you will see the diagonal crossing of an old railroad bed. Directly on your left will be a rock wall which was part of the railroad bed. As the bed crosses the trail, follow it to the right. This is not a cleared trail and, consequently, you will be climbing over and under logs. Follow the bed for about 1/3 mile and you will hear and see the falls. Pass through a thicket of small spruces to a deep gorge. The remains of an old trestle can be seen and to the left, the waterfalls.

Trainloads of logs crossed this trestle on their way to sawmills in the valley. On the return trip, keep your eyes open for other remnants of this industry that once flourished here. Other railroad beds can be seen at various places along the trail. Old skidways intersect your path and meander back into the hills where they aided in transporting the forest's harvest.

Keewaydin Trail to White Rocks Cliff, 3.2 miles round trip. Take Vermont Route 140 east two miles from Wallingford. Turn right on a dirt road and follow signs to White Rocks Picnic Area of the Green Mountain National Forest. Keewaydin Trail starts at the far end of the parking lot by the picnic area.

Driving north on Route 7 toward Wallingford, you can see the limestone of the White Rocks Cliffs to the east gleaming over the valley. A short but demanding hike offers a spectacular view of the valley and surrounding countryside from the top of the escarpment.

The blazing that you will follow is blue, indicating that this is an approach to the Long Trail. Soon the going will become more strenuous as you begin a relentless mile-long ascent. A few hundred feet after beginning your ascent, you will hear and see a small stream cascading down to the left of the trail. A refreshing side-trip can be made to a small waterfall that comes into view. From here it's up through birch and hardwood forest with an attractive stand of hemlock and spruce at a turn in the trail.

If it has rained recently, the going will become quite muddy from now until just near the Long Trail junction. At 1.1 miles from the trailhead you will reach the Long Trail and relief. Go south on the Long Trail for 0.2 miles, following the white blazes. Occasional dips and rises make this a gentle part of the hike. A sign and cutoff for the White Rocks Cliffs soon appears. Go right for 0.2 miles, following this trail down through ledges and pine forest, then climb up again to the edge of the cliff.

Looking west, Tinmouth is the most prominent mountain in the foreground, with the Adirondacks looming off in the distance. At the base of the cliffs, the talus from the cliffs fans out in a wide, white apron.

Pico Peak via the Long Trail, 5.5 miles round trip including side trips. From Rutland, go east on U.S. 4 approximately nine miles to Sherburn Pass. The Long Trail and the Long Trail Lodge are readily visible. Park your car at the trailhead.

This rather strenuous day hike combines several pretty views with an interesting trail. Easy access to the trailhead and the obvious markings characteristic of the well-kept Long Trail allow the hiker to concentrate on the country around him. Varying steepness and convenient accessibility to water sources make it a pleasurable hike.

Start hiking the Long Trail southward, following the white blazes. The first half mile in from the pass is rather steep, giving no rest to weary legs and pounding heart. Soon, though, the trail becomes more gradual in its ascent. At 0.6 miles a spur trail is encountered leading right to the top of the alpine lift of a ski center. From the lift site, you can see Deer Leap mountain to the north and Blue Ridge mountain to the northwest.

Return to the Long Trail heading south and at 1.1 miles, a small permanent stream is seen at the side of the trail. At this point the stream returns to the earth in sinkhole. Continue gradually upward to a spring off the trail on a short spur at the 2-mile mark. The water is cold and delicious.

A short 0.1 mile from the spring takes us to the Pico Junction. This is the north end of the loop to Pico Peak. Bear right onto this trail and continue for 0.4 miles across increasingly steep terrain. At 3,967 feet, the summit of Pico Peak affords a beautiful view to the north. Killington Peak is visible toward the south from here through a chair lift clearing.

Continue east along the Pico Loop and down 0.4 miles of steep terrain to Pico Camp. The camp clearing on Pico's east slope offers excellent views toward Killington in the south and Mount Ascutney in the southeast. Approximately 100 feet north on the Long Trail which meets the Loop Trail here, is another spring, making this scenic camp a superb lunch stop.

The return trip takes you northward on the Long Trail (white blazes) for 0.3 miles to Pico Junction and then back down the way you came.

Leicester Hollow Trail to Silver Lake, eight miles round trip. From Brandon, head east on Vermont Route 73 to Forest Dale. A mile beyond Forest Dale, the trailhead can be seen on the left side of the road.

This is a long but easy day's hike in the northern section of the

Green Mountain National Forest. The trail is an old carriage road, unmarked but obvious. It follows the sloping valley made by the Leicester Hollow Brook, which is a babbling stream of clear and delicious water. You will cross this stream several times during the hike. Follow the gradual slope of the valley until four miles from the start of the hike, when you come to Silver Lake. The quiet and beauty of this lake is preserved by its designation as a walk-in area only. No camping is permitted near the lake. A short distance from the lake is a small camping area to accommodate those inclined to stay nearby.

Snake Mountain Trail, four miles round trip. Head east on Vermont Route 125 from Middlebury. In six miles, East Street exits through the farmland on your right. As East Street becomes a dirt road, Snake Mountain will become visible on the right.

Take the fourth right-hand turn off East St. onto another dirt road. You are now heading toward and along the base of the mountain. The Ray Torrey farm soon appears as the first farm on the right side of the road. Please stop here to tell Mr. Torrey that you are going to use the trail, since you will be crossing his private land. He asks this courtesy to monitor use of the trail and extends his welcome to friendly hikers.

Now continue up the road past a field on your left. At the end of the field is an old barn with a farm road entering past it. Pull off to the left side of the road, without blocking entrance to the farm road. Since you have received the owner's permission, disregard the "No Trespassing" sign and follow the road in.

Snake Mountain is located in the westernmost part of central Vermont. Its height of 1,287 feet seems insignificant with respect to the three- to four-thousand-foot peaks to the east. Don't be deceived by this, though, because its isolation from the other mountains, and its proximity to the lower Champlain valley and New York's Adirondacks, makes the easy walk up it a worthwhile excursion. Snake Mountain doesn't derive its name from venomous slithering creatures lurking on the trail, but rather from the undulating nature of the short ridge.

Walk past the old barn and through the field behind it, and begin to appreciate the beauty of old, rolling New England farms. Follow the road into the woods at the far end of the field. The crossing of a small stream here makes the going wet and muddy, making some form of waterproof boots a must. Your ascent now begins and in about 200 feet, you will bear left at the junction of another log road. The trail is unmarked but obvious as the road is kept in good shape by frequent dirt mounds diverting the water down to the left.

The forest is open for most of the hike, with stands of white birch decorating the woods. Bear left at all major log road intersections. Soon the road begins to snake (pun intended) more directly up the slope and ultimately will follow the top of the ridge. After about 1.8 miles the trail levels off on the summit.

The rock escarpment now becomes visible on the left. Cut over at any of the several footpaths to the top of the cliff. An old foundation covers part of the top. Many years ago, an owner of the top of Snake Mountain tried to build a house here, but gave up because of vandalism. At one time an inn also was located here. Its wooden wreckage lies 100 feet to the east in the woods.

From your vantage point you can see to the west, north, and south along the Champlain Valley. The southern part of the lake is clearly visible, with the Adirondacks looming up behind it on the far side of the valley.

Battell Trail to Mount Abraham and Lincoln Peak, 7.2 miles round trip. Take Vermont Route 17 east from U.S. 7 for seven miles to the town of Rocky Dale. From Rocky Dale, head southeast toward Lincoln. In four miles you come to a left turn toward Jerusalem. Pass this and take the next public road to the left. Park at the beginning of the road.

Mount Abraham and Lincoln Peak are located at the northern end of the Presidential range of the Green Mountains. Both are located on the Long Trail. The Battell Trail serves as a relatively easy access route, making this a pleasant day's hike.

The history of the naming of Mt. Abraham and Lincoln Peak is rather involved. At first, early settlers called Mt. Abraham Potato Hill, because of its seeming similarity to a large potato mound. This name proved to be unacceptable to writers and mapmakers describing the area however, and soon the name Lincoln Mountain was adopted. This was not to honor the president, as one might think. The mountain was named after General Benjamin Lincoln, the famous Revolutionary War figure. Colonel Joseph Battell, a man determined to work toward the preservation of existing forest land in Vermont, bought the mountain and some surrounding land in the late 1800's. He decided to bring "Honest Abe" back into the picture and renamed the peak Mount Abraham. So that the general would not be cheated of his namesake, the next peak to the north, which Battell also owned, was named Lincoln Peak.

The Battell Trail is blazed in blue. It follows the old road winding gradually upward along a relatively easy grade. In two miles, you come to the white-blazed Long Trail. A short distance north, the Battell Shelter, a sturdy structure for six to eight people, is encountered. Cold spring water can be found 100 feet to the east of this. Continue north on the Long Trail as it leads toward the summit. The going becomes a bit more difficult now because you must negotiate a rocky trail that winds among outcroppings of ledges. At 0.8 miles from the Battell shelter, you will reach the 4,052-foot summit of Mount Abraham.

North, south, east and west, the bare summit offers a panoramic view. The White Mountains of New Hampshire are clearly visible to the east. Directly to the west, Mt. Marcy can be seen as the highest point in the Adirondacks which rise over Lake Champlain. The Green Mountains are visible from Killington in the south to Mt. Belvidere 50 miles to the north.

Continue north on the Long Trail. The trail re-enters the woods as you descend into the sag between Mount Abraham and Lincoln Peak. In 0.7 miles, you will cross the minor summit of Little Abe and in another 0.1 miles, you will be on the 3,975-foot summit of Lincoln Peak. The uppermost station of the Sugarbush Valley Gondola is located here. The cleared areas that surround this structure offer wide views. During the summer season, this spot may be a bit crowded because the gondola is in operation, bringing less ambitious mountain lovers up to this beautiful summit.

Forest City Trail to Camel's Hump (return by Burrows Trail), 7.5 miles round trip. Take Vermont Route 17 east from U.S. 7 to a point about five miles northeast of South Starksboro. Go north on a road branching off Route 17. Follow this road for five miles to Huntington Center. Here, head due east on a road that goes off to the right for 2.8 miles, where it forks. Park near the fork. Half a mile up the fork to the left is the Burrows Trail. To the right, the Forest City Trail begins.

Camel's Hump, at 4,083 feet, shares the honor of being Vermont's third highest mountain with Mount Ellen. Although the mountain in profile deserves its name, far more fitting is the earlier French name, Le Leon Couchant (the Reclining Lion).

Camel's Hump has long had an aura of superstition and disaster about it. Tales of buried treasure on its summit caused many a wealth-seeker to climb the mountain looking for the mysterious caves where the treasure was to be found. In the 1930's, a college student fell from a cliff and died; in 1944 an Army Air Force bomber crashed into the mountain's southern edge, killing nine and leaving the lone survivor to wait 40 hours for rescue.

But such tales aside, the wide and far-reaching views from this summit make the peak a worthwhile, though long day's hike.

Heading right at the fork, the Forest City Trail follows a logging road. You will cross over two small brooks and at 0.3 miles, come upon "Forest City," an old CCC camp. In 0.6 miles, bear right from the logging road and follow the trail as it makes its climb gradually up the side of the mountain. In 2.2 miles the trail intersects the Long Trail with its familiar white blazes. Go north on the Long Trail.

The ascent from here to the summit is a steep and rather muddy one, although views to the north and east are rewarding. After 1.9 miles on the Long Trail, the summit is reached. To the south, Mounts Ethan and Ira Allen are near. Past these is Lincoln Peak and, far off to the left, Killington and Pico Peaks. To the north, the mountains as far as

Belvidere — distinguished by white scars from its asbestos mines — and Owl's Head in Canada, are visible. To the east, Mt. Washington and the White Mountains dominate the lower Vermont mountains and valleys, while westward, Mount Marcy rises over the Adirondacks with Whiteface standing alone to the north. Most of Lake Champlain is visible.

Continue hiking the Long Trail north for 0.3 miles to where it intersects the Burrows Trail. Head left and downward on Burrows following the ridge between Camel's Hump and Bald Hill. The descent increases to a moderate slope through the forest. At 2.4 miles from the summit, the trail intersects a private road near a house. Follow the road right, to a private residence. This is the end of the Burrows Trail; your car is parked half a mile farther down the road.

MOUNT MANSFIELD

The Abnaki Indians who lived in the valleys near Mount Mansfield spoke of it as "Mose-O-De-Be-Wadso," an Algonquin name meaning "mountain like the head of a moose." Indeed, the naming of the several peaks follows this anatomical suggestion. From south to north there is the Forehead at 3,940 feet, the Nose at 4,062 feet, the Upper and Lower Lips at 3,964 and 4,030 feet respectively, the Chin at 4,393 feet and the Adam's Apple at 4,060 feet. The Chin is the highest point in the Green Mountains.

Other legends have the profile belonging to a human. One story tells of Mishawaka, crippled son of an Indian chief, who died after pulling himself to the top of the mountain to uphold the family's name. A more humorous story tells of a man named Mansfield who slid off Camel's Hump as the camel knelt for water.

Many trails of varying difficulty cover this fascinating mountain. Most lead to or include spectacular panoramic views.

Bear Pond Trail, 2.3 miles. Take Vermont Route 108 northwest from Stowe to Smuggler's Notch. The trail heads west off the road at Smuggler's Notch. It is said to contain the steepest half-mile of trail in Vermont and should only be attempted by very experienced and surefooted hikers.

Hell Brook Trail, four miles round trip. Take Vermont Route 108 northwest from Stowe to the Big Spring parking area near Smuggler's Notch. The trailhead is across the road from the north end of the parking area.

If you're in bad shape, or out for an easy day, this is not the trail for you. If, however, you want to clear out your lungs, tone up your leg muscles, and get a real workout, then this, the second steepest trail in Vermont, is where you should head.

Follow the blue blazes up, up, and up. If you're hoping for a break in your ascent, forget it until you reach the top of the ridge about 1.3

miles away. Hell Brook plunges to the left of the trail for most of the ascent. Frequently you can catch glimpses of waterfalls and cascades as the noisy water makes its way over outcroppings and ledges.

Several small tributaries of Hell Brook must be crossed, offering a good excuse for a rest and drink of cold, clear water. Because of these stream crossings, the trail often becomes quite muddy, making water-proof and sturdy hiking boots a necessity.

At several points along the trail outcroppings of rock are undercut to form natural shelters for hapless hikers caught by a surprise rainstorm. At one point, the trail leads under such an overhang and makes the going difficult over large boulders that litter its entrance.

After 0.9 miles, a junction with Hell Brook Trail Cutoff to Taft Lodge (also blue-blazed) is encountered. Stay to the right on the Hell Brook Trail and in 0.4 miles you will meet a triple trail junction. The Bear Pond Trail heads off to the right, while the Hell Brook Trail goes ahead and then west around the summit of Adam's Apple. Go left onto the Adam's Apple Trail. The 0.1 mile ascent to the summit of Adam's Apple is steep but not as taxing as the previous trail was. Soon the forest gives way to low shrubs and finally the round bare summit.

The view is splendid to the north and east, but the summit of the Chin blocks the view to the west and southwest for the most part. Lake of the Clouds lies just below you to the north. A few feet deep, this lake is trapped on the very top of the Mansfield ridge.

After a rest, head toward the Chin by going down into Eagle Pass between Adam's Apple and the Chin. Rock cairns guide your way into the low shrubs and soon you follow blue blazes again to the junction of the Long and Hell Brook Trails. Follow the white-blazed Long Trail now, upward to the Chin. The going soon becomes very steep and tricky, requiring you to climb over many ledges. In 0.2 miles, all the misery pays off as you come out in the Arctic-Alpine environment of the Chin's summit. Please stay on the trail here, since this flora is rare for the Green Mountains and its delicate roots cannot withstand the boots of the many hikers visiting it.

Look around you in any direction at the breath-taking panorama. Northward, all the Green Mountains are clearly visible to Big Jay and Jay Peak. Especially clear weather even allows Montreal's Mount Royal to be seen. To the west, all of Lake Champlain is visible, framing the Adirondacks behind it. To the east, the Worcester Mountains are clearly seen and Mount Washington and the White Mountains lie in the south-east. The Green Mountains as far as Killington lie in sight to the south. Closer up, Smuggler's Notch lies in the valley at the base of Spruce Peak, the nearest mountain to the west.

The return trip can be made via a seldom-used trail that cuts off some of the steepness of the Hell Brook Trail. Follow the Long Trail back down the way you came and stay on it past the Hell Brook and

Adam's Apple Trail junction in Eagle Pass. In 0.6 miles from the summit, you will come upon the Taft Lodge. Take the Hell Brook Cutoff Trail to the right of the Lodge for 0.7 miles to the junction with the Hell Brook Trail. This footpath is blue-blazed but not always obvious, so you'll have to keep alert for markers. It is also partially overgrown, but its very gradual descent is a welcome relief from the steep ups and downs encountered since the beginning of the hike. At the end of this trail, follow the Hell Brook Trail downward.

The going will be just as miserable as when you came up. In 0.9 miles from this junction, you're back to the Big Spring.

Sunset Ridge — Laura Cowles Trail Loop (to Cantilever Rock and the Chin), 5.7 miles round trip. Take Vermont Route 15 east from Burlington to Underhill Flats. From there, go east on a paved road for 2.8 miles to Underhill Center. Go another mile to a right turn to the Mount Mansfield-Underhill State Recreation Center and Camping Area. Leave your car at the camping area parking lot and proceed along the old road for one mile. At a sharp turn in the road, the Sunset Ridge Trail — blue blazes — is seen going off to the left.

This footpath is a very common westward approach to the summit of Mt. Mansfield. It offers challenging hiking with good views and some astounding sights along the way. Novice hikers should beware, though. This is not a simple trail. Steep ascents and descents on often slippery ground are the name of the game.

One-tenth of a mile from the trailhead, the junction of the Laura Cowles Trail appears. Bear left onto the Sunset Ridge Trail and begin a climb to Lookout Rock, 0.3 miles away. In 0.1 mile, you come across the Cantilever Rock Trail heading off to the left.

Take the Cantilever Rock Trail 0.2 miles to its end at the base of a cliff. Above you, you will see a strange geological phenomenon indeed. A horizontal needle of stone extends 40 feet from the cliff without support. Discovered in 1960 by Clyde H. and Clyde F. Smith, this rock has an estimated weight of 75 tons. It extends straight out 60 feet above the base of the cliff. A wooden ladder provides access for closer inspection.

Follow the Cantilever Rock Trail back to the Sunset Ridge Trail. Go left and upward. The going now becomes wet, steep, and slippery. The path begins to wind up and across exposed ledges. Great care is needed not to slide, and often, hiking the side of the trail with the support of nearby trees is necessary.

At 1.6 miles, you come to the junction of the Story Trail on the left. Stay right on the Sunset Ridge Trail and soon you will intersect the Laura Cowles Trail again at its upper end. Bear left, and at the 1.8-mile point, meet the Long Trail. Bear left on this white-blazed trail and in 0.2 miles, you will reach the summit of the Chin.

The return route takes you back down to the junction of the Sunset Ridge Trail and the upper end of the Laura Cowles Trail. Now follow the Laura Cowles Trail downward to the left. The trail is very steep and care is advised to avoid hazardous spills. Open ledges are crossed, but soon the trail takes refuge in the forest again. Small stands of trees decorate the way as you continue your steep descent. In a little while you will encounter a small brook that meanders and crisscrosses the trail. Do not, by the way, let the occasional orange blazes fool you. Stay on the blue-blazed trail to the junction of the Sunset Ridge Trail, and return to your car the same way you came up.

Forester's Trail, 5.4 miles round trip. Take Vermont Route 100 to Eden Mills. Head north on the asbestos mine road for about 4.5 miles to where the road makes a sharp right toward the town of Lowell. From the Warner Farm (Tillotson Mill), the trail starts on the left-hand side of the road.

Belvidere Mountain is a 3,360-foot peak in northern Vermont. The Forester's Trail is a footpath direct to its summit that is maintained by the Vermont Bureau of Forests and Parks. Though an access route to the Long Trail, this trail is unblazed but quite obvious. The going tends to be of moderate difficulty and the view in the end is worth the trip.

The trail heads west in a continuous but reasonably gradual ascent for about 1.5 miles. Then the going gets steeper as you make the ascent into the Belvidere Saddle. At 2.5 miles, the Forester's Trail intersects the white-blazed Long Trail. Just before this point, a clear spring appears. Bear left past the Long Trail, remaining on the Forester's Trail. In 0.2 miles you will be on the summit.

There is a fire lookout tower and a watchman's cabin on the summit. From the firetower's top, the views stretch for many miles. To the south, Camel's Hump is visible. Jay and Big Jay peaks are prominent to the north. To the northeast, some Canadian peaks near Lake Memphre-magog are visible in the distance. The east offers a view of the North-eastern Highlands of Vermont, and to the west, the Cold Hollow mountains loom near. Looking down to the eastern base of Belvidere, an active asbestos mine can be seen. The mine at the southern base is defunct.

Massachusetts

Hiking in Massachusetts means walking through history as well as along the trail. Reminders of its 356 years are strewn throughout the towns and countryside of this 8,257-square-mile commonwealth which separates rural New England from the crowded Greater Northeast Metropolitan Area. Hawthorne's House of the Seven Gables, Revolutionary War battlesites, memories of famous Americans from John Adams to John Kennedy, are just a sample of the literary and political heritage that Massachusetts has given to the country.

The state's terrain is as varied as its history. To many people, Massachusetts is simply Boston and Cape Cod. But the scenery changes from the Cape's summer playground of beaches and bays to what has been called the "Switzerland of America" in the Berkshires, to the lush woodland where Thoreau spent two years contemplating Walden Pond.

Geographically, the state can be divided into four regions. The coastal lowlands, including Cape Cod, Boston, and the primary urban areas, offer sandy beaches, four bays, and a surprising amount of good walks and scenery through woods, fields, and streams. The area is basically flatland, with a few rolling hills and an occasional rocky area.

Westward, the plateau or eastern upland area, more than 1,000 feet above sea level, comprises most of the state and is a land of low, rounded hills, valleys, short streams, lakes, and ponds, Thoreau's Walden among them. Mount Wachusett (2,006 feet) is the highest point in this area. It is located in a state reservation of the same name a few miles southwest of Leominster. There are excellent views from its summit, which can be reached either on foot or by car.

The Connecticut Valley area, running parallel to the Connecticut River and Interstate 91, contains the most fertile land in the commonwealth. Here there is rich, red soil and plenty of water from the river.

The most rugged areas of the state are the western uplands. They are dominated by the Taconic Range on the New York border, the Hoosac Range, and the Berkshires, all of which run north-south. Actually, the Berkshires are part of Vermont's Green Mountains. The area is one of clear blue lakes and deep valleys; the mountains themselves are hilly, long ridges. There are no "empty" mountains here — all are forested to

97

the top. The highest point in the state, Mount Greylock (3,491 feet) and the Appalachian Trail are found in this area.

Massachusetts wildlife in general is typical of that in most of eastern North America. Cape Cod is a bird watcher's delight, however, particularly in migratory season when the coast becomes a major flyway. Autumn migration is especially rewarding for observers since birds that migrate inland as far as the Mississippi River in spring tend to return south along the coast. Some years, more than six million birds have been counted in a single night.

The only thing we can say about Massachusetts weather is that it changes a lot, as is true for almost all of New England. There is more snow in the west, while seacoast chill makes eastern Massachusetts winters damp and penetrating. Temperatures are extreme in both summer and winter, so the best time for hiking is probably autumn when the air is clear and cool.

Fall color, particularly spectacular in the Berkshires, is at its prime the second and third weeks of October. (The Cape changes seasons less colorfully; nonetheless fall is also a good time to be there. More later, about cranberries.)

Compared to many other states, Massachusetts has few large wilderness areas, but it does contain a widespread network of smaller areas designed chiefly for day hikes.

The trails of Massachusetts reflect both the natural beauty of the area and its historical significance. The hiker can walk on well-marked trails through areas described by the explorers and pilgrims of the early 17th century or by the poets, philosophers, and naturalists of the mid-19th century.

In the eastern part of the state in particular, the hiker can be guided through wildlife sanctuaries or along trails designed to emphasize unusual or delicate ecosystems. Since the state is so densely populated, the integrity of these environments grows a little more precarious each year in the unprotected areas. Many of the labeled or guided nature trails are short but interesting and will help you understand more of the terrain you see on longer hikes.

There are more than 90 private and 26 state campsites in Massachusetts, along with 64 day use areas. Public fees at state sites range from $4.00 a night for full improvements and hook-ups to $1.00 for simple tent sites. Parking at day use areas is $1.00. Campsites cannot be reserved in advance and maximum stay limits are two weeks. Regulations insist that children under 13 are not left unattended while adults go hiking through the woods.

There are 21 state parks in Massachusetts, 27 state forests, and four state leased areas with recreational facilities. In addition, there are approximately 10 unimproved parks and 67 unimproved forests. Although the improved parks have marked trails, don't neglect the old forest workers' roads in these areas. (By the time you read this, there probably will be more improvements than we saw — the Massachusetts Department of Natural Resources has a habit of opening new facilities and trails regularly.)

If you live in Massachusetts, and are a senior citizen, you can get into state parks free. Massachusetts residents over 65 are entitled to use all recreational facilities of the Division of Forests and Parks except campsites, at no charge.

Massachusetts state trails are divided into foot, bridle, recreational vehicle, and bicycle trails. The Department of Natural Resources is currently compiling a bicycle atlas for the state. Many of the trails it describes — up to 55 miles long — are also suitable for hiking.

The state trails are well marked and color coded to assure that no hiker gets run over by a horse. Foot trails are marked with blue triangular hardboard markers, bridle trails with red, R.V. trails with orange, and bicycle with green. The triangular shape serves both as a blaze and a directional pointer.

When there are six inches of snow, bridle trails may be used for hiking. Also, bicycles are usually allowed on R.V. trails and on the forest and park road system.

The Massachusetts Trustees of Reservations, incorporated in 1891, maintains 41 reservations throughout the state — areas of particular geological, botanical or animal life interest. Many of these areas provide splendid scenery ranging from waterfalls and sandy beaches to pine forests and part of a dinosaur footprint. Most allow hiking but no camping. Many of these reservations are indicated on good road maps. Otherwise, write the trustees or ask at a tourist office.

The Massachusetts Audubon Society also maintains 25 sanctuaries. All but two of them have day use trails. The Massachusetts Audubon Society is the oldest in the world and the largest in any one state. If you're a birder, make your way to the Back Bay area of Boston, where the organization's main store is and records are kept, and learn something about Massachusetts' birds that should make your hikes even more enjoyable. For information on the sanctuaries and maps, write to Society headquarters in Lincoln, Massachusetts 01773 or stop at the sanctuaries.

Finally, the Massachusetts Division of Fisheries and Game manages more than 20 wildlife areas, primarily for the benefit of hunters, on which hiking is also allowed. Ask for the dates of hunting seasons on various species and remember to wear bright clothing if you venture in at those times.

TRAILS IN THE COASTAL LOWLANDS

The main attractions of southeastern Massachusetts are the sandy beaches and scenic harbors along the coast, particularly on Cape Cod.

This historic peninsula ends at Provincetown, a thriving artists' colony close to where the Pilgrim Fathers first landed.

Historically, Cape Cod has been known as a center of the fishing and whaling industries as well as for Pilgrim settlement. Today, for many hikers, the name conjures up visions of beaches crowded with sunbathers and fishermen, supported by an endless string of resorts, motels, and gift shops.

To some extent these visions are justified, although the situation has improved somewhat with the creation of the National Seashore. But the natural plant and animal communities encountered on the Cape are as diverse as those anywhere in the mountains, and well worth the trip. The trail system on the Cape is designed chiefly as a series of short nature trails operated by the National Park Service and by several conservation organizations interested in the area.

The hiker here must adapt to a number of unfamiliar conditions, one of which is property rights. An area which appears on a topographical map to offer an uninterrupted stroll along a sandy beach may in fact be fenced off or posted with no-trespassing signs. One wonders if Thoreau would have felt frustrated if his walk across Cape Cod in 1849 had been stopped short by a chain link fence which seemed to originate somewhere in the depths of the Atlantic Ocean and terminate at an asphalt road.

More important than property laws to the integrity of the Cape, though, are the laws of nature which govern the ecology of the dunes and the surrounding communities. Although the admonition, "Take nothing but pictures, leave nothing but footprints," may suffice as a guideline in a more stable environment, the dune communities, like the alpine zone, may be too fragile to withstand the impact of the hiker's boot. All the trails are well marked and should be followed. When walking along public beaches, the hiker should avoid jumping off or climbing on the dunes or in any way disturbing the vegetation whose roots stabilize the sand. Lugsoled hiking boots are not only unnecessary, they are undesirable. Sneakers are recommended; and it is advisable to carry a canteen.

In addition to the National Park Service trails described below, the Massachusetts Audubon Society, the Trustees of Reservations, and several of the local towns maintain sanctuaries, museums, and nature trails on Cape Cod. Hikers might enjoy reading Henry Beston's *Outermost House*, a description of his Thoreau-type hermitage on the outer banks of the Cape in the 1920's, or Thoreau's own *Cape Cod*, before beginning to walk. In addition, *Wildflowers of Cape Cod*, by Harold Hinds and Wilfred Hathway, makes a delightful hiking companion on a trip to the seacoast anywhere from Maine to Long Island.

One more point: Besides its scenery, Cape Cod is particularly well known for its cranberries. The annual harvest each fall means that workers must toil almost around the clock to harvest and process the fruit within 24 hours from the time it is picked from the cranberry bogs. Massachusetts produces 100 million pounds of cranberries a year, with a healthy percentage of these coming from the Cape. If you're here in season, watch the work that goes on as the berries are first submerged, then cut and gathered. You'll have a lot more appreciation for the next can you take from the grocery shelf.

There are also numerous bicycle trails on the Cape, eight miles of which start at the beginning of the Beech Forest Trail in the Province Lands area (see below). The Park Service is seeking to expand these, so check with them, whether or not you have a bicycle, since some of these trails may be used for hiking.

CAPE COD NATIONAL SEASHORE

The Cape Cod National Seashore was authorized in 1961 to "keep intact the charm and beauty of the old Cape for future generations." Although it was not able to start with unspoiled wilderness, the project does seek to save as much open space as possible. To date, the government has acquired 24,477.85 acres of a proposed 44,600 total for the completed project.

There are four official areas of the Seashore, open for visitor use: The **Province Lands, Pilgrim Heights, Marconi Station Area**, and the **Nauset** or Coast Guard Beach Section. The *Province Lands*, 4,400 acres at the tip of the Cape, were originally set aside in a conservation act by the Pilgrim fathers. Here are some of the most beautiful sand dunes on the Atlantic. The **Beech Forest Trail**, one mile, made up of the Beech Forest Loop and the Pond Loop is reached by turning right from U.S. 6 toward the Province Lands Visitor Center, at the traffic light on Race Pond Road. The Beech Forest Parking lot is on the left about ½ mile up.

The beginning of the Beech Forest Trail is marked by a box filled (hopefully) with a nature guide and trail map. Although the trail is clearly marked, some less thoughtful hikers have left the beaten path to climb up and down the dunes which surround the pond. The effects of their action and the subsequent erosion are obvious; the moving sand dunes threaten the Beech Forest and parts of the trail. Where the trail itself climbs the dunes, rustic log steps have been installed to minimize the erosion.

Although the forests of Cape Cod are now dominated by pines and oaks, early settlers found extensive beech forests such as the one encountered on the Beech Forest Loop. Forest fires, cutting, and overgrazing destroyed the soil, however, resulting in forest more suited to the dry, sandy environment. Six species of pines may now be found in this forest, two of which, Scotch Pine and Austrian Pine, are not native American species.

At *Pilgrim Heights*, two self-guided trails begin, both of them ½ mile loops. These include the **Pilgrim Spring Trail**, an interpretive path emphasizing natural and political history; and **Small's Swamp Trail**, on which you'll encounter blueberries, beach plum thickets, and bearberry heaths. To reach the trailhead, turn right off U.S. 6 about 1½ miles north of the North Truro turnoff at the Pilgrim Heights Area sign.

The lofty bluffs of the *Marconi Station Area* offer some particularly memorable views as well as a scale model of the first telegraph nearby. Access to the **Atlantic White Cedar Swamp Trail**, 1.25 miles, is gained by turning right at the light 5.2 miles north of the Salt Pond Visitor Center and following the signs to the Marconi Station parking lot. The trail begins at the observation platform next to the lot where a leaflet may be obtained which describes the plant communities. This is the most interesting and varied of the nature hikes on Cape Cod. After passing through a succession of dry upland communities, the trail leads downslope to the white cedar swamp. A raised boardwalk winds through the cedar grove.

The longer **Great Island Trail**, eight miles round trip, is also in this area. Turn west off Route 6 at the Chequesset Neck Road sign for Wellfleet. Turn south at the Town Pier sign, 0.2 miles farther on. Follow along the harbor coast 3.3 miles to a parking lot.

The box at the starting point may or may not contain a map and trail guide, but before beginning your hike, check the tide schedule as the spit connecting Great Beach Hill with Jeremy Point may be submerged when the tide is high. A canteen on this hike is essential.

The trail leaves the parking lot, dropping through a wooded section to the tidal flat. At high tide, this section of trail may be submerged, forcing you to walk along the bank.

Walking on loose sand is more strenuous than on a firm woodland trail. The impression of slipping back half a step for every one forward can become depressing when the sun is hot and your feet are wet, so be prepared.

At Great Island, the trail divides. A short spur to the left takes you to the site of the 18th century Smith's Tavern. Archeologists from Brown University have excavated this site; do not add your efforts to the project. It is illegal to remove any artifacts from the National Seashore. Return to the main trail via the same spur.

The trail leads across the height of Great Island. The forest is dominated by pitch pine. At one point the trail leaflet reads "note the fine grove of white pine." But white pine has needles in bundles of five, and if you look closely, you will discover that at this point pitch pine is the rule.

The trail then drops to near sea level where a large lush saltwater swamp must be skirted before climbing up Great Beach Hill. From the south end of Great Beach Hill, Jeremy Point is still 1.2 miles away along a narrow spit. This section should be attempted only if you are aware of the condition of the tides. From here it is possible to return the way you came or by walking along the beach on the Cape Cod Bay side of Great Island.

The *Nauset*, or *Coast Guard Beach* section, has four trails. The **Nauset Marsh Trail**, reached from the parking lot at the Salt Pond Visitor Center, is a one-mile trail emphasizing salt marsh plant and animal cycles. The **Fort Hill** or **Red Maple Swamp Trail**, ½ mile, is reached by turning right on Governor Prence Road near the Fort Hill sign, and continuing to the parking lot across from the Captain Penniman House. This trail is designed especially to point out the life cycles of swamp plants.

The **Buttonbush Trail**, 4 miles, begins to the left of the Salt Pond Visitor's Center as you face its front door. It is constructed for the enjoyment of those who are blind. A guide rope follows the trail, not only leading the way, but signaling, through the use of plastic disks or pieces of garden hose, when a trail sign or difficult section of the path occurs. Signs are in both large print and Braille, and visitors are encouraged to touch the various trees and shrubs as well as smell, hear, and feel the changes in environment that occur over the course of the trail.

Camping is not allowed within the National Seashore. Numerous private campsites, however, can be found on the length of the Cape. Many of these are open only during the summer and some cater only to enclosed rigs such as travel trailers and pickup campers. Nickerson State Park on Mass. 6A just east of East Brewster is the best bet for Cape Cod, with camping on a first-come, first-served basis.

Access to **Martha's Vineyard** is by daily ferry service during the summer and weekend service November through March from Woods Hole. There is also summer boat service from Hyannis and Falmouth. There is a state forest here where nature trails are still being developed, but the coves, beaches, cliffs, ponds and woods make Martha's a delightful place just to walk without specific guides. Woods people will like the north shore; those looking for more varied ocean scenery should head south.

There is also a quarter mile trail up **Indian Hill** to a firetower from which you can get an excellent view of the whole area. To find the tower, follow Vineyard Haven Road west for 100 yards from Tisbury. Turn right on Indian Hill Road and continue ½ mile to a crossroad. Turn right and go ½ mile to Christiantown, an Indian burial ground. The trail begins at the rear of these grounds.

For the current status of trails in **Martha's Vineyard State Forest**, stop at the office of the forest superintendent.

The *Barnstable County Agricultural Society* maintains about 110 miles of intersecting trails on the Cape. Basically bridle paths, most of

these are also suitable for hiking and are marked by paint or plastic
streamers. The area is flat, although there are occasional hills, and most
trails pass several lakes and ponds.

The trails are long, but broken up by roads and interesting trails so
you can plan a trip of almost any length. (Camping on private property
is not advised without permission.) Following are the trailheads of the
nine primary trails. Maps are available for 50 cents from: The Cape Cod
Animal Hospital, West Barnstable, Mass.; Govone Grain and Feed, Mass.
130, Forestdale, Mass.; Maushop Farm, Cotuit, Mass.; Flying B Ranch,
Pine Lane, Barnstable, Mass.; and Circle B. Ranch, Mass. 28, Hyannis,
Mass.

Dopple Bottom Trail, 67 miles. Continue south on Mass. 130 past the
junction with U.S. 6. The trail begins on the east side of the road
opposite the southeast end of a bypass connecting the two highways in
Sandwich. The trail is marked in orange.

Mashpee Pond Trail, 40.1 miles. Marked in red, this is a cutoff of the
Dopple Bottom Trail, beginning 2¾ miles east of the Dopple Bottom
trailhead.

Hathaway Ponds Trail, 19 miles. Near the Chamber of Commerce
Building in Barnstable, the trail begins on Iyannough Road, second road
on the right beyond a power line southeast of the junction of that road
and U.S. 6. The trail is marked in blue.

Cotuit Highlands Trail, 59 miles. This path leaves the Dopple Bottom
trail 5-5/8 mile from its beginning heading southwest. It is blazed in red.

Town Line Trail, 16 miles. Leave the Dopple Bottom trail 5.5 miles
from its start. This trail is also marked in red.

Mystic Lake Trail, 14 miles. This trail, marked in red, heads south six
miles along the Dopple Bottom Trail.

Race Lane Trail, 12 miles. It begins where the Dopple Bottom Trail
ends, near Clay Hill and is also marked in red.

Mill Pond Trail, two miles. From the junction of U.S. 6 and Mass.
130, go east 4 miles to the second cloverleaf. Follow Chase Road, which
crosses here, north. The trail starts in the town of Sandwich, on Chase
Road, a short distance north of County Road. This is a fairly rugged,
wooded, trail, marked in blue.

Wequaquet Lake Trail, 52.8 miles. The trail begins at the northeast
corner of Wequaquet Lake in Barnstable. It is marked in red.

MILES STANDISH STATE FOREST

Miles Standish State Forest, 2.1-mile trail (with an additional one
mile spur trail). Access to this state forest south of Plymouth is from
Mass. 58 in South Carver via Federal Furnace Road, then right on South
Carver (watch carefully or you'll miss the signs); or, from the north, by
following signs south on Long Pond Road (Exit 39 of U.S. 3) from
Plymouth. Park Headquarters is on South Carver Road.

The area is comprised chiefly of irregular, low-relief (200 feet or so) rolling hills, forested by open growth pine and oak.

The hiking trail starts from the parking lot at the headquarters and circles East Head Pond, a pretty little man-made reservoir. A mile-long spur leaves the loop trail at the north end of the pond and follows roughly north along the shores of Long Pond and Three Corner Pond.

Although the parking lot may have been full of sportsmen unloading their trail bikes, the hike around the lake escapes the exhaust fumes and the roar of these machines, which have for the most part been routed away from the "pedestrian" area. The trail does cross both bicycle and bridle paths, and, for a short stretch on the northern spur and on the west side of East Head Pond, it follows the paved road.

Several campgrounds are maintained within this state forest by the Department of Natural Resources; check at park headquarters. During the "off season," camping is restricted to "enclosed units." The trails are closed Saturdays during hunting season.

SWANSEA AREA

Three walks around the Swansea area provide views of rocks and caves of historical, as well as geological and esthetic interest. A quarter-mile walk from the junction of Pearce Road and Wilbur Avenue (Mass. 103) will take you to **Hiding Rocks Cave**, where the son-in-law of Indian Chieftain King Philip was cared for by white women. The ensuing friendship of the Pocasset Indians quite possibly affected the outcome of King Philip's War. There is a rock outcropping a few hundred yards west from the intersection on Wilbur Ave. Go through the metal gate by the rock and continue north for about 100 yards to where there is a long rock on the right. The cave is here.

Margaret's Rock and **Devil's Rock Trails**, 2 miles. Roger Williams supposedly lived in a cave on Margaret's Rock for a year after fleeing Boston, here developing a friendly relationship with King Philip. On Devil's Rock, there are depressions, possibly fossil dinosaur tracks, which supposedly are the footprints of Satan himself. Access to these rocks involves a drive over a Swansea Water Department road. Check with the department to obtain permission before using it. From U.S. 6, this road may be reached by going south about ¼ mile on Bushee Street. The road is on the west side just after a road leading to an old house. Drive ½ mile across sandbank fields until you see a path entering the woods on the west side of the field.

Leave the car and take the path until you see a large outcropping of rock on the other side of a brook. This is Devil's Rock. Climb it from the west and come down by the path on the south that starts just east of the north end of Devil's Rock. After about 1/3 mile, this path will reach a stone wall surrounding an open field. Pass through the break in this wall and, keeping the woods on your right, walk until you reach a path into the woods. This leads a few hundred feet to Margaret's Rock.

Abraham's Rock and Lion's Head Rock are geologically interesting pudding stone boulders more than 100 feet high. To see them, leave your car in the Christ Church parking lot in Swansea Village and take the path at the back of the lot. Walk north until you are at a point on the north side of a field just beyond a stone wall. Keeping the wall on your right, follow it to its end where another trail enters. Turn left on this trail. It leads directly to Abraham's Rock. The easiest way to climb the rock is up the south side and down at the northeast corner. From just north of the rock there is a yellow-marked trail going north which should be followed to a wood road leading east and then turning north. On your left are the *Wildcat* and *Kitten* rocks. The road you are on will end at a path entering from the left. Go east on this path to another path that climbs the west end of Lion's Head Rock.

AMES NOWELL STATE PARK
This park is reached via an unnamed side road in Abington. Follow Mass. 139 south 2.3 miles from where it intersects Mass. 37 in Holbrook, to Hancock St. Park signs on your right lead to the park.
This is basically a wooded area with several paths and a small pond. Trails include the **Bridle Path**, 1¼ miles, heading north from the clearing behind the gatehouse and ending on Mass. 139 just north of Hancock St., and the **West Shore Trail**, 1 mile, leading west from the clearing and continuing to the northwest shore of the pond. From the pond another trail may be followed about 1½ miles to Quincy Street about ½ mile south of the Brookfield Shopping Center.

THE PEREGRINE WHITE PARK AND WILDLIFE SANCTUARY
The Peregrine White Park and Wildlife Sanctuary includes rocky woodland, swamp, and Cleveland Pond. Access is from the end of Linwood Street in Abington. There are some dirt roads leading south from Chestnut Street to the granite quarries. In addition, there are three trails (actually two paths and a wood road) of 1.25, 1.3 and one mile starting from the parking space near the park entrance.

WORLD'S END PENINSULA
World's End Peninsula in Hingham is a privately owned area with a beach and a unique figure-eight shaped drumlin. A drumlin is an unstratified, glacially formed hill. The neck of this one measures about 500 feet in width. There is one trail on which hiking is encouraged, but picnicking is not allowed.
BLUE HILLS RESERVATION
Blue Hill (635.5 feet) is affectionately referred to by Bostonians unable to get any farther away for a weekend as one of the "great hills" of the east. Only 15 miles south of Boston, the reservation is more than five miles long, with a total number of hiking trails probably exceeding

any other park in Massachusetts. Although Blue Hill is objectively not very high, it is the highest point around and affords some excellent views.

To reach the trails from Mass. 128, exit (heading southeast) at Interchange 64 (Mass. 138), and proceed to the Howard Johnson's on the left. Park here and begin the hike a few hundred feet north on the left of Mass. 138. At this point, the summit is ½ mile away.

If you drive north ½ mile from here to the ski area parking lot you can follow one of the ski slopes or trails to the top.

For a longer hike, (about two miles round trip), drive east on Blue Hill Street (it becomes Hillside Street just south of the Howard Johnson's), and start from the parking lot just beyond Hoosicwhisick (Houghton) Pond about 1½ miles from Mass. 138.

The maze of trails, some of which are also used as bridle trails, cross more than a dozen lesser hills in the reservation. A topographical map is useful here, both as a guide in sorting out the numerous paint-blazed trails and an aid in identifying the ponds, swamps, hills, highways and other landmarks visible from the numerous outlooks.

Although these are not considered to be strenuous hikes, the trails are not always the wide, smooth paths usually encountered in eastern Massachusetts. Often, they are genuine rock and root mountain trails on which many hikers find sneakers insufficient.

It is generally desirable to carry water and a trail lunch, since it is very easy to fall into the "one more peak" syndrome, after reaching the first "summit."

Norfolk County, where Blue Hills is located, has a generous amount of rocky terrain, affording some excellent outlooks and interesting rock formations. The **Warner Trail**, 34 miles, traverses the southwestern ridge, extending from the Canton Junction railroad station in Canton, to Diamond Hill in the northeast corner of Rhode Island. It is the longest continuous trail in eastern Massachusetts.

Access to the north end is via either U.S. 1 in Norwood or U.S. 95, Exit 11. From either of these, take Neponset Street east toward Canton. Turn left on Chapman Street and right on Sherman Street, following Sherman to the station.

The trail is generally marked with round metal discs or by white blazes. It is meant to be walked as a series of day hikes and so no facilities for camping are to be found. The trail alternates between stretches running along streets and roadways, with stretches along old and often abandoned wood roads. More of a walk through rural Massachusetts than a wilderness hike, the Warner Trail nevertheless passes scenic ponds and fascinating rock formations, and it gains a number of hilltops with good views. The section from Diamond Hill to Mass. 1A south of Wampum Corners is reportedly not well maintained or completely marked and should not be attempted unless you are accompanied by someone who has traveled the trail in the past.

PLUM ISLAND STATE PARK

Plum Island is actually a peninsula containing the 74 acre **Plum Island State Park** and part of the **Parker River National Wildlife Refuge**. Access to the refuge is from Mass. 1A in Newbury. Follow signs to Plum Island Turnpike, go east, turn north on Northern Boulevard, and follow it to Refuge headquarters. The park is at the southern end of the island.

This is a prime area for beach walkers and birders. Nearly seven miles of uninterrupted sand beach awaits those who may have been frustrated on Cape Cod. When walking along these ocean beaches, do not climb up the dunes or wander off into the surrounding plant communities. To do so would disturb not only the vegetation but also the nesting areas of numerous waterfowl and shorebirds. To protect these nesting places, most of the area is closed to the public from March 1 to June 30. Also, because it is a wildlife refuge, parts of the area are closed to the public; and hiking, other than on established trails, is not permitted. Special permits are required to enter some areas. For more information and permits, contact: Refuge Manager, Parker River National Wildlife Refuge, Newburyport, Mass. 01950.

THE PLATEAU AREA

Purgatory State Reservation:

Purgatory Chasm is a half-mile fissure in solid rock with sheer walls rising upward from 70 feet. The **Purgatory Chasm Trail**, ¾ mile, is reached by driving six miles south of the Massachusetts Turnpike (U.S. 90) on Mass. 146. Exit at the sign to Purgatory Chasm and drive ½ mile west to the parking lot on the left.

The trail is actually a low-grade rock scramble entering the Chasm behind the refreshment stand next to the parking lot.

The gorge, at times appearing deeper than wide, is shaded by large hemlocks which cling precariously to the top and sides of the 70-foot-high cliffs. Jutting rocks form overhangs of tremendous proportion. The floor of the Chasm is made up of car-sized boulders over or around which the trail wanders. With a flashlight in hand, you may find your hiking time doubled or tripled as you poke your head into or crawl through the numerous grottos formed by this jumble of rock.

The Chasm ends even more abruptly than it began in a low, flat swampy area where the trail turns left and climbs up sloping ledges with several overlooks into the Chasm. Small hemlocks with their roots anchored in crevices appear to offer some security for those who venture near the edge of these overlooks, but they are not meant to substitute for a handrail, so don't use them to lean into the gorge. Also, other hikers may be below you, so be careful not to "accidentally" kick anything over the edge. The trail ends not far from where it began.

The **Memorial Trail**, 0.3 miles west of the Chasm parking lot, is a well-marked loop circling through the mixed oak forests adjacent to the Chasm. As you approach the west side of the Chasm, the oak forest gives way to evergreens. When the trail turns sharply left, you can leave it and walk back along the top of the west side of the Chasm and to the parking lot, or continue on to the point where the trail began.

Mount Wachusett (2,006 feet) in the Wachusett Mountain State Reservation near Princeton and Westminster, is the highest point in central Massachusetts, with magnificent panoramic views of the surrounding low country from its summit. The **Jack Frost Trail** to the summit, 1.08 miles, is reached by driving north 1.3 miles from Princeton Center on Mountain Road and turning left at Westminster Road. Continue for 0.8 miles to Administration Road, turn right, and drive 0.4 miles farther to a wood road on the right which is the beginning of the trail.

The trail name is painted above a brook; from here follow the light blue blazes up steep ledges, through hemlock forest, and up again, to join the Mountain House Trail (turn left) which may be followed to the summit.

The **Mountain House Trail**, one mile, coming from the east, begins close to an old shack on the west side of Mountain Road, 2.4 miles north of Princeton Center. It is unmarked and steep, but easy to follow.

The **Harrington Trail**, 1.5 miles, which joins the Mountain House and Jack Frost Trails at the summit, is reached by driving from Princeton Center 1.4 miles north on Mountain Road. Upon reaching a Y crossing, turn left, and turn left again after 0.8 miles. The Harrington Farm appears in 0.7 more miles. The trail begins near the brook at the back of the house.

This trail is longer than the others and in places involves climbing over rocks. At one point, you have a choice between climbing over rocks or following the **Mountain House Link Trail** for a short distance before rejoining the Harrington.

CONNECTICUT VALLEY

The **Metacomet-Monadnock Trail**, some 300 miles, is the longest continuous trail in Massachusetts (98 miles). Beginning in northern Connecticut, southwest of Springfield, it stretches north through the Connecticut Valley in Massachusetts, crossing the Connecticut River between *Mount Tom* and *Mount Holyoke*. At the northern end of the state it climbs *Mount Grace* before passing into New Hampshire where it ends on Mount Monadnock.

There are few shelters or other established places for camping on the trail, although there are some campsites. But the trail crosses numerous highways and roads and can be readily hiked in a series of day trips.

USGS maps are useful here, but the route of the MM Trail is not generally marked on the maps, and where it is, it is usually not labeled as such. *The Guide to the Metacomet-Monadnock Trail*, published by the Berkshire Chapter of the Appalachian Mountain Club, describes the trail in detail. It is available from the Appalachian Mountain Club, 5 Joy Street, Boston, Massachusetts 02108.

Weekend or day trips can be planned coupling the MM Trail with side trails and forming pleasant loops in any of the state parks it passes through.

The **Mount Grace Summit Loop**, 1.8 miles, may be reached from Mass. 2, by going north on Mass. 78 to Warwick. Turn left (west) on Northfield-Warwick Road. The trail begins one mile up on an old wood road.

This route follows the MM Trail to the summit of Mount Grace (1,617 feet), then descends the north slope, returning via the **Round the Mountain Trail** to the starting point.

Beginning on the abandoned wood road, the trail follows white paint blazes a few hundred yards to a point where it turns sharply right up the hill. This turn is marked with two blazes, one above the other; as are succeeding turns. The trail then contours along the slope until it meets **Snowshoe Trail**. Here it turns sharply left and climbs the ridge to the summit of Little Mount Grace, drops, skirts another small peak and then climbs steadily up to the summit of Mount Grace.

Mt. Monadnock to the northeast and Quabbin Reservoir to the south may be visible from the firetower. Continuing north from the summit, the MM side trail called the **Winchester Trail** drops for ½ mile to meet the **Northside Trail** (same as Round the Mountain Trail), 2.5 miles. Turning left, this trail again follows the contours around the base of Mount Grace, meeting the old woods road and returning to the beginning.

The summit of Mount Holyoke (930 feet) may be reached via a combination of the MM Trail and the **Halfway Trail**, 2.75 miles round trip. From junction with Mass. 116, drive northwest on Mass. 47 for 2.7 miles to the entrance of the Joseph Allen Skinner Park. Turn right, drive ½ mile and park near the turn by the gate. Walk up the Summit Road for ½ mile.

Just before the Halfway House clearing you will reach a sign on the right that says "To Summit." From here it is a steep climb up the Halfway Trail to the MM Trail, which continues level and then over ledges to the summit. The Connecticut River Valley, Mount Greylock to the northwest, and Vermont's Mount Ascutney to the north are visible on clear days. The return trip is via the MM Trail, continuing on after it passes the Halfway cutoff to where it passes the Skinner Park graveled road. Turn right here, and follow the road to a point ½ mile from your car. There are good views of the river valley along the MM Trail, but be careful, as in some places loose rocks on the trail are a problem.

THE WESTERN UPLANDS

The Berkshire Mountains are the major feature of this area, stretching from Mount Everett at the southern boundary of the state to Mount Greylock on the north, only 40 air miles apart.

A major feature of the Taconic Range (generally meaning the ridges west of the Housatonic River and of the Green River farther north), is **Mount Everett** (2,602 feet). Views from Everett's summit stretch from Mount Greylock to Bear Mountain in Connecticut. The upper part of the mountain and Guilder Pond, at 2,042 feet the highest natural body of water in the state, form the Mount Everett Reservation. In the interests of conservation, swimming, fishing, and camping are prohibited in this area. There is a narrow, gravel road which leads to two parking and picnicking areas close to the summit which may be reached from Egremont by following Reservation signs.

The **Elbow Trail**, 5.8 miles round trip (including AT Trail link) leads to the Appalachian Trail and the summit.

It may be reached from the intersection of Mass. 41 and Mass. 23 in South Egremont. From that point, go south on Route 41 to a sign that says the Berkshire School is 3.2 miles ahead. Turn toward the school, drive past the athletic fields, turn right, drive between a cement building and a brick building, and continue uphill to a turnaround near a brook. The Elbow Trail leads west from here, and in 1.1 miles turns into the white blazed Appalachian Trail on the left. In another 1.15 miles, you will pass the picnic area over lovely Guilder Pond, then travel through woods and along an abandoned summit road before reaching the open plateau at the top. The road was abandoned after being flooded in 1927, when ecology advocate Walter Eaton urged that the money be used instead for the Everett link of the Appalachian Trail.

Bash Bish Falls, the most exciting waterfall in the state, is located in Mount Washington (a town, not a mountain), south of Mount Everett (at the state's southwest corner where it borders New York). Although best in spring when the snow melts, the falls are majestic any time of the year. Supposedly, they are the home of a childless Indian maiden, rejected by her husband, who jumped into the water to join her mother, a witch, who lived there.

To reach the 8-mile, round trip trail to the falls from the South Egremont junction of Mass. 23 and Mass. 41, follow Mass. 41 south to a fork, turn right and follow the signs to Mount Washington and Mount Everett. Signs along this route direct you to the parking area for Bash Bish Falls. The trail starts at the rear of the parking lot and is well marked with blue and white triangular trail signs.

Lenox Mountain (2,123 feet) provides some fine views from its summit. The **Firetower Trail**, also known as the **Trail of the Ledges**, 2½ miles, begins at the duck pond west of the Pleasant Valley Sanctuary superintendent's house on West Mountain Road. The trail is red blazed.

Mount Greylock (3,491 feet) is the highest mountain in Massachusetts and the center of the Mount Greylock State Reservation. It is located at the state's extreme northwest corner. Three automobile roads and several trails lead to the war memorial and excellent views on its top. The **Mount Greylock-Mount Prospect Loop**, 12.1 miles, combines part of the Appalachian Trail with parts of three other trails to reach Mount Greylock and Mount Prospect (2,690 feet) plus Mount Williams (2,951 feet) and Mount Fitch (3,110 feet).

Access is from the center of Williamstown where U.S. 7 forks north from Mass. 2. Go east on Mass. 2 for 1.7 miles. Turn right on Luce Road (which becomes Pattison Road) and watch for the Appalachian Trail signs and white blazes on the right between the Williamstown and Mount Williams Reservoirs.

There are three camping areas with lean-tos along this route. Since much of the trail follows ridges, it is advisable to carry water. The trail follows the white blazes of the AT all the way to the summit of Greylock. In the first 1½ miles, it climbs 1,500 vertical feet up the north ridge of Mount Prospect, turning left where it meets the blue blazes of the **Mount Prospect Trail**. The trail then descends slightly, crossing the Notch Road (one of the three auto routes to the top), and climbs over Mount Williams and Mount Fitch to the War Memorial on the summit. On a clear day, it is possible to see Connecticut, New York, Vermont, and New Hampshire.

The route continues southwest from the summit down Rockwell Road, leaving the AT where the **Hopper Trail** forks right. The Hopper Trail drops steeply soon after passing Sperry Campground. After about a mile, take the right cutoff to meet **Money Brook Trail**, and, shortly after that, you will reach another lean-to. A few hundred yards beyond the lean-to, turn left on Mount Prospect Trail, which climbs 1,200 feet in about a mile to the summit. The trail then descends to the north and meets the AT before returning to the start.

Mount Busby (2,566 feet), also known as Spruce Hill, is on the western end of the Hoosac Range in Savoy Mountain State Forest. To reach the **Busby Trail**, which starts on Shaft Road, take Mass. 2, ¾ miles east of the Mohawk Trail West Summit, and drive for two miles before turning right at a fork. In another ¾ mile is the Forest Service Building and about 100 yards beyond that, the trailhead. The trail follows a wood road, then a grass trail to the rocky summit, where views extend to Mount Greylock.

The **Dorothy Frances Rice Wildlife Sanctuary**, on South Road, one mile south of Mass. 143 in Peru, offers several color-coded nature walks through 273 acres of woodland. Visitors are not allowed in the sanctuary after dark.

Squaw Peak (1,642 feet) is a quarter-mile open crest offering sensational panoramic views. **Profile Rock**, just south of its northern summit, takes on the aspect of an Indian head in the early light. North of Profile Rock is **Inscription Rock**; and **Devil's Pulpit** is a lofty formation on the east. Squaw Peak is part of the **Monument Mountain Reservation**.

To reach the **Indian Monument Trail** on that reservation, 1¼ miles, drive to the parking and picnic area at the base of Squaw Peak on U.S. 7, 2½ miles south of Stockbridge. The trailhead is 1/3 mile south along the highway on the right, where a sign indicates "Indian Monument." Although the trail crosses many others on its way to the summit, always take the course on the right.

Laura Tower (1,465 feet) is part of the **Beartown Mountain** area near Stockbridge. The **Laura Tower Trail**, 0.8 miles, starts at Memorial Bridge in that city, and follows yellow markers to a place where two alternate trails both climb to the summit and its steel tower.

Bartholomew's Cobble, a plant and bird sanctuary maintained by the Trustees of Reservations, has many footpaths for those interested in botany and geology. It is one mile west of the traffic light in Ashley Falls.

Umpachene Falls is actually an eight-acre park in Marlborough, centered around the long series of waterfalls.

Access from Mass. 57 at New Marlborough is by turning south on Southfield Road and going four miles to Mill River village. Then, go left on Clayton Road, cross the bridge and turn left again. Turn left once more 1.4 miles from Mill River village, and cross the bridge to the picnic area at the foot of the spectacular falls. Although the path by the falls soon disappears into "no trespassing" areas, the falls are worth the visit just to look at them.

10

Rhode Island

Rhode Island is a boating, fishing, sports, and cultural paradise. The state recreational emphasis is not on hiking, however. There are 57 parks in the state, only nine of which have trails. You can still find places to walk, though. With 40 miles of coast (384 miles if you count the land along the bays and the shores of 36 islands), there are plenty of informal beach and shore walks.

Or visit Newport, site of international yacht races, jazz and folk festivals, to gape at the mansions of the nineteenth century shipping magnates and industrialists who spent their summers here. Your first walk can be the *Cliff Walk*, a particularly lovely three-mile stretch between the craggy Atlantic Coast and the lush splendor of fine Victorian houses. Cornelius Vanderbilt built his opulent 70-room "Breakers" here, and William Vanderbilt settled nearby at "Marble House," one of the most ornate buildings in America.

Most of these extravagant creations were considered second or even third homes. But Rhode Islanders have long been devoted to such luxury and fun. Providence, for example, was the site of the first world championship baseball game in 1844. Newport saw the first public roller skating rink in the country in 1866. Golf, polo, and tennis matches have been held here as well.

Which isn't to say that Rhode Islanders are entirely a frivolous lot. Originally founded by Roger Williams as a refuge from Massachusetts persecution, the state has always been proud of its native resourcefulness. The Old Slater Mill in Pawtucket, for example, one of the first successful textile mills in the U.S., is credited with starting America's Industrial Age.

New England clambakes can be found nightly up and down the state's shores. The Indians covered seafood with seaweed and cooked it right on the beach. If you're lucky, you'll find someone upholding this tradition. If not, enjoy it from a steaming pot. Either way, don't miss this treat.

Rhode Island is known for its commercial and sport fishing. White marlin, mackerel, swordfish, perch, flounder, squeteague, and tuna are just a few of the species you might find on the end of your hook.

In 1734 Rhode Island set aside public lands for the improvement of oyster beds. Steps have also been taken to protect shellfish.

You'll find milder weather in Rhode Island than in the rest of New England, partly because of the warm air from Narragansett Bay. There are fewer extreme temperatures. January averages in the 30's, July in the 70's. The coast though, is vulnerable to hurricanes.

The state contains 1,234 square miles and may be divided geographically into the coastal lowlands and the northern uplands. The coast consists of sandy beached peninsulas almost separated from the mainland by salt marshes and ponds. To the west are rough, tree-covered hills. Roughly 2/3 of the state is heavily forested. Much of the southeastern section of the state is actually a series of bridge-connected islands. Here the shores are high, rocky cliffs, and inland from the shores are rounded, grassy slopes.

There are many inland waterways in Rhode Island, several small but swift rivers, waterfalls, lakes, ponds, and reservoirs. Many of the so-called rivers are actually salt water arms of the bays.

NORTHWEST REGION

The Walkabout Trail, eight miles (plus six miles of side trails). It is in the George Washington Management Area on the north side of U.S. 44, two miles east of the Connecticut-Rhode Island state line and 22 miles west of Providence. The trail is a circuit starting and ending in a picnic area on the second fork to the left after entering the Management Area. Originally cut and marked by a group of Australian sailors, this trail has been improved by the Rhode Island Department of Natural Resources. White rings mark an eight-mile main trail and there are also yellow, blue, and peach-blazed side paths. The yellow hike is eight miles, the peach, two miles, and the blue, four miles. An extension of the trail leads to Pulaski Memorial State Park. Reservations for camping should be made with the Rhode Island Division of Conservation, 83 Park St., Providence, R.I. 02903. The department can also give you information on the current development state of new trails.

SOUTHWEST REGION

There are several intersecting trails in three connecting parks in this area, maintained by the Appalachian Mountain Club and the Rhode Island Department of Natural Resources. The parks are the Arcadia State Park, Dawley State Park, and Beach Pond State Park. They are about 30 miles south of Providence via Interstate 95. Dawley is just east of the Interstate and the others are west near the towns of Arcadia and Escoheag.

Breakheart Trail, 14.3 miles. The trail starts at the bridge below Fish Ladder Dam at Breakheart Pond in Arcadia State Park. It is marked with yellow blazes and passes through deciduous woods, pine groves, and swamp before ascending Penny Hill (370 feet) for a panoramic view.

The trail follows wood roads as well as paths and has at least one side trail. The trail ends at Falls River Bridge, where it connects with the Ben Utter and Escoheag Trails.

Ben Utter Trail, 4.3 miles. Begin at the Falls River Bridge, two miles north of RI 165 on Escoheag Hill Road and the westward extension of Austin Farm Road. This trail, marked with yellow blazes, passes the remains of a vertical sawmill and an old grist mill, goes through the Stepstone Falls picnic area, which has both a spring and toilet facilities, and culminates at Stepstone Falls.

Escoheag Trail, two miles. From the Escoheag Post Office on RI 165, take Escoheag Hill Road north 0.9 miles to the first road on the right. Here a sign directs you to the Ledges picnic area where the trail starts at the south end of the parking place: The white-blazed trail passes through two valleys, some forest area, ledges and open country before ending at Falls River Bridge.

John B. Hudson Trail, 1.6 miles. The trail begins at RI 165 about 2.5 miles west of RI 3 and follows a logging road and a brook south and ends at Breakheart Pond where there is an unusual dam. The trail is marked with yellow paint, and one mile from Appie Crossing a white-blazed side trail leads to two overnight shelters.

Arcadia Trail, 3.4 miles. The trail, marked with yellow blazes, begins at the Tefft Hill Camping Area, one mile east of Arcadia Picnic Area on a dirt road and ends at Appie Crossing. It passes the Arcadia State Park picnic area and bathing beach, so it is not the place to go for solitude (although you might have a nice swim). There is, however, an overnight shelter on the trail and another on a side trail going west just north of Arcadia Pond.

Tippecansett Trail, 45.5 miles. The trail starts opposite the shelter near the parking space at the Stepstone Falls Picnic Area, which is 2.5 miles north of RI 165 via Escoheag Road. This trail heads south, passing through several types of woods and sections of mountain laurel. The yellow-blazed trail intersects several other trails, including some that began in Connecticut and three highways before ending at Narragansett Trail just south of Yawgoo Pond.

The Rhode Island Recreation Map, published by the Rhode Island Department of Natural Resources, shows hiking trails in the state parks as well as on other property. State game and other natural areas with hiking trails include the **Carolina, Great Swamp**, and **Burlingame Management Areas**, and the **Kimball Bird Sanctuary**.

State parks with hiking trails include **Colt, Diamond Hill, Goddard, Lincoln Woods** and the **Ninigret Conservation Area**.

11

Connecticut

Connecticut is rolling hills, covered bridges, country barns, colonial houses — and miles and miles of trails. The hiker can definitely find variety here; everything from a few hours' jaunt to a major backpacking outing, thanks to the combination of an extensive system of state park pathways and a far-flung network of privately maintained trails.

Connecticut's 5,009 square miles may be divided into three main regions: The Western Highlands, the Central Lowlands, and the Eastern Highlands. The northwest is the ruggedest section of the state, although the Appalachians are less impressive here than in other regions of the chain. There are almost no high peaks; Bear Mountain, at 2,316 feet is the highest place in the state. Instead, the mountains take on the appearance of a series of rolling crests.

The mountains of this section are part of the Taconic range that leads directly into the Berkshire area of Massachusetts. The hillsides are covered with timber, and rich farmlands fill the valleys. To the southeast, the country becomes lower but remains wild. This is the Litchfield Hills area. Mohawk Mountain (1,680 feet) is the highest point. In the southwest the Litchfield Hills become gentler with many lakes, ponds, brooks, and miles of rolling, forested country.

The Connecticut River Valley forms the Central Lowland. This is basically level farm country with a steep, hilly section near Meriden.

The flat, wooded hills of the Eastern Highlands surround narrow valleys that widen near the Rhode Island border. Although the soil here is not deep, there is some farmland, with forest growing in areas where farms used to be.

There are 90 state parks in Connecticut. At least 20 of the major parks provide hiking trails, and the Department of Environmental Protection administers over 1,500 campsites. Camping season is from April 15 to September 30. Certain sites are designated each winter, on the basis of both geography and use, to be winter campsites. Write to the Chief, Parks and Recreation, Department of Environmental Protection, State Office Building, Hartford, Connecticut 06115, to find out what the policy is for any particular winter. Camping is generally not allowed in the spring because heavy use of the land can upset the ecology,

119

compress the soil, and cause erosion as the land thaws. Reservations are taken by the department from January 15 through April 15. After that date, requests should be sent directly to the specific park. Most sites are $2.00 per night per campsite, although a few are $3.00, and, without reservations, are available on a first-come, first-served basis. There are no electrical, water, or sanitary hook-ups at state campgrounds, and at the other extreme, the Department warns that "in general, campsites in Connecticut campgrounds are not suited to the use of sleeping bags as the only form of camping equipment," although some park managers permit such use.

One nice service of the park system is an emergency service for out-of-state travelers who have been unable to find lodging or campsites; temporary space in an open field or parking lot may be assigned until 8:00 the next morning. Participating parks, indicated in the park directory available from the department, are located on or near major highways.

In addition to the park trails in Connecticut, the major trail network of the state is the blue-blazed system maintained by the Connecticut Forest and Park Association, which has been creating trails since 1929. They are marked by oval trail signs at state highway crossings and blue arrows where they cross other roads, (on the trails themselves, double blazes indicate turns).

Many of these trails are quite long. These are the so-called "through trails." We will describe access routes and end points as well as the main features of these trails, but topo maps or the maps in the Connecticut Forest and Park Association's "Connecticut Walk Book" (available from them for $5.00 at 1010 Main Street, East Hartford, Conn. 06108) would come in handy on longer trips.

Camping at undesignated points on these trails is prohibited. Most trails intersect the state parks, where camping is often allowed, or the state forests, which provide a few open shelters. Otherwise, you must become just a hiker, not a camper, and rely on the motels, tourist homes and farmhouses encountered on the intersecting roads.

Even on the short trails in Connecticut, rough, rocky terrain may be encountered. Therefore, good hiking boots should be worn. Water should be carried, particularly on the rockbound trails of the central part of the state, and in other areas, to avoid bothering private landowners.

THE WEST

Mattatuck Trail, 35 miles. The trail is a varied and interesting route, passing waterfalls, lakes and streams, and crossing two mountains, Mohawk and Mount Prospect, as well as Black Rock State Park and Mattatuck State Forest. It also passes a sewage plant and a gravel pit. [Access is at Mad River Road on Route 69 in Wolcott. The trail heads northwest to end at the Appalachian Trail, just past Mohawk Mountain.] There are several side trails. The section connecting Black Rock State Park with the Mattatuck State Forest is historically significant. King Philip, trying to keep the colonists from expanding their territory, chased settlers along this path to keep them from moving farther into Indian territory.

The **Quinnipiac Trail**, 21 miles, starting in North Haven, is reached by going north on State Street 0.1 mile north of the intersection of Route 22 and Bishop Street. At this point, Banton Street begins on the east. Follow Banton to its end; the trail begins 0.1 mile south of here. It ends on Conn. Route 68 near the Cheshire Reservoir.

The trail follows a series of trap rock ridges, passes through the **Quinnipiac River** and **Sleeping Giant State Parks**, presents good views from **York Mountain, Mount Sanford**, and several parts of the **Sleeping Giant's** body, and travels by lovely Roaring Brook Falls. Aside from the viewing points, most of the trail is wooded.

The **Paugussett and Pomperaug Trails**, 9.7 miles, travel northward along the east bank of the Housatonic River. There are a few steep climbs with some nice views along the ridges, gorges, and brooks. The biggest portion of the trails are on wood roads, and there is a campground (inaccessible by car) near the end of the Pomperaug after the two paths combine. Access to the Paugussett is in a grove of hemlock at the Well in Indian Well State Park on Conn. Route 110. It connects with the Pomperaug in 4.4 miles. The Pomperaug starts at a point reached by following East Village Road 0.2 miles west of East Village. (This town is in the middle of an area bounded by Routes 110, 11, and 134). The trail goes north from here, merges with the Paugussett just before crossing the river, and continues north to Kettletown State Park.

Another trail following the Housatonic is the **River Trail**, 0.7 miles. From the junction of the Warren Turnpike (Conn. 341) and U.S. 7, follow the turnpike 0.8 miles to where the trail starts heading west.

Pine Knob Loop Trail, 2.5 miles. From Cornwall Bridge, go 1.1 miles south on U.S. 7. Access to the trail is from the parking lot on the west of U.S. 7 at this point. One of the most scenic trails in the state, the Pine Knob Loop looks out over river vistas from the Housatonic Meadows State Park and Housatonic State Forest.

Macedonia Brook State Park, near Kent, has several trails worked into a connecting system. To get there, take Conn. 341 northwest from Macedonia. Turn right into the park on Brook Road, turn right again at a fork with Fuller Mountain Road. The **Red Trail**, 0.3 miles, starts at a point on the left of Keeler Road about 500 feet north of the Gorge, a well-marked landmark on Brook Road. It runs into a **Green Trail**, 0.5 miles, which started on Fuller Mountain Road, just west of the park entrance, and a **Yellow Offshoot**, 1.1 miles, leading to a shelter. **Pine Hill Tree Trail**, a blue trail, 1.2 miles, and another yellow trail form separate connections between Keeler Road and the Appalachian Trail.

The terrain in the park is interesting because the rock it is on, Becket

Gneiss, is very hard and has worn down very slowly. Interspersing are several streams and springs. The highest peak in the park is **Cobble Mountain** (1,350 feet) which is reached on the Appalachian Trail. There are about 15 miles of trail throughout the park, making several different hiking loop combinations possible. There is a campground.

Mohawk Mountain (1,683 feet), in **Mohawk State Forest** was never used by the Mohawk Indians: it was used by other tribes as a lookout to see if the Mohawks were coming to attack them. It is a woody, hilly area with several ledges on the hills and some interesting features such as unusual plantlife growing in a glacial pothole, or bog. The park is 10 miles west of Torrington on Route 4. There are about 15 miles of trail and several shelters throughout the park. Five trails begin or cross Wadhams Road at about 3,000 3,750, 4,000, 5,500, and 8,000 feet east of Mohawk Mountain Road. One goes south at about 2,750 feet to Mattatuck Road. There is a second trail beginning on Mohawk Mountain Road about 500 feet south of the point where Allen Road runs into Mohawk. Trails also intersect Toumey Road, about 3,000 feet west of Mohawk Mountain Road, and Mattatuck Road, from its intersection with Mohawk and a place about 3/4 mile east of there. These go to Route 128. A trail along the east Branch of the Shepaug River begins on Eli Bunker Road about 500 feet south of the bridge over the river; and travels east from there to a road that connects with Milton Road.

The **Burr Pond State Park**, 3.3 miles, five miles north of Torrington on Route 8. Hikers can enjoy a lovely path encircling an 88-acre pond. Historically, this area was the site of industrial progress: sawmills, a tannery, and Gail Borden's first condensed milk factory. The trail may be followed in either direction from the beach near the concession stand.

The **American Legion State Forest**, off Route 44 in Barkhamsted (on Conn. Route 81 near the south end of Barkhamsted Reservoir) and north of Pleasant Valley, is characterized by mixed hardwood forest and rugged, steep terrain. Among the wildlife here are game and song birds, the pileated woodpecker and the white tailed deer.

The **Henry Buck Trail**, 1.5 miles, begins near a foot bridge on West River Road, 2.5 miles from Pleasant Valley. The trail is famous for its beautiful rock formations. It also passes an old cheese-box mill, climbs the Tremendous Cliffs, passing near the highest point in the forest (1,100 feet), and ends at West River Road, 0.3 miles north of the starting point.

The American Legion Forest and People's State Forest adjoin one another.

People's Forest, named "of, by and for" the 400 individuals and organizations who contributed the funds to buy the land, is on the west branch of the Farmington River, in the town of Barkhamsted, off Route 44, north of Pleasant Valley.

There is a network of short, pleasant trails here. In general, they are on moderate grades through the evergreen and deciduous timberland, with elevations ranging from 500 to 1,000 feet. There are also four backpacking shelters (some of them also reachable by road). They are along Greenwoods Road near the crossing of the Jesse Girard Trail, 1/3 of the way south between Warner Road and the Agnes Bowen Trail (south on the Agnes Bowen Trail near the Jesse Girard Trail and near the first picnic area on Route 341 coming from the Nature Museum).

The red marked **Elliott Bronson Trail**, 1.5 miles, travels through forest and across a 60-foot cliff. It starts at the parking area near the Nature Museum and continues to a picnic area on East River Road near Route 181. The **Jesse Girard Trail**, 1.3 miles, marked in yellow, offers some particularly spectacular sights, especially in winter. The trail climbs over stone steps to a ledge overlooking Farmington Valley. This is lovely enough in itself, but in winter the right wall of the stairs catches water which freezes into a wonderful wall of blue-green ice formations, a spectacular sight well worth a winter walk. The trail begins at Barkhamsted Lighthouse and Indian village three miles north of Pleasant Valley on East River Road, or at the end of the connecting trail coming off the Jesse Girard Trail. It ends on Greenwoods Road near the Big Spring. (Greenwoods Road is reached by following Route 181 south of East River Road and turning right at the first fork. Big Spring is on the Charles Pack Trail just southeast of the Greenwoods Road end of the trail).

The **Charles Pack Trail**, 1.9 miles, yellow marked, begins near King Road on Greenwoods Road and ends on Greenwoods Road near Big Spring. Finally, the blue **Robert Ross Trail**, two miles, runs from the end of Warner Road to the Nature Museum.

Sleeping Giant State Park, taking its name from the fact that from New Haven Harbor its woods and ridges look like a giant lying on his back, is reached via Whitney Avenue (Route 10) or the Hartford Turnpike. It is located largely in the town of Hamden. Indian legends say that the giant is an old chief sleeping after stuffing himself with oysters. Another legend says that it is the spirit Hobbamock, under a spell of eternal sleep for changing the course of the Connecticut River.

More important to the hiker than who the giant is, though, are the quiet woods, pine groves, rocky crags, and cascading waterfalls among the trails. There are several trails besides the Quinnipiac Trail already discussed. Next to the blue Quinnipiac, the **White Trail**, 2.8 miles, is the roughest. It starts where the Yellow, Orange, Violet and Green trails converge and covers the major heights, traveling over the right slope of the giant's left leg and the right knee, steeply descending to the base of the knee, climbing the right thigh, and crossing the waist and the shoulder to the chin. There are good views along the way and the trail ends at the Picnic Area Road.

The **Tower Path**, 1.6 miles, is an easy, wide trail leading from the park entrance to the Stone Tower via the neck and chest.

The **Green Trail**, two miles, is made up of old woods roads. It travels through the Inner Mountain Valley, and across the waist to join the White Trail on the shoulder. The **Violet, Yellow and Orange Trails** fall somewhere between the White and Blue Trails and the Tower Path in difficulty. All start, as does the Green Trail, at the Picnic Area road. They end at a place two miles east of Mt. Carmel Ave. From Whitney Ave., turn north on Chestnut Lane and follow it to the second sharp turn where the trails converge. The Violet Trail travels through wooded country, passes the remains of an old quarry, and provides good northwest views, (there are north views in fall and winter after the leaves have fallen). 3.2 miles. The Orange Trail travels across the waist and along the right leg. From it you can see the Inner Mountain Valley. 2.4 miles. The Yellow Trail involves some steep switchbacks, is basically shade and has some nice views. 2.2 miles.

There are several trails in the region around Waterbury, many of which intersect the Mattatuck Trail. The **Whitestone Cliffs Trail**, 3.7 miles, climbs the steep side of the cliffs for some excellent views of the Naugatuck Valley. Access is at the intersection of Echo Lake Road and Thomaston Road. (Echo Lake Road runs from Route 63 just south of Watertown to the railroad bed). The trail follows an old trolley bed at first that is picked up on the east side of an iron bridge. The trail returns to the starting point.

The **Jericho Trail**, three miles, begins off Echo Lake Road 0.9 miles west of the Whitestone Cliffs Trail, follows and crosses Jericho Brook, traverses many ravines and hills, and joins the Mattatuck at Crane Lookout ¼ mile south of U.S. 6 on Mattatuck Trail.

The **Lone Pine Trail**, three miles, travels through woods, over a ledge and comes within 100 yards of the Quinnipiac Trail. Access is on Summit Road, 0.3 miles past Route 69 in Prospect. The trail ends at Route 68 near the Quinnipiac.

The **Hancock Brook-Lion Head Trail**, three miles round trip, passes through hemlock woods, climbs to the top of Lion Head, and follows a ridge with some nice views. The trail starts just east of the Hancock Brook bridge in Waterville at the end of Sheffield Street. (Waterville is reached by following Route 13 from Waterbury to Thomaston Road, turning northeast about two miles.) For a time, the trail follows a blue trail.

The **Roy and Margot Larsen Wildlife Sanctuary of the Connecticut Audobon Society**, in Fairfield, has 6½ miles of walking trails passing through woods and meadow, and by marsh, pond, and swamp. Included is a walk for the blind. The entrance to all trails is through the Parking lot of the Connecticut Audobon Center at 2325 Burr Street, Fairfield.

The **Naugatuck Trail**, 4.8 miles, begins 1.1 miles west of Route 63 on

Beacon Road (Route 42). It leads along wood road and path, past a good viewing ledge, through a gorge and through woodland to end on Route 8 where Egypt Brook meets the Naugatuck River. There are several side trails.

CENTRAL REGION

The **Metacomet Trail** covers 45 miles from the Hanging Hills of Meriden to the Massachusetts state line where it becomes the Metacomet-Monadnock Trail and continues to Mount Monadnock in New Hampshire. Access to the first section is on U.S. 5 in Berlin, across from the Puritan Restaurant. Highlights include views from Ragged Mountain (754 feet), Bradley Mountain (685 feet), Pinnacle Rock, Rattlesnake Mountain, South Rattlesnake, and Chimney Point; as well as caves, reservoirs, rock climbing opportunities, and Penwood State Park.

The **Shenipsit Trail** is a through trail, (with the exception of 11 miles), between East Hampton and the Massachusetts line. Access is on the north side of a gravel road reached in the following manner: Turn northeast at Y-shaped intersection in Cobalt at intersection 0.1 mile north of where Route 66 meets Route 151. In 0.8 miles, turn right and drive 0.5 miles to where trail intersects with dirt road. The trail travels through the Meshomasic and the Shenipsit State Forests. The gap is between Bolton and Crystal Lake Road between Conn. Routes 6 and 85 in Ellington. To reach the point where the trail resumes, go to Rockville, travel 3 miles north on Route 83 to Crystal Lake Road (Route 140), turn right, travel to where Lake Bonair meets Hopkins Road. This is where the trail begins again. 30 miles.

In Simsbury, the Great Pond State Forest includes a pine forest with every age of white pine from one to 100 years old. The forest is also a haven for migrating birds, particularly waterfowl. There are almost five miles of well-defined hiking trails and wood roads, beginning at the parking lot. The park entrance is at Great Pond Road in Simsbury.

Devil's Hopyard State Park, 5 miles south of Colchester on Route 82, includes Chapman Falls, the Eight Mile River's spectacular 60-foot plunge, several interesting glacial formations, shady woodland, and a view of the hills. There are more than 15 miles of hiking trails and connecting logging roads and paths, many of which start near the covered bridge.

The Westwoods Area in Guilford is an open area partially owned by the state of Connecticut, but largely private property. Access is through Peddlar's Park. (To go through Peddlar's Park, leave Route 95 at exit 57, travel south on Route 1, turn sharply right in 5/8 mile on Peddlars Road which runs to Moose Hill Road.)

There are basically four color-coded, circle-marked trails leading north and south, and two rectangle-marked east-west trails. The east-west blue base trail bisects the north-south trails which, from east to west are orange, white, yellow and violet. The blue trail starts at Bishop's Pond and runs to Moose Hill Road. It is the primary access to the north-south trails, except for the **Charles Hubbard Memorial Trail** (marked with orange H), 2.5 miles, which intersects the orange trail. The Charles Hubbard starts south of the Bishop's Pond parking lot, and permission from the property owner on the premises is required to enter. (The Connecticut Forest and Park Association Walkbook lists Bernard N. Kane, 138 State St., Guilford, Conn. 06437 as chairman of this section in 1976 if information is needed for advance permission). A Green Trail, also starting from Bishop's Pond, runs to the north of the blue trail. The trails are harder farther west, with the green nature trail presenting the fewest problems, the orange and the white, 5.12 miles, being more difficult, and the yellow the most rugged. (The violet trail on the west is an exception. It is fairly easy).

The **Cockaponset Trail**, 7.3 miles in the Cockaponset State Forest near Clinton, passes through woodland, across several brooks, along the Pataconk Reservoir shore and up to a high ledge with only a limited view. It begins 2.6 miles east of Route 81 at the intersection of Route 148 and Filley Road, and ends at Beaver Meadow Road ¼ mile west of Route 9.

The **Mattabesett Trail**, 39 miles, is a through trail offering a woodland area of brooks, bogs and ledges, and some excellent ridgetop walking. It starts near the Connecticut River at Seven Falls Roadside Park on Route 9A. To reach the trailhead on Brainerd Hill Road, take Route 9 to the Spencer Road cutoff one mile southwest of Higganum. Follow Spencer Road about 1¼ miles to the trailhead. The trail ends 200 yards north of the Metacomet trailhead on U.S. 15, 2.5 miles southwest of Berlin.

EASTERN REGION

The **Nipmuck Trail**, 21.5 miles plus 5.75 miles of Pudding Lane Branch, stretches south from Bigelow Brook in Yale Forest (near U.S. 171 at North Ashford) to close to Fenton River, about half a mile northeast of Springhill, where it splits into two southern branches: one 0.8 miles west of Route 195 on Pudding Lane in Mansfield, and the other on a dirt road north of the picnic section of Mansfield Hollow Dam Recreation Area. The trail passes through several different types of terrain. On the Pudding Lane section, be careful not to bother the animals at the University Animal Diseases Farm. If you are coming from the south, after the trails have merged and about 9½ miles from Mansfield Hollow, the trail leads onto private property past a "No Trespassing" sign. This is a fairly recent route, so ignore the sign. About 1 mile farther north, is an area known as "Murder Lane." An old cellar hole is all that is left of the place where the crime was committed.

The **James L. Goodwin State Forest and Conservation Center** is a unique place. Formerly a forestry operation, it now includes several forest demonstration areas, as well as the Conservation Center which shows how land use in Connecticut has changed over the years. Reached off Route 6 just east of Clark's Corners, the center has only camping sites for supervised youth groups, except for one lean-to available to backpackers who have registered at the center. Trails include an old railroad bed **(Airline Hiking Trail)** crossing the grounds for about 3.66 miles; a yellow-marked 1.12-mile trail, a white-marked one-mile trail and a red-marked .86-mile trail. In addition, there are about three miles of the blue-marked Natchaug (through) Trail here.

The Natchaug Trail leaves Goodwin and travels through the **Southern and Northern Natchaug Forests**, stretching from U.S. 6 in Phoenixville – near Pine Acres Lake ¼ mile northeast of Clark's Corners to U.S. 44 in Eastford. Interesting features include some large anthills near Black Spruce Pond, the lean-to at Orchard Hill, a scenic climb up Goodwin Brook Falls, rivers, brooks and a chestnut "skeleton." About 11.6 miles.

The **Mansfield Hollow State Park** is built around a reservoir and offers trails passing through stone foundations, former pastures, and what is left of former homesteads in the area. The trails are easy and many hikers have found bits and pieces of stone knives, arrowheads, and other archeological evidence of habitation by the Nipmuck Tribe. It is also possible to watch the dam operations. The trails are not named, but there are about three miles of pathways through the park.

The **Pachaug State Forest** just north of Voluntown, is the largest state forest in Connecticut. Take Conn. 138 west to the firetower on Trail Roads or go north on Route 49 to Forest Headquarters. Unfortunately, at one time the forest's 24,000 acres were also among the most thoughtlessly lumbered in the New England area, although today, careful management is restoring the growth. White pine, hemlock and coastal white cedar are present, which add to the possibility of improving the forest's condition. About 100 additional acres are being converted to conifer type each year. An interesting feature of the park is the Rhododendron Sanctuary. It usually blossoms around the Fourth of July and is an unusual type of area. The highest point in the park is the Mount Misery Overlook (441 feet) which provides views of the forest and the town. It is reached via the Firetower Road or on the Nehantic Trail. There are 20 campsites in the area, although none are available on the trails.

The park contains two short trails as well as sections of four through trails. The white blazed **Castle Trail**, 1.5 miles, connects the **Quinnebaug Trail** at the Phillips Pond Picnic Area with the **Nehantic Trail**, passing the ruins of an old castle on Stone Hill Road.

The **Canonicus Trail**, 2.5 miles, also white blazed, starts south of the Shetucket Turnpike at the Pachaug Trail and leads into Rhode Island, to the Escoheag Hill Lookout Tower.

The **Nehantic Trail**, 14 miles, starts near the camping area at Green Falls Pond, crosses ledges, climbs Mount Misery and Stone Hill, and ends at the parking area in Hopeville Pond State Park.

The **Narragansett Trail**, (20 miles, 16 in Connecticut), begins at Lantern Hill on Route 2, 2.5 miles east of Route 164. It travels through woods and ravines, and passes several brooks and lakes. From the high points, the Atlantic Ocean is visible. The trail ends near the town of Canonchet in Rhode Island.

The **Pachaug Trail**, about 15 miles, starts one mile into Rhode Island on RI 165 at a beach area on the yellow Tippecansett Trail. The trail passes Beach Pond, Dawley Pond, Mount Misery and ends, after going by Pachaug Pond, at the Pauchaug River near Route 138. There are several good picnic areas along the route.

The **Quinebaug Trail**, 9.7 miles, begins at the Lowden Brook Picnic Area on the Pachaug Trail and follows the Pachaug Trail for 0.4 miles. When the Pachaug turns south, it continues west, intersects the Castle Trail, passes through Hell's Hollow and follows Spaulding Road north to end at Plainfield Pike on Route 14A about ½ mile east of Smith Road.

The **Mashamoguet Brook State Park** is 5 miles southwest of Putnam on Route 44. Its most famous feature is the Wolf Den where Israel Putnam, who was later to find fame in the Revolutionary War, shot the last wolf in the area. The wolf had been preying on local farms for several years. Near the Den are several interesting rock formations, the Table Rock and Indian Chair, which provides a good view of the valley from its "seat." There is an interesting interconnected system of 12 numbered trails in the area, most under or just over a mile long. Trail 12 goes to Indian Chair and passes close to the Wolf Den. Trail 2 passes close to Table Rock. There are three camping areas: between Trails 1, 2, 7 and Wolf Den Drive; off a road extending Trail 3 from Wolf Den Drive; and near the entrance to the park. There is also swimming and fishing in the area.

The **Rocky Neck State Park**, in East Lyme, juts out into Long Island Sound, even dips beneath the surface. To get there, take exit 72 south from U.S. 95 into the Park. It includes a 3/4 mile expanse of white sand along clear water, abundant fish and wildlife, and wooded trails. There is also a scenic marsh. The trails lead to natural formations, such as Rocking Rock, Baker's Cave or Tony's Nose and are not at all difficult walking. There are also several historic sites on the park grounds, including a shipyard, salt works and tannery, as well as several campsites.

New York

There is a popular concept that the East Coast is made up of wall-to-wall houses and elbow-rubbing people, and has barely enough room for a walk in the park, let alone wilderness hiking. It isn't so. Take New York. The state is riddled with trails, including those traversing one of the biggest "wild" areas in the east and, if public policies don't nibble too much at its edges, there is enough such "unspoiled" land to last for generations. The Adirondack State Park, in particular, includes an area comparable in size to the Grand Canyon, Yellowstone, Glacier, Yosemite, and Olympic National Parks combined. And, less than an hour's drive from New York City, Bear Mountain and Harriman State Parks provide hundreds of hiking trails, five to 20 miles long, with mountains and views of the Hudson River. (That's all we're going to say about that park, though. There are already a lot of people in it.)

The wealth of trails in New York is due to a fairly enlightened public policy history in the state. Hiram Bingham, governor in the early years of the century (also the first white man to discover the lost city of Macchu Picchu in Peru) brought conservation ethics to that executive office. More recently, Nelson Rockefeller used his long tenure to help expand protection for the state's wild country.

In 1972, for example, the Adirondack Park Agency's "Master Plan for State Owned Lands in the Adirondack Park" was approved. This plan places strict controls on public use and management in the area.

There are three basic geographic zones in New York, with three different types of forest and trail. The western and central parts of the state are characterized by limestone glens where the trails often follow deep winding gorges cut into shale with hundreds of waterfalls, chutes, pools, and small parks scattered throughout the area. Then, there is the Rip Van Winkle country of the Catskills, where hardwoods dominate the mountains. And finally, there are the mountains of the northern Adirondacks. These are mixed hardwood valleys that change to a birch zone on the slopes and end in alpine tundra on the peaks.

The Adirondacks have long been a favorite area for the famous and the literary. Poets Ralph Waldo Emerson and James Russell Lowell and scientist Louis Agassiz formed a "Philosophers' Camp" there in 1858.

Colden Dike – rugged, trailless route up Mount Colden in the Adirondack High Peak Region.

James Fenimore Cooper used the Lake George area as background for his novels. Mark Twain had a summer camp on Lower Saranac Lake.

Because of this early publicity they brought to the area, and the willingness of the government in the early days to sell land, much of the park-to-be fell into private ownership and remains so today. Although it is the largest park in the U.S., 60 per cent of its land is still privately held.

The dominance of private ownership gives the park a different flavor from that found exclusively in government-owned parks. For instance, it does seem unusual at first to find a whole town, complete with high school, dime store and newspaper office within park boundaries.

You can usually expect clouds to be hanging over the Adirondacks, with rapid changes from rain to gloom to sun to rain. And on trips to the east end of Lake Ontario you should keep in mind the phenomena of lake-effect storms — violent rains in summer and massive snow storms in winter. Weather in the Glens country is consistently nicer and more predictable, while the Catskills are a milder version of the Adirondacks.

Seasons are characterized by muddy springs leading to bugs by the bucket that diminish greatly in number by early summer. Summers are wet and hot until middle or late August, when the weather turns dry. Late August through early October is the best hiking time — the ground is as dry as it's going to get, the bugs have nearly vanished, and trees have begun to show their fall color.

There are snakes in the Catskills, the southernmost area described in this guidebook, but you aren't likely to see many unless you wander out at night, when reptiles seek the warmth of pavement or open ground, or unless you develop a compulsion to turn over rocks. If snakes know you're coming, they tend to get out of the way. Bites come from stepping on one by accident, reaching or stepping into hidden spots where they're lying, or just being short on alertness. If you do meet one, let it leave or back off slowly to avoid problems.

Except for a few limited areas, the Adirondacks are snake-free.

Commercially valuable hardwood forests in the Adirondacks have been cut, recut, and cut again. Remaining are extensive stands of beech, but their elephant-gray trunks are being attacked today by beech rust disease and so also may decline soon in numbers. White pine, the lumberman's only remaining resource of any quantity, is under heavy pressure. Oak, the common ridgetop plant of extensive sandy hills, suffers from the gypsy moth and a slightly hostile climate, so the oak trees are generally scrubby. Spruce bud worm attacks the spruce and some other conifers, while the fragrant cedar is hunted for tourist gifts and handcrafts. Thanks to Dutch Elm disease, few of those stately giants remain, but maple, common to the lower valleys, makes New York one of, if not *the*, biggest maple sugar producer in the country.

If this gives a depressing picture of the state of health in New York forests, good. Foresters and conservation people have, for a long time, taken each separate problem and treated it on a cost/value basis to come up with justification for more cutting and less expenditure. (This attitude is apparent not just in New York. Areas to the east have had enough gypsy moths since the late 1800's to make the death of the oak and serious damage to other hard woods a long-time major threat.) But even when the massive elms began to die en masse, few people seemed to care. New Brunswick is currently encountering the same problem. That Canadian province has had little Dutch elm disease impact as yet, but forestry officials seem to think it won't bother their trees.

In spite of all the problems the New York forests have, though, there is still a huge forest – there are even some areas of big timber left – and it's big enough (if managed well) to absorb many invaders, even lumbermen, for at least the next 300 years.

The state Department of Environmental Conservation operates 45 campgrounds in the Adirondacks and the Catskills. Permits are issued on arrival and reservations are not accepted in advance. The fee is $2.50 per night per site, but is collected only during busy summer months. The Department also maintains 200 "Open Camps" along the 1,000 miles of trail and near canoe routes in the Forest Preserve (state owned sections) areas. These camps feature "Adirondack Lean-Tos," fireplaces and pit privies. If you plan your hike carefully around use of these sites, you can lighten your backpacking load since you won't need a tent.

TRAILS IN THE WEST – ALLEGANY STATE PARK

Each region has a distinctive character, well worth getting to know. Although our emphasis here will be on the east, the western region deserves at least a few days of roaming around. Letchworth State Park near Geneseo and the Allegany State Park in the southwest contain extensive tracts, but small parks – all of them based on a gorge or limestone glen natural formation – are more typical. Notable among these parks are those in the *Finger Lakes* region.

FINGER LAKES REGION

The Finger Lakes are 11 lakes with the long and narrow shape of fingers. The Iroquois Indians believed the five largest were formed by the Great Spirit pressing his hand upon the earth. **Buttermilk Falls** and the **Robert H. Treman State Park** west of Ithaca on N.Y. Route 13 are particularly scenic. The Park includes **Enfield Glen**, whose three miles of hiking trails pass 12 waterfalls; as well as fine walks along gorges cut into interesting shapes. The famous **Watkins Glen** region, at the south end of Seneca Lake (accessible via N.Y. Route 14) also offers rugged rock patterns, glens, waterfalls, and gorges in addition to lakes and varied plantlife. There is a three-mile trail running the length of the

Glen, and an Indian trail along the rim.

Some 5,300 acres of unspoiled marshland offering several miles of hiking trails can be found in the **Montezuma National Wildlife Refuge** at the northern tip of Cayuga Lake. The area attracts numerous species of waterfowl.

Take the Seneca Falls exit from Interstate 90 about 25 miles west of Syracuse and drive east on Routes 5 and 20 to the refuge entrance. Hiking trails are closed in May and June to protect newly hatched birds.

The 350-mile Finger Lakes Trail, almost complete, connects the Red House in Allegany State Park with the Catskills. Part of the National Scenic Trail system, it will eventually connect with the Appalachian Trail, the Long Trail of Vermont, and the Bruce Trail of Canada. It is not a wilderness trail, but it does pass through calm woodlands and fern coated areas, and it passes several spectacular waterfalls. Particularly scenic is the section bordering the Finger Lakes. Although most of the trail is finished, some sections (including a spur north to the Adirondacks) are still under construction, and a few segments still need sponsorship.

Further information on the Finger Lakes Region is available from the Finger Lakes Conference, c/o Frances Jacobi, 71 Superior Road, Rochester, N. Y. 14625, the State Department of Environmental Conservation, Albany, N. Y. 12201, or the State Bureau of Parks and Recreation.

Interesting walks may also be had at **Letchworth State Park**, which stretches southwest to northeast in a narrow ribbon between Portageville on N.Y. Route 19 and Mount Morris on N.Y. 36. This beautiful area has an unusual tree plantation, lovely bridges, and borders on the great gorge of the Genesee River, the "Grand Canyon of the East." Indian traditions, such as archery contests, are kept alive here too.

There are about 20 miles of hiking trails in Allegany State Park, which borders Pennsylvania's Allegheny National Forest and is accessible via N.Y. Route 17 east of Jamestown.

There are so many trails in the west region, basically similar, but each with a distinctive flair, that the best thing to do is just hoof around the glens and gorges and find them. It's fun to come upon big waterfalls, carvings, and gorges without warning.

THE CATSKILLS

The Catskills, in the southeastern part of the state, have a gentler quality than the land in the west, although there are steep-sided valleys, rocky glens, ridges, and ravines next to the rounded mountain tops. These mountains are part of the same Allegheny plateau that widens throughout Pennsylvania and West Virginia, becoming the Poconos and other ranges.

The Indians called the Catskills the "Land in the Sky," the Dutch "Wildcat Mountain." The Dutch word evolved into "Catskills," but it was not until fairly recently in New York history that the area was fully explored. As late as 1918, for example, there was still confusion as to exactly how to get to the summit of Slide Mountain. Recent years have brought not only increased knowledge of the area, but macadam and concrete highways and trails to all the major peaks.

Access to the Catskills is via N.Y. Route 23, 212 and 28 west of Interstate 87 between Athens and Kingston.

The trails of the Catskills are well marked and passable all year. Intersections are indicated by signboards and trail routes by circular markers in red, blue, and yellow. Many of the trails cross private land. When this is indicated, camping, fishing, picnicking, and hunting are often prohibited according to the owner's wishes.

The Catskill trails may be divided into those of the northern area and those in the central area. Northern trails include the **Indian Head-Hunter Mountain Range Trail**, 23.19 miles. Access is via N.Y. 23A west of Interstate 87 north of Kingston. Drive ½ mile west of the New York City Police Camp and turn south at Tannersville on Platte Clove Road 0.4 miles. The trailhead is south of a bridge across the East Branch of Echoharie Creek. The trail, heading west, is marked in red with a lean-to at 14.2 miles. It passes over the ridges of Indian Head, Twin, and Sugarloaf Mountains, Plateau, and Hunter Mountains. There are several good views as the trail follows these ridges for most of its length. It crosses N.Y. 214 and ends at Spruceton Road. Carry a canteen on this trail during the dry season.

The yellow-blazed **Echo Lake Trail**, 2.8 miles, turns off the Indian Head Trail 1.65 miles west of its eastern terminus and continues to the Echo Lake lean-to, a pretty lake, and a clear spring.

At mile 4.2 on the Indian Head Trail (from its eastern end), at Jimmy Dolan Notch, a blue-blazed trail, 2.7 miles long, heads north to Platte Clove Road ½ mile west of the Police Camp. This side trail involves a steep descent and after 2.2 miles turns right to follow red blazes.

A trail to Pecoy Notch begins at Platte Clove Road near the turn to Twin Mountain House. It follows blue markers and may be followed south to Indian Head or to Sugarloaf or Twin Mountains.

Mink Hollow Trail, 11.7 miles, leads from Lake Hill on N.Y. 212 northeast to Tannersville. It is marked with blue blazes and heads northeast three miles to an old mill, past a lean-to in another three miles, then across slopes of Sugarloaf, Twin, Indian Head, and Plattkill Mountains.

Hunter Mountain (4,040 feet) is the second highest mountain in the Catskills. There are four trails to the firetower on its top. The blue-marked **Becker Trail**, 2.4 miles, is reached by following Stony Clove Road (N.Y. Route 214) one mile north of the Devil's Tombstone Campsite. There is a spring on the trail. The multi-coded **Spruceton Trail**, 3.7

Author Henley on the "Waltzing Matilda" Bridge at cliff base in Avalanche Pass at Mount Colden in the Adirondacks High Peaks.

miles, begins eight miles east of West Kill where Spruceton Road meets a truck trail. Follow a blue-blazed trail to Old Hunter Road, then continue on a red-blazed one. After you pass a spring and a lean-to, begin following the yellow-blazed trail. At the Colonel's Chair and Hunter Village, a blue trail branches off to a spring while the yellow trails leads to the observatory. The **Shanty Hollow Trail** starts at the Colonel's Chair but follows the yellow markers to a recrossing of the Spruceton Trail. At that point, you may follow a blue-blazed side trail to a spring, then follow yellow markers past a lean-to and eventually to Devil's Tombstone Public Campsite.

The Phoenicia and Willow Trails provide access to **Mount Tremper** (2,720 feet). The **Phoenicia**, 2.15 miles, is shorter, steeper, and easier to reach by car. It starts on N.Y. Route 28 about a mile east of Phoenicia Village, heads south, following red markers, and passes one lean-to. The **Willow**, 4.6 miles, begins west of the Willow Post Office on N.Y. 212 at a cross road. The trail follows the crossroad west, then turns left.

The **Diamond Notch Trail**, 4.5 miles, leads from Lanesville north to the Hunter Mountain Trail. Access is on Stone Clove Road (Route 214) at the Lanesville highway bridge and Hollow Tree Brook. Follow the dirt road on the east side of the brook north, and where the road ends, follow the blue markers. There is a spring and a lean-to on the trail.

The **Escarpment Trail**, 24 miles, in the **North and South Mountain area**, is one of the oldest trails in the Catskills and provides continuous views of the Hudson Valley and Kaaterskill Clove. The North and South Mountains are famous for their rock formations, bear dens, blueberries, and a high glacial swamp pothole of black alder, which becomes full of red berries in the fall. They also contain the Sleepy Hollow made famous by Washington Irving. The blue-marked trail begins on the north side of the intersection of Kaaterskill Creek and Route 23A. Several side trails along the route lead to lookouts and waterfalls. Lean-tos may be reached off a side trail at 13.77 miles by turning onto the yellow trail at 23.05 miles.

The **Blackhead Range Trail** climbs four miles to the summit of Blackdome Mountain (3,980 feet) and offers spectacular views at its end. The red-marked trail begins at the intersection of Maple Crest Road and Elmer Barnum Road; it follows east on the road, follows the Old Town Road to the left, and turns left again on a footpath to the summit.

Central area trails include the **Phoenicia-East Branch Trail**, 9.85 miles, which passes through woodland and along streams mostly on wood roads, with no steep climbs. It begins near the Woodland Valley Club, reached by following the macadam Woodland Valley Road south from a point on Route 28 about one mile west of Phoenicia. The trail is marked in yellow and ends on the highway to Claryville.

The **Giant Ledge-Panther Mountain-Fox Hollow Trail**, 8.9 miles, begins at the eight-mile point of the Phoenicia-East Branch Trail and climbs to Giant Ledge (3,200 feet) and Panther Mountain (3,710 feet). There is a lean-to 125 feet to the left of the trail at the 6.3-mile point. Follow markers at the trailsite.

The **Wittenberg-Cornell Slide Trail**, 8.9 miles, explored by naturalist John Burroughs, leads to Slide Mountain (4,180 feet), highest peak in the Catskills, as well as to Wittenberg (3,720 feet) and Cornell (3,880 feet). It is a famous trail, with good views, hard climbing and, unfortunately, thousands of travelers every year. Access is at Woodland Valley where the Wittenberg Trail intersects a macadam road. The trail is marked in red; there are lean-tos at 1.45 and 6.05 miles, and there are several springs.

There are two trails to the **Belleayre Mountain Observatory** (3,375 feet). The **Hanley Corners Trail**, 3.55 miles, originally a bridle path, is the easiest. It begins in Hanley Corners, reachable from Fleischmann's on N.Y. Route 28 by turning south on Railroad Avenue, crossing an iron bridge and the railroad tracks and continuing straight ahead. The trail is marked in red. The **Lost Clove Trail**, 3.05 miles, also marked in red, begins at Esopus Creek. To get there drive ½ mile south on the road to Oliverea from Big Indian Village on N.Y. Route 28.

The **Pine Hill-Eagle Mountain-West Branch Trail**, 14.25 miles, crosses not only Belleayre, but also Balsam (3,620 feet), and Big Indian (3,680 feet) Mountains. Access from the east is in Pine Hill Village at the foot of Pine Hill. Access from the west is West Branch Highway. The trail is marked in blue. A yellow blazed side trail at the halfway point directs you to a lean-to.

The **Seager-Big Indian Mountain Trail**, 4.1 miles, starts at the Seager Post Office and heads north to end at the Pine Hill-Eagle Mountain-West Branch Trail, following the valley of the Dry Brook. There is a lean-to at 3.2 miles.

The **Oliverea-Mapledale Trail**, 6.85 miles, travels west from the town of Oliverea to where Mapledale Road intersects the Dry Brook. Access is at the bridge over Esopus Creek in Oliverea. The trail passes between Balsam and Haynes Mountains, intersects the Pine Hill Mountain-West Branch Trail at 2.65 miles, is red-marked and has three lean-tos at 1.3, 3.85, and four miles.

The Delaware Trails are a system of five trails in Delaware County immediately west of Catskills Park. The **Trout Pond Trail**, 5.4 miles, marked in blue, is reached from Route 17, westbound exit 93, or eastbound exit 92. Turn northeasterly on Russell Brook Road and follow it about five miles to the start of the trail. There are two lean-tos, at 0.9 and 1.4 miles. The trail ends at the start of the Campbell Mountain Trail.

The **Campbell Mountain Trail**, 4.1 miles, climbs up Brock Mountain and has a lean-to at 1.1 miles. It is also marked in blue and ends at the beginnings of the **Little Spring Brook** and **Pelnor Hollow Trails**.

The **Little Spring Brook Trail**, marked in yellow, travels 0.6 miles to the end of the state land, but a town road may be followed another 1.1 miles from this point to Cat Hollow Road.

The **Pelnor Hollow Trail** continues four miles before the state land ends. The town road here may be followed 1.5 miles to Berry Brook Road. This trail is blazed in blue and has a lean-to at 3.1 miles.

The **Mary Smith Trail**, 4.5 miles, begins 0.8 miles into the Pelnor Hollow Trail or from the Holiday Brook Road and Parking Area 1.2 miles farther east. It leads to Mary Smith Hill Road.

There are six trails to the **Balsam Lake Mountain Observatory** (3,720 feet). The **Neversink-Hardenburg Trail**, 14.7 miles and marked with yellow blazes, starts at the bridge over the east branch of the Neversink, ½ mile south of Claryville and heads to Hardenburg.

The red-marked **South Approach**, 2.75 miles, starts at the 11.2-mile point on the Neversink-Hardenburg Trail, and leads to the observatory. There is a lean-to at 2.35 miles.

The **North Approach**, 3.05 miles, begins two miles east of the Belleayre Post Office at a point where the Pakatakan-Dry Brook Ridge-Beaverkill Trail meets Millbrook Road. The red-marked trail ends at the 11.2-mile mark on the Neversink-Hardenburg Trail.

The **Long Pond Trail**, 3.9 miles, leaves the Neversink-Hardenburg trail at the 2.1-mile mark and leads to the Long Pond lean-to and lake.

Also intersecting the Neversink-Hardenburg Trail is the **Pakatakan-Dry Brook Ridge-Beaverkill Trail**, 14.1 miles, near Margaretville. It is reached via the new Route 28. Turn left at the Agway Farm Store and take the first left-hand road. The trail starts on the right in 1/8 mile. **Pakatakan Mountain** (3,100 feet) is a landmark along the trail. There are intersections with other trails leading to Balsam Lake Mountain. There is a lean-to at 7.9 miles. The trail ends at the 11.2 mark on the Neversink-Hardenburg Trail.

THE ADIRONDACKS

Most of northern New York is included in the Adirondack region. The mountains here are far more rugged than the Catskills, with peaks of open rock to 5,344 feet, hundreds of little lakes, hundreds of miles of trail and many kinds of physical environments. This is the biggest hunk of wild real estate not under restricted access or commercial control in the east. It's still possible to hike, camp, swim, climb, and just look around without paying for it here.

The history of the Adirondack forests is the history of invasion by water, attack on the timber, and slow settlement. From the time Albany was settled in the mid 1600's until now, lumbering has been the primary activity throughout the Adirondacks, with the tourist trade trying to come in second since the turn of this century and gradually catching up.

Adirondack hikers are faced with a variety of terrain, ranging from sandy hills with conifer cover, to the alpine conditions of the High Peaks region. Typically soggy from early spring until mid-summer, the trails have a lovely black goo between stretches of sand, gravel, and boulder.

In the High Peaks region of the Mac Intyre Mountain Range are the open rock summits of the "46." The name refers to the number of peaks over 4,000 feet high, (or at least once thought to be over that height until a resurvey lowered some of them). Most are found in the region south of Lake Placid, with Mount Marcy as the center. Marcy, at 5,344 feet, is both the highest point in the state and the most heavily trafficked. Characteristic of overused trails, there is the "herd" path up Marcy from Heart Lake. It is deeply rutted and widely tromped, with deep holes bypassed by equally muddy bypasses.

The northern approaches to the Marcy area are probably the most used. Firewood, campsite openings, and just plain peace and quiet are in short supply during the "prime" summer vacation period. We'd highly suggest any visits to the area be out-of-season.

Since climbing the "46" peaks is an addictive project claiming a goodly number of trail stompers, we should mention the *Adirondack High Peaks* book put together by the Adirondack Forty-Sixers Club. It's a fine collection of advice, and information of practical and historic interest. We'll also add that, given all the people on the trail during those peak user weeks, bushwacking the "46" off-trail has become more and more popular. Thanks to the structure of the peaks, it's fairly easy to navigate. (We won't mention once climbing the wrong mountain in a six-hour battle with jackstraw [blowdown] and second growth in the Sewards on the west side of the High Peaks Region.) Slide scars, ridges, and streams provide a wealth of navigable routes, with, of course, a few tough tangles of bush to bust here and there. Most of the jackstraw blowdown from an old hurricane has now collapsed. Once, though, it was possible to cover a fair bit of mountain by clambering over the top of downed timber 10-15 feet deep.

Many of the "46" peaks are listed as trailless . . . but in fact there are frequent paths to, or to be found at, the summit. Sometimes the path merely means that a lot of people have made the same mistake. Usually some feature of the mountain has forced hikers into the same spot and collectively they've established a route out. But any of the peaks can be climbed off-trail – depending on how serious the climber is. In some cases, it can get to be a highly technical rock climb, in others, a matter of getting all the bush-busting a human body can stand. Add black flies to the project, and peaks like Street and Nye that look like little lumps become something a lot of climbers tend to talk about with red-eyed fervor about conquering. Anyone planning such trailless jaunts to the Peaks area should base his outing on a set of topo maps. And, for the sake of keeping up the blood supply, some good insect repellent.

One fairly unique kind of natural route throughout the Adirondacks is formed from the big slide scars left when the thin soil slips off the steep-sided humps of anorhosite. Mountains like Giant, Gothics, and Big Slide are well noted for their characteristic markings, and the routes up them vary from "better than the scrub" to serious rock climbing challenges. The west face of Giant, the slides of Gothics, and several others are rock climber routes, not hikers' pathways. Marshall, Seward, Colden, and McComb have scars that can be used as routes . . . but with caution. Rain, or snow (which can and has fallen in every month of the year) can make them dangerous.

Streambeds are not normally a good make-do route in this area. They are far too rocky and cluttered to make decent time on. It's often easier to get above the stream a distance to where the ground may be more even. Ridges sometimes work well, but old blowdown can make them rough. Best bet is normally to get away from the rugged little stream and into standing trees on or just under the ridge lines. But there is no real rule of thumb to go by. Movement becomes a matter of finding the least resistance when making your own way.

The Northville Placid Trail

This 133-mile, blue-marked trail is destined to be part of the National Scenic Trail cutting across the northern U.S. For now, it connects the lower (southern) Adirondack village of Northville to the High Peak region and Lake Placid.

The trail begins at the western end of the bridge over the Sacandaga River in Northville. The first nine miles of the trail follow N.Y. Route 30 from Northville to Benson Center. Since the trail was first laid out in 1922, these miles are preserved as part of the trail for historic purposes, but if you have the time it's a good idea to walk them. The scenery along the Stony Creek Valley is worth lingering over.

These nine miles and the next 24, going on to Piseco, constitute the trail's first section in brochures compiled by the state Department of Environmental Protection. The path is bordered by wild forests. The second section, 17 miles long, follows a logging road north to Spruce Lake, then cuts through country that was not opened until the trail was put through. It still imparts the atmosphere of true wilderness. The third section, about 26 miles, from West Canada Lake to Stephens Pond Junction, is rolling upland. At one time, it was heavily lumbered, but wild growth is returning. The next 17 miles, between Stephens Pond Junction and Long Lake, are wild country with steep ridges. The trail follows streams and around lakes. The next 13 miles, from Long Lake to Shattuck Clearing, is primarily through open woodland. (If you want to avoid some walking here, you can take the mail boat from Long Lake Village to Plumley's Landing.) The final section, about 25 miles, to Lake Placid, follows old logging roads over a fairly easy grade.

*The last bit up Mount Colden in the Adirondack
High Peak Region with Marcy Dam below.*

There are no stores selling supplies between Piseco and West Canada
Lake or between Long Lake and Lake Placid. Otherwise, accommodations, restaurants, and stores are available at various communities along
the way. There are lean-tos and open camps at fairly short intervals, and
temporary camping is permitted at undeveloped sites on state-owned
land.

Turn-back or alternate routes out are few and far between, on the
northernmost portion of the trail and, once Long Lake is left behind,
the hiker is committed to keep going – with no civilization except the
ranger station at Duck Hole before reaching Lake Placid.

Spring, by the way, is not the finest time to do this trail. Beavers,
bogs, and bugs can put some pressure on a hiker's patience. Late summer or autumn gives the feet a more solid trail and a much more kindly
population of bugs.

One particularly interesting place should be pointed out: the remains
of Noah Rondeau's "town" on the Cold River, right in the middle of a
40-mile stretch of woods. Rondeau, who died in 1967 at the age of 84,
was a hermit. He lived at his "Cold River City," complete with a long
hut called the "Town Hall," a shorter hut called the "Hall of Records,"
and three wigwams: his "Wife's Kitchenette," the "Pyramid," and the
"Beauty Parlor." This "Mayor of Cold River" would venture out only
once each year, at Christmas, to get his mail and to play Santa Claus.
Otherwise, his only contacts for years were the growing number of
"46ers" and other hikers who "discovered" his city in the woods.

The High Peaks

Giant to Seward: Actually, there is no direct trail between Giant
(4,627 feet) and Seward (4,361 feet). Since the main division of the
High Peaks is between three passes running north-south, any crossing
from east to west is going to run into all kinds of trouble: Up, down,
around . . . and over half of the "46." But this is as good a way as any
of providing a sequence for describing some of the High Peak Trails,
(and quite a challenge for anyone who wants to try to make the crossing).

Beginning on the east side of Giant, as a warm-up, is the longest
ascent in the High Peaks, five miles, going up from about 1,000 feet to
over 4,600 by way of Rocky Ridge Peak. The yellow-marked trail begins on the northwest side of Route 9, just outside of New Russia and
heads southwest to the summit. Watch for the trail sign. This is a fairly
new trail, but not nearly as well kept up as others in the region. There
is one lean-to about ¾ mile from the start.

From the summit of Giant, the whole High Peaks region sprawls out
to the west. (If you did intend to make the crossing you might recon-
sider while standing above the first pass through the mountain below
Giant.) There are several trails down Giant – one marked in red, along

the ridge to the northeast (about 6¾ miles); one to the north and down into Keene, (about 5¼ miles); and one straight down the Slide scar. The ridge trail is a fine one for early spring since the snow melts early. The north trail gets you down but isn't very interesting. And the path down the slide scar is a job of work, recommended to experienced climbers only. It's steep and mossy, wet, and dangerous. Once off the bedrock, it's still a long way down a boulder-chocked stream bed to the highway below Roaring Brook Falls. This trail is called the **Roaring Brook Trail**, and is 3.57 miles long.

Chapel Pond, in a mountain pass on Route 73 at the end of the southernmost route down Giant Mountain, is a fine site for rock-climbing and a popular base for heading up Giant or into the Dix Range west of Route 73. Camping is not permitted in the Chapel Pond area, though, so hikers should plan to get well up the **Dix Trail** or otherwise off Giant before nightfall.

The trail up **Mount Dix** (4,857 feet), 6.7 miles, begins at the top of the hill along the southerly approach to the Ausable Club which heads west from Route 73 north of Chapel Pond. A sign indicates the trail and parking area. This trail is very steep and marked in blue.

A popular off-trail route, not marked, but with pathways worn by use descends Mount Dix on the east, turns south, climbs **Hough Peak** (4,300 feet), **South Dix** (4,000 feet), and **McComb Mountain** (4,405 feet), for a magnificent view of Elk Lake and the mountains in back of it. Descent from Dix Mountain to the **Elk-Lake-Dix Trail**, red-marked, is south and west by way of Slide Brook. There is a lean-to on the south slope of the mountain where the trail begins. This trail may be taken south to Elk Lake, a 2.33 mile gradual descent to Elk Lake Road, or it can be followed north, passing a lean-to at Lillian Pond at 1.33 miles, intersecting, at 3.66 miles, a yellow alternate trail access to Dix from Route 73, and continuing north, 6.12 miles past Hunter's Pass and back to Chapel Pond.

The **Trail to Marcy from Elk Lake**, 10.96 miles, is one of the longer approaches to that peak. Camping is not permitted on the first 6.5 miles northeast from Elk Lake; the land is privately owned. The first lean-to on this route is at nine miles, and the trail is marked in blue.

An easy trail up Marcy from the southwest is by way of Calamity Brook from the ghost town where Tahawus used to be. This trail also known as the **Upper Works Trail**, 10.11 miles, is reached by taking N.Y. 28N, 9.1 miles east of Newcomb, turning right, turning right again at the first fork, passing the Sanford Lake bridge and the huge titanium open pit mine on the right, and continuing on to the end of the road where you can park.

The trail begins on red markers, crosses Calamity Brook on a suspension bridge at 1.18 miles, crosses a blue trail from Indian Pass at 1.7 miles, crosses the brook again and follows blue markers to the right as

Avalanche Pass and Lake in the Adirondack High Peaks.

they follow the brook. The trail begins to climb gently, then steeply northeast, then gently before descending to cross the brook again at 2.79 miles. The trail climbs again, goes around Calamity Pond, passes a monument to David Henderson, an iron works manager whose death was the "calamity" after which the stream, mountain, and pond were named, and reaches several lean-tos and the red markers at 4.46 miles. Take the red markers left to pass Lake Colden and climb Marcy. The trail rises 3,600 feet from the ghost town.

The **Van Hoevenberg Trail** up Marcy, seven miles, is the previously mentioned "herd trail" from the Adirondack Lodge at Heart Lake south from N.Y. 73 at North Elba. The trail passes three lean-tos, has some good views and follows Marcy Brook for a time. Markings are in blue. Since the top of the mountain is a rocky cone, watch for rock piles or paint blazes as markers at the summit. (More about Heart Lake below.)

The **Indian Pass Trail**, about seven miles, runs from the Tahawus ghost town north through the cleft between the MacIntyre Range and MacNaughton to Heart Lake.

Another pass, **Avalanche**, is a good route for the return trip. From Tahawus, follow the yellow markers to the first lean-to. Then continue north, following the red. The trail is a gentle, winding trek for almost four miles, passing two lean-tos, with plenty of drinking water available. The last half-mile rises steeply to a lookout rock where most of the mile-long stretch of thousand-foot-high cliffs on the west wall of the Pass can be seen. (There are several rock climbing routes up this face.)

The trail drops down into regions of huge boulders toward the north end of the Pass. Hunt around a little and you'll probably find some ice, even in mid-summer. Cold air running out from under the boulders is refreshing as you walk through. Also at the north end of the pass is a blue-marked trail to the left going to Scott Pond, one of the more remote-feeling sites we've ever been in.

Beyond the boulders of the Pass, the main trail north follows a gentle valley for several miles with a lean-to near an old lumbering operation clearing and dam. This area was a one-time fur trappers' haven.

The last camp south of your destination at Heart Lake is Rocky Falls lean-to, 2.25 miles before the end of the trail.

Heart Lake is owned and operated by the Adirondack Mountain Club. It has many rentable lean-tos, and some foodstuffs and supplies are available at the new Hikers' Center along with showers and phones. It is a starting point for several trails.

Returning to Tahawus is a matter of choosing a trail. You can go over **Algonquin Mountain** (5,110 feet) to Lake Colden and then down, or to Lake Colden via Avalanche Pass. Either is a fine example of Adirondack Trail, but the popularity of Lake Colden might discourage you from planning to camp there. Both trails are marked in yellow. They split just after passing MacIntyre Brook with the Avalanche Pass

Trail on the left, and rejoin shortly after the Avalanche Pass Trail passes Avalanche Lake and intersects a blue trail on the right. The blue trail leads into the Algonquin Mountain Trail. Follow this to a red trail on the right, take it around Flowed Land Lake and turn right on the blue trail which follows Calamity Brook. At the junction with the red trail going straight ahead, take the red back to Tahawus.

Tahawus to Indian Pass is a nine mile round trip; to Heart Lake another 10.2 miles; return via Lake Colden is 21 miles for complete circuit.

To go from the **Tahawus ghost town to Duck Hole**, (6.45 miles), follow the yellow markers north from Tahawus 1.59 miles to an intersection with the red markers, just north of Henderson Lake, but south of the Henderson Lake lean-to. Follow the red blazes along an inlet to the lake. The trail does not begin to rise until you've walked a mile and a half and then only gently. The trail turns right to go around Little Hunter Pond and then goes up a short, steep grade. The trail then descends, steeply at first, then more gently onto a level section. The trail continues to rise and fall along easy grades, passing Upper and Lower Pond and skirting an arm of Duck Pond, before ending at the Northville-Placid Trail described above. Turn left on this trail half a mile to reach a lean-to and the Duck Hole Ranger Station.

The route up Seward is not a trail (there aren't any) but there is a popular path that can be followed if you use caution. The hurricanes have made the going in this region difficult; the climb is not for the inexperienced climber without equipment. Sometimes it is hard to predict what areas will be passable from the map, and you may spend hours going around something you didn't know was there. Do not attempt this without maps, plus a compass, food, first-aid kit, and whatever you need to spend an unexpected night in the woods. From Duck Hole, the route follows the light-duty road to the west just over three miles (there are lean-tos about ¾ mile farther along this road), and takes off to the northwest up Mount Seymour (4,120 feet), down to the north, back to the road and another lean-to, and up toward Seward to the southwest. The trail turns south, then southwest again. From Seward, you may wish to continue south for exploration of Mount Donaldson (4,140 feet), and Mount Emmons (4,040 feet). It's 4½ miles from Seward and Donaldson as the crow flies, but plan on covering at least double that amount.

Cranberry Lake Area

The Cranberry Lake Area is southeast of Route 3 in the western Adirondacks. Access points from that highway are at Wanakena and the town of Cranberry Lake. The region offers 50 miles of interconnected hiking trails in one of the largest wilderness areas in New York. Three outstanding features of the lake are worth noting: The big swing bridge at Wanakena, some big pine at High Falls, and the old bobcat dens on Cat Mountain off the southeast tip of the lake. (There actually was a bobcat a few years back — it followed one of the authors all the way from Cat Mountain Ranger Station down to the lakeshore). There has been relatively little civilization buildup here; beyond the trails and canoeable waters, unbroken forestland reaches south past Beaver River. The trails themselves tend to be far less stomped down than those in the High Peaks. Some are even obscure in autumn.

There are 13 lean-tos along the trails, and there is a public campsite just east of Cranberry Lake Village. Permits are not required for stays of less than three nights at undeveloped sites or lean-tos. For longer stays, see the forest rangers in Cranberry Lake or Star Lake.

The Loop, actually a series of truck trails and connecting paths, starts in the village of Wanakena. It forms a 16-mile hub from which several other trails branch out over the region. Follow the red-marked **High Falls Truck Trail** for the first mile and a half south, then fork left to follow the blue **Leary Trail** for 2.7 miles. Rejoin the truck trail and follow it east for another 1.75 miles, at which point there are two lean-tos and the magnificent sight of High Falls. (The blue-marked **Plains Trail** cuts across the Loop here, heading north to Glasby Pond, and shortens the Loop by 2.2 miles). The main trail then becomes red-marked for 4.7 miles east and then north to **Cowhorn Junction**. Just past Cowhorn Junction, follow the yellow trail left 1.5 miles to the red-marked **Cat Mountain Trail**. This will lead west past the edge of Dead Creek Flow and join the **Dead Creek Flow Truck Trail**, also red-marked, back to Wanakena. The yellow-marked **Buck Pond Trail**, three miles, leaves the High Falls Truck Trail on the right, 5.5 miles into the Loop and heads south to Buck Pond. Continue on a yellow-blazed path three miles to Cage Lake where the trail winds east to Muir and Woh Ponds.

Proceed south from here via the blue-blazed **Five Ponds-Wolf Pond-Sand Lake Trail** two miles to Sand Lake. Or head north five miles past Little Shallow, Washbowl, Big Shallow, Little Five, and Five Ponds. There are two lean-tos along the route. The **Big Deer Pond Trail**, blazed yellow, leaves the Loop at Cowhorn Junction and travels two miles southwest of Big Deer Pond.

The **Cat Mountain Trail**, 2.05 miles, is a short, steep climb to spectacular views from atop Cat Mountain. It begins on the Loop near Dead Creek Flow at the point where the 0.2-mile yellow Janack's Landing Trail cuts off. Follow the red markers right up the hill.

The **Six Mile Creek Trail**, 4.2 miles, joins the South Flow section of Cranberry Lake to the Loop at Cowhorn Junction. It is marked in blue, has a lean-to on the north shore of Cowhorn Pond, and has two side trails: a red-marked one leading right three miles to Ash Pond a mile north of Cowhorn Junction and one leading left to Olmstead Pond (2.2 miles) and a lean-to.

These Cranberry Lake Trails do not connect with the Loop, and the first three are accessible only by water. The **Clear Pond Trail**, ½ mile, starts at Hedgehog Bay on Cranberry Lake and leads to Clear Pond. It is marked in yellow.

The **Curtis Pond Trail**, 1.2 miles, starts at the southeastern end of East Inlet on the lake and is red-marked. It heads southeast to Curtis Pond.

The **Darning Needle Pond Trail**, 2.4 miles, follows Chair Rock Creek south to Darning Needle Pond, starting at Chair Rock Flow on Cranberry Lake. It is marked in yellow.

The **Bear Mountain Trail**, 2.4 miles, forms a loop, starting at the public campsite near Cranberry Lake Village. It travels over the mountain and has several views of the lake. There is a lean-to 0.6 miles from the public campsite on the red-marked trail.

Moore's Trail, two miles, is a particularly fascinating trail as it follows the Oswegatchie River along a section of waterfalls and rapids, west from Wanakena to Inlet. It is marked in yellow.

Old Forge – Big Moose – Fulton Chain Region

The Old Forge-Big Moose-Fulton Chain region, off N.Y. Route 28 in Herkimer County offers the hiker miles of forestland, large lakes, mountains and streams. Public campsites are scattered through the region, and there are lean-tos on the trails.

In the Old Forge region, the blue-marked **Big Otter Lake Trail**, eight miles, serves as a starting point for several other trails. Basically the fire truck trail from the parking lot ½ mile north of Thendara to Big Otter Lake's southern border, the trail connects to a red trail which goes by a lean-to at Pine Lake before continuing west 9.56 miles to the village of Brantingham. There is also a short (¾ mile) trail to the outlet of Big Otter Lake at the junction of the red and blue trails.

The **Lost Creek Trail**, five miles, marked in red, goes by Big Otter Lake and connects to the East Pond Trail. It starts seven miles from the beginning of the Big Otter Lake Trail, turns northeast, and stops in a dead end.

The yellow **East Pond Trail**, 3.8 miles, passes through sparse forestland and open fields to connect with the Black Foot Pond Trail. It starts 1½ miles east from the beginning of the Big Otter Lake Trail, turns northeast and leads to East Pond, where there is a lean-to.

The **Black Foot Pond Trail**, one mile, another dead-end, leaves the East Pond Trail 3.6 miles east from its beginning. It is marked in red and leads to the Old Mica Mine at Black Foot Pond.

The **Moose River Mountain Trail**, ¾ mile, leaves the Big Otter Pond Trail to the south two miles from its beginning, and climbs up Moose

The Great Range from the ledges of the Giant Ridge Trail in the Adirondack High Peaks.

River Mountain for a pleasant view. It is marked in red.

The **Middle Branch Lake-Cedar Pond-Middle Settlement Lake Trail**, 8.8 miles, is marked in yellow and leaves the Big Otter Lake Trail to the south after 6.5 miles. It provides access to the bodies of water for which it was named as well as Lost Lake, Pine Lake and several lean-tos, before leading to Old Browns Road which may be followed left to Route 28.

The **Nicks Lake-Remsen Falls-Nelson Lake Trail** is an 18-mile network of trails reached either one mile south of the Village of Old Forge on Bisby Road or via the Nicks Lake Campsite. It follows Nicks Lake Creek, the Moose River, and Nelson Lake and has a side trail to Bloodsucker Pond. There is a lean-to at Remsen Falls. The trail is marked in blue.

The **Scusa Access Trail**, 3.75 miles, begins on the west side of Route 28, 3½ miles south of Thendara, and follows red markers. It is a short trail, basically providing access to the Brown Tract Road after ¾ mile, the trail to Cedar Pond by way of Grass Pond after one mile, and the way to the parking lot south of Thendara at this last intersection.

The **O'Kara-Cedar Pond Trail**, 1.75 miles, runs from the Old Brown Tract Road to the lean-to at Cedar Pond. It is marked in red, with a short yellow loop trail going to Grass Pond in ½ mile.

The **Woodhull Mountain Trail** leads to the Woodhull Mountain firetower after following a truck trail for six miles. It starts east of McKeever at a gate and follows the Moose River's south branch, before climbing the last 2.5 miles to the top.

The Big Moose region is northeast of the Old Forge section, and includes several trails accessible only by ·boat, or by boat and aircraft. The **Beaver River Flow** area, just north of Big Moose, for example, includes the **Trout Pond-Salmon Lake-Clear Lake Trail**, 5.5 miles, which begins on the north shore of the Big Trout Pond Reservoir. There is a lean-to on this blue-blazed trail at Salmon Lake. The **Norridge Trail**, six miles, also marked in blue, leaves from the south of the hamlet of Beaver River which is a community reachable only by railroad or boat. It ends at Twitchell Lake after passing through three miles of hardwood forest and three miles of low hills.

There are three trails reachable by boat on Big Moose Lake. The **Gull Lakes Trail**, one mile, leaves from the north shore of the inlet and is marked in blue. There is a lean-to between the two Gull Lakes. The **Russian Lake Trail**, ¾ mile, also marked in blue, leads from East Bay to Russian Lake's western shore, where there is a lean-to. The **Andes Creek Trail**, ½ mile, leads from the northeast edge of the lake at Andes Creek Inlet to a lean-to.

These trails are reachable by car: The **Cascade Lake–Queer Lake Trail**, 1.6 miles, begins one mile northwest of Eagle Bay Village on Big Moose Road. The red-marked trail follows the road to Cascade Lake for one mile, then becomes a foot trail going upwards to Queer Lake. The **West Mountain Trail**, 2.5 miles, begins on Higby Road near Big Moose Lake and follows Constable Creek east, intersecting the Hermitage Trail, the Windfall Pond Trail, and an alternate trail around Constable Pond, before reaching the Queer Lake Trail and a yellow trail to Chub Pond. (The trail to Chub Pond is one mile).

The **Hermitage Trail**, marked in red, connects the West Mountain Trail to the Queer Lake Trail. The yellow marked **Windfall Pond Trail** splits after about 1½ miles, with the blue trail reaching Windfall Pond in another ½ mile and Cascade Lake 1½ miles after that. The yellow trail continues on to Queer Lake, reaching it after a total of four miles.

The **Bald Mountain Trail**, one mile, leaves the Rondaxe Road parking lot and climbs to the firetower on Bald Mountain for some magnificent views. It is marked in red. The **Scenic Mountain Trail**, 4.5 miles, also leaving the Rondaxe parking lot, heads northeast past Fly Pond and Carry Pond, climbs to 2,100 feet, descends 95 feet to Mountain Pond, and follows a ridge east to the Bubb Lake Trail and Route 28, with many excellent viewpoints along the way. This trail is marked in blue.

The **Bubb Lake Trail**, one mile, starts one mile west of Eagle Bay on Route 28 and leads north to Bubb Lake and Sis Lake, following blue markers.

The blue-marked **Safford Pond Trail**, 3.75 miles, connects the Orvis School parking lot (on Big Moose Road eight miles north of Eagle Bay) to Safford Pond. The **Snake Pond Trail**, one mile, also blue-marked, leaves the Twitchell Lake road one mile north of Big Moose and continues northwest to Snake Pond.

Moose River Recreation Area

The Moose River Recreation Area in western Hamilton County consists of land made up of both plains and mountain ridges. Although it is now a wilderness area, at one time it was heavily lumbered; therefore there are several abandoned logging roads throughout the area in addition to trails. Entrance from the east is via Route 28 from Indian Lake Village to Cedar River Road, turning left and continuing past Cedar River Flow. From the west, there is a road going south from Route 28 just east of Inlet. This leads into the west entrance at Limekiln Lake. Everyone entering the area must register with the caretaker at the gate, who will assign camping sites at any of the 23 designated spots along the Primary Road. Permits are required for stays of longer than three nights, and no camping is allowed on the two private land segments contained within the area. Roads are narrow, occasionally steep, and unimproved. They might be closed if the weather is bad. Trailers are not permitted past the gate.

Since these trails do not have official names, we will describe them by the points they connect. Not all are color-marked, therefore we suggest that you bring topo maps (USGS Quads Old Forge and West Canada Lakes) with you when hiking this region.

The trail to **Wakely Mountain**, about 2.7 miles, leaves the Cedar River Road about ½ mile before the entrance to the area. There is a blue-marked trail, about nine miles, connecting the Cedar River entrance to two lean-tos just past Squaw Brook (about 4.5 miles), and near Interior Headquarters at **Cedar Lakes**. From Interior Headquarters, the blue trail may be followed north two miles to **Lost Pond**, or southwest along Cedar Lakes, and past **Cat Lake** and **Mud Lake** to the Interior Headquarters and lean-to at **West Lake**. From West Lake, a red trail, about seven miles, goes south, then east to another lean-to after about ¼ mile, a third lean-to just across South Lake (½ mile), a fourth lean-to just past Mud Lake (another ½ mile), and a fifth in another two miles. The trail extends, after the sixth lean-to at **Pillsbury Lake**, to a yellow trail, about two miles, which may be taken back to the Cedar Lakes lean-tos.

From West Lake, the red trail continues west along West Lake, past a lean-to after about 1.6 miles at **Brooktrout Lake**, and to a junction where a ½-mile side trail leads south to **Deep Lake**, another one mile

trail leads to **Wolf Lake**, and the trail itself continues on past Wolf
Creek to a ¼-mile side trail on the left leading to **Falls Pond** and junction with the Primary Road near Campsite 20. Between Campsites 18
and 19, a trail goes northeast for two miles, then south and east again
for three miles to reach Sly Pond. A trail leaves Campsite 16 to reach
Beaver Lake in 1.5 miles; while a trail going west, 1.75 miles, starts
between Campsites 5 and 6 on the Primary Road to reach **Mitchell
Ponds**. From Campsite 23, a 2.5 mile trail leads to **Horn Lake**. Another
trail branches off ¾ mile from the beginning of this trail, which passes
near **Balsam Lake**, and to **Stink Lake** in about 2.25 miles. There is a
trail, about one mile long, leading from the western terminus of the
Primary Road to **Red River** near **Rock Dam**.

Blue Mountain Lake

Blue Mountain, almost 4,000 feet above sea level, is the dominant
feature of the **Blue Mountain Lake Region**, on Routes 28 and 30 in
Indian Lake. Known to the Indians as the "Hill of Storms," the mountain towers over the east shore of the lake. The region has several lakes,
ponds, and mountain summits in addition to 44 miles of trails and 12
lean-tos. There are public campsites at Lake Durant, Forked Lake, and
Lake Eaton. The Northville-Lake Placid Trail, which we have already
discussed, also passes through this region.

The **Owls Head Mountain Trail**, 3.1 miles, red-marked, leaves Long
Lake on the north, near the end of Endion Road. (Turn left after
crossing lake — do not go toward Lake Eaton Campsite.) The trail
climbs 1,060 feet to the summit.

As you drive north on Route 30, the **Sargent Ponds Trail**, 4.3 miles,
is reached via a macadam road on the left as you pass Blue Mountain
Lake. The road follows the lake to the beginning of the trail in 1.35
miles. The trail goes around Chubb Pond, goes by Helms Pond, and
follows the Helms Pond outlet to Upper Sargent Pond. The trail is
marked in red.

The view from **Blue Mountain**, two miles, is a spectacular one of
waterways and forestland. The trail to the summit begins near the
Adirondack Museum on the east side of Route 30. It is marked in blue
and climbs 2,000 feet.

The **Tirrell Pond Trail**, 3.25 miles, goes around Blue Mountain, and
connects the hill behind the museum with the Northville-Lake Placid
Trail, via red markers. From Blue Mountain Lake Village, the distance
around the mountain, ending on Route 28 near Lake Durant, is 8.7
miles.

The **Wilson Pond Trail**, 2.9 miles, connects a parking lot across from
Eagle Lake on Route 28 with the lean-to at Wilson Pond and a fine view
of Blue Ridge. The red-marked trail passes Grassy Pond and the inlets to
Rock Pond and Slim Pond, and includes a climb up a ridge.

*Henley on Whiteface Mountain in the Adirondack
High Peaks.*

The **Cascade Lake Trail** connects the cemetery on the south end of Blue Mountain Lake Village with the Northville-Lake Placid Trail which may be followed to the Lake Durant Public Campsite. It is 2.8 miles to the Cascade Pond lean-to and 3.35 miles to the trail junction.

Schroon Lake

The Schroon Lake Area, off Routes 9 and 74, is east of Blue Mountain. This section, too, has miles of unbroken forestland, along with several mountain peaks, rolling hills, lakes and ponds. There are over 30 miles of marked trails here, and many more unmarked but familiar to locals. There are public campsites at Eagle Point on Schroon Lake, Paradox Lake, Putnam Pond, which is three miles south of Chilson, and Sharp Bridge which is 16 miles north of Schroon Lake on the Schroon River. Most of the area's ponds and lakes are stocked with fish.

The **Peaked Hill Trail**, 2.25 miles, connects Legoys Bay across from the Paradox Lake Campsite with Peaked Hill and some interesting views. The blue-marked trail travels to Peaked Hill Pond and through a ravine.

The **Arnold Pond Trail**, 1½ miles west of Eagle Lake Causeway on Route 74, is a steep climb over a quarter mile to some good trout fishing at Arnold Pond. **Otter Pond**, also good for trout, is reached from a small bay on Eagle Lake's east shore via a trail about ½ mile long. Both the Arnold Pond Trail and the Otter Pond Trail are marked in blue.

The **Severance Hill Trail**, 1.7 miles and marked in yellow, connects Route 9, 1½ miles north of Schroon Lake Village, to the top of Severance Hill (1,693 feet) where there are good views.

The yellow-marked **Gull Pond Trail**, .75 mile, and **Spectacle Pond Trail**, 1.6 miles, are reached off a road following the eastern shore of Schroon Lake. To reach this road, travel two miles east from Route 9 along the Crane Pond Road and turn right. The Gull Pond Trail is reached in 1.7 miles, the Spectacle Pond Trail in 2.7 miles.

The **Goose Pond Trail**, .75 mile, also marked in yellow, is reached off Crane Road near Alder Pond. A mile to the east is the **Pharaoh Mountain Firetower Trail**, 2.75 miles, which ascends 1,257 feet to the 2,557 foot summit. The 30-foot tower may be used if an observer is on duty, but even from the mountain top itself, the views of the high peak country in the north and the countryside of the Schroon Lake Region all around are rewarding. The trail is marked in red. There is a lean-to along the blue-marked trail that forks to the left after 0.7 miles.

The Short and Long Swing Trails travel among many of the ponds of the region. The **Short Swing Trail**, 9.7 miles, connects Route 74, 0.2 miles west of the Paradox Lake Campsite, to a point on the same road 1.4 miles east of Paradox Village. It passes Alder Pond, Crane Pond, Glidden Marsh, Oxshoe, Crab, Horseshoe, Lilypad and Honey Ponds as well as passing near Pine Hill. There are lean-tos at Oxshoe and Lilypad Ponds and north of Tub Mill Marsh. Most of the ponds have good trout fishing; Crane Pond should also be good for bass and northern pike. The trail is marked in blue and coincides for the first four miles with the **Long Swing Trail**, 11 miles, (including the four that overlap with the Short Swing Trail). The Long Swing Trail turns off to the left on yellow markers after Glidden Marsh, and continues on to Pharaoh Lake, Grizzle Ocean and Putnam Pond before ending at the Putnam Pond Campsite. Pharaoh Lake, and Grizzle Ocean offer brook trout fishing; Putnam Pond should have yellow perch, northern pike and bass.

The **Treadway Mountain Trail**, marked in red, begins west of Putnam Pond near the Mud Pond Outlet. There are some good views at the top of the two-mile climb.

The **Rock Pond-Clear Pond Trail**, 3.25 miles, leaves the Putnam Pond Campsite and travels to Heart, North, Rock, Lilypad and Clear Ponds along a yellow trail. There are lean-tos and trout at Rock, Lilypad and Clear Ponds. To return to the campsite, follow the blue trail south from Clear Pond, past Mud Pond and the Treadway Mountain Trail, to the yellow trail from Grizzle Ocean. Turn right and follow it to the camp. The left fork is the Putnam Pond Trail, continuing to the west shore of Putnam Pond. The **Bear Pond Trail**, 2.5 miles, adds an optional loop to the Rock Pond-Clear Pond Trail, going from Heart Pond to Bear Pond to Rock Pond along blue markers.

The **Lost Pond Trail**, 1.7 miles, connects the Putnam Pond Campsite with the lean-to at Lost Pond. The trail is yellow-marked and the pond should be stocked with trout. The **Berrymill Pond Trail**, 4.9 miles, also starts at the campsite and travels to New Hague, passing Berrymill Pond where you should find some good northern pike, as well as two lean-tos. The trail is marked in blue.

The **Pharaoh Lake Trail**, 2.3 miles, travels along the east shore of Pharaoh Lake, connecting the Long Swing Trail on the southeast shore to the lake's outlet, and a ½-mile trail to two lean-tos and the Pharaoh Mountain Trail. The Lake and Pharaoh Mountain provide some fine scenery and there are four lean-tos along the shore. The trail is marked in yellow.

Lake George

The Lake George Region, near the eastern border of Adirondack State Park, offers the spectacular sight of mountains surrounding lovely Lake George. The area in general is populated — motels, hotels, amusement, and historic areas do not a wilderness make — but the 50 miles of marked hiking trails in the region should get you away from most of the crowds and, at any rate, the surroundings here are so beautiful you feel friendlier toward the few people you do meet.

The **Tongue Mountain Range Trail** is actually an 18-mile trail system along the top ridge of **Tongue Mountain**. Access is on Route 9N at Clay Meadow or at the top of the Tongue Mountain Highway, or, from the lake, there is access at Five Mile Mountain Point and at the point of the

Tongue. There are two lean-tos on the main trunk of this system. Views are tremendous, but care should be taken to carry a canteen and take precautions against rattlesnakes in the area. Basically, it is enough to wear high boots and to watch where you place your hands when climbing.

Tongue Mountain takes its name from the fact that, from the air, the ridge actually looks like a tongue extending into Lake George. The main section of the trail starts at Route 9N on the summit and is marked in blue. It is 15.3 miles long. After an easy climb of about 2/3 of a mile, a yellow trail cuts to the left for a one-mile trip to Deer Leap. After 0.8 miles the trail begins to have some good viewpoints as it slopes up fairly gently. At 1.25 miles, **Brown Mountain** is reached with views of the Northwest Bay and the High Peak Region. The trail is fairly easy from here, crossing the Huckleberry Mountain ledges, and climbing **Five Mile Mountain** where there is a lean-to at an elevation of 2,258 feet. As the trail descends from here the views are magnificent.

There is an intersection with a red-marked trail which may be followed 1.9 miles to the right to reach Clay Meadow, or 1.35 miles down a steep descent to the left to Five Mile Mountain Point on the lake. At 5.5 miles, a yellow trail to the left leads about 1,500 feet to a lean-to. (Actually, this side trail *should* be taken — the view from this point should not be missed.) The trail continues along the ledge and across a plateau, leading through heavy forestland to **French Point Mountain**. There are two "knobs" to this mountain. The trail goes around some steep ledges and descends into a notch. There is a steep climb out of this notch to the north spur of **First Peak** at 7.75 miles. The south spur is reached at 8.9 miles, and, at 10.45 miles the Point of the Tongue, where the trail turns around and passes through an interesting marsh filled with birdlife before ending at **Clay Meadow**.

The view from **Black Mountain** includes Vermont's Green Mountains, Lake Champlain, the Lake George Islands, the High Peaks Region, and the Hudson Valley. It is a rocky mountain that rises almost out of the water's edge, with the **Black Mountain Firetower Trail**, 2.75 miles, reachable only by boat or by way of the trail network described below. It begins at Black Mountain Point on the east shore, two miles north of the Glen Island headquarters, and for the first ¾ mile is fairly easy. After another quarter mile, a mile of switchbacks rise steeply to the tower, which may be entered if the observer is on duty. The trail is marked in red. Another, less scenic approach to Black Mountain, but one that is easier and reachable by land, comes from the east. Drive to the road to Hulett's Landing which intersects Route 22 between Whitehall and Ticonderoga, and follow this road to the red-marked trail within two miles of the summit.

To the east of Lake George are nearly 30 miles of interconnecting trails leading, again, to mountain summits, along the shore of the lake,

At Marcy Dam in the Adirondacks.

and by several ponds. Rattlesnakes have occasionally been seen in this
area, although very rarely; care is advised. The main branch of this trail
begins one mile north of Hogtown on Shelving Rock Road, and follows
yellow markers most of the way. At the beginning of the trail, the
yellow markers may be followed south for 5.8 miles to Pilot Knob,
passing the summit of Buck Mountain with some good views at 2.5
miles. The red trail may be followed northwest about 4.5 miles to
Shelving Rock Mountain, where a yellow trail leads 0.6 miles up the
summit. Or the yellow trail may be followed north 3.38 miles, eventually rising fairly steeply up Sleeping Beauty Mountain where the Lake
George Region as well as the Green Mountains may be seen. At 2.2
miles, a red trail climbs just over a mile to Bumps Pond, and another ¼
mile to the Bumps Pond Overlook. From the Pond, it rejoins the yellow
trail in 0.1 mile, and follows it to Fish Brook Pond, which should be
stocked with trout. At 5.56 miles, a red trail again leaves the yellow,
this time to follow the notch north of Erebus Mountain to Lake George.
It passes a lean-to just north of Fish Pond, and reaches Lake George in
three miles.

Another spur trail cuts off at 5.64 miles, leading to Greenland Pond
in one mile; Milman Pond is passed, and at 8.4 miles a blue-marked trail
leading past Lapland Pond leads to Pike Brook Road in 2.25 miles.
There is a lean-to at Lapland Pond. The trail continues past Round Pond
and Black Mountain Pond to a junction with the Black Mountain Firetower Trail, the end of the yellow markers, and a meeting with the
three-mile red trail from Fish Lake Pond to Lake George. The trail continues south about three miles following picturesque Red Rock Bay, to
Shelving Rock Mountain, and from there, to the beginning.

The **Prospect Mountain Trail**, 1.13 miles, is at the southern tip of
Lake George. Access is via Montcalm Street west from Fish Lake Village
to Smith Street. Go south about ½ block on Smith Street to where a
sign indicates the trailhead. This red-marked trail is a fairly easy climb
to the summit, following an old funicular railroad bed part of the way.

13

Worlds of the Wild . . . on Night, Caves, Rock Climbing and Igloos

An image of sunlight filtering through the trees on a soft summer morning is inevitably evoked whenever somebody uses the words "forest, outdoors, or wilderness." And during a short span of the year, into limited areas of sunlit forest, pile people by the incredible thousands. They end up not liking each other, sometimes not even liking that classic sunlit forest. Yet few of that hoard ever explore very far into the other worlds of the wild that are only a few hundred feet, a few hours, or a season away.

The more hiking, and then backpacking, you do, the more eager you get for experiences somewhat more rugged, scenery more remote.

Bugs, storms, exertion, and other such inconveniences become less important, though we've never found a backpacker able to ignore them completely. Exploration of "managed" wilderness, usually in state and national parks, costs least in terms of equipment, skill, mental and physical requirements. There are other worlds that cost more, but they often provide more, too.

Pick anything not summer, or day, or flat ground.

NIGHT TRIPS

Take a night, for instance, and get out to watch for meteors, auroras, and the shadows of hunting bats. Sneak around listening for a beaver chomping up some tree near his pond. Join the social world of the raccoon, possum, deer, bear, bobcat, and rattlesnake . . .

It's a good idea to plan your first night sortie during full moon; pack along a carbide lamp or good battery unit, too, for focusing on something specific — an owl, maybe — or for extracting yourself in case the moon gives out.

Know the area by day first, and ask knowledgeable locals about area snake species and any large known dens. Make no unplanned changes of

159

route, since someone back in civilization knows just what you are up to, right? And adapt. Move very slowly, prepared for the eyesticker branches, holes, bogs, and other menaces.

Listen. And in the event of an encounter with a bear, ranger, or other irate critter, be cordial, respectful, and very, very cooperative.

Fear, an element too few people lay on the table and examine or admit, has a valuable and constructive place in night or any of the other worlds of the wild. Accept it and use it. It improves eyesight and hearing and cleans off the mental debris that normally stands between humans and direct meeting with the wilds. Fear shared with others can also deepen friendship.

CAVING

Also dark, and far more demanding, is the realm underground. The wild world of caves offers dramatic experience and exotic scenery. There is nothing in the northeast that can compare with the giant caverns in the southern states and Mexico, but size is not the only criterion for beauty.

Caves are scattered all over the northeast, from the limestone cave systems of mid-eastern New York to mountain crevasses and small passages in every sort of rock from granite to sandstone. Any backpacker will eventually encounter one big enough to give him one heck of a hassle — and one heck of a thrill. We can't prepare you thoroughly for caving in this brief chapter, but if we can impress the need to be prepared, then we've made a good beginning.

Careful preparation is even more important in this activity than in above-ground hiking. The cost of doing something wrong is much greater, as Tom Sawyer could have told you. In report after report, accidents have happened to the "casual caver," who ventured into a cave on the wrong terms.

Carbide and electric lamp and candles, fireflies, and anything else that provides light should be a prime supply. Know as much as possible ahead of time about the layout of the place: deep pits or unstable formations, likelihood of flooding from swollen streams outside after sudden rains, and the chances of someone innocently locking the cave gate while you are inside. Never venture into a cave without at least one experienced spelunker in the party, and make sure equipment is familiar to everyone, familiar by use, not by sight.

A cave crew faces all the forms of wilderness imaginable, from rock climbing to histoplasmosis, fear and exposure, with a healthy physical pounding thrown in. The crew should have a leader of skill and experience recognized and accepted by the entire party. And each member should attempt to learn the leader's skills without getting in the way. Shifts of reliance can happen without warning, and the sudden demand for survival from all members of the party is one of the potential prices of invading the underground world.

Depressing? Caves sound like trouble? Good; they are. They are also a fascinating, delicately balanced ecological system that can be destroyed by a single uncaring, unprepared party. Thousands of years of development in life forms and formations can be ended in seconds. That harsh, even cruel wilderness underground is as fragile as it is powerful. Going in prepared to preserve it is fully as important as going in prepared to come out.

Caving also assumes some knowledge of climbing around on rock, and cliffs and mountain rock are another of our finest worlds of the wild.

ROCK CLIMBING

Rock climbing has boomed in the last few years, thanks partly to all those glamorous, active people in the soda commercials. Most backpackers have tended to initiate themselves to rock climbing by coming upon a huge boulder unaware and clambering onto and over it helter skelter. We figure out we've done something wrong when we find ourselves in a spot we can't get out of without considerable difficulty.

Trial and error may be an effective learning technique, but real danger can be greatly reduced by a little knowledge, caution, good equipment, and some careful thought about how to proceed from one point on a mountain to the next.

Climbing is a sport to develop slowly. Never attempt more than can be retreated from in safety. College outing clubs, climbing schools, and how-to books are well distributed throughout the country. Anyone lacking the initiative to learn from those sources shouldn't bother adding the world of vertical real estate to his wilds. And the more skilled you are, the freer you will be to enjoy the flavor of the wind from those sheer heights.

Night, caves, and rock climbing are the obviously dangerous worlds ... dramatically and explicitly so. Yet the sunny glen can bust a leg, or sudden illness drop a hiker. And there is demonstrable danger in an automobile, driving to and from the site of a wilderness outing. Dangerous situations can't and need not be avoided. The important thing is to face them with knowledge, respect ... and curiosity.

There is such endless variety to the worlds out there, demanding and rewarding all at the same time, that no person can ever hope to delve into them all. That classic sunlit glen is a different world, too, in different hours of the day, in different seasons, and from different vantage points. The woods from clifftop is a different woods, for instance, than the forest in a valley, beside a meandering stream. Try the rain, the night, the snow, and dawn, but be alert for the demands of nature and respect them.

WINTER

Of the scores of worlds defined by the changes in nature one deserves special space here. Of all the changes, the most complete is that produced by winter.

Winter is criminally short-changed by outdoors people. In fact I've spent 75 per cent of my life avoiding frosty feet and chapped lips, convinced that the suffering just wasn't worth it. And if you have to suffer, it might not be. The shock of discovering that it's possible to get around more easily in winter than in summer and to be *comfortable* out in that intimately nasty, body-threatening cold opens up a whole gigantic wilderness.

Snow ... beginning its career as almost invisible needle crystals drifting down, quickly becoming the star-shaped "flake," then becoming crusted into big fat flying wads of frozen winter. It is the base element of winter recreation, danger, and, quite surprisingly, the prime source of comfort.

Using snow, we've designed a whole flock of devices for moving through winter ... snowshoes, long and short skis, sleds, toboggans, snowmobiles, and hunks of cardboard for sliding down handy slopes. Even delta wing kiters are out there now. But most of our devices are designed for a fleeting contact with the white stuff, quickly dropped in favor of toasting toes at an indoor fire.

Out there in the gloomy threat of frostbite, however, is a world that can be enjoyed for surprisingly long periods in relative comfort.

"Ideal" winter weather, that sunny spell with snow bowing down the trees and snow fleas speckling the drifts around tree trunks, usually follows the worst weather imaginable. To really appreciate those ideal days, though, you have to be out in the woods before it clears, out when the wind is blowing and the snow is sweeping down with blind fury. Of all the perfections nature is capable of letting us savor, one of the finest is that still, cold, clear period of hot sun and silence right after a storm.

By way of cross-country ski, snowshoe, or ice axe and crampon, it's possible to get "out." You can camp, then, in a nylon tent with catalytic heat, or you can try a first-class traditional alternative ... learn how to build an igloo.

IGLOOS

There are plenty of advantages to this sort of lodging. Perhaps closest to the backpacker's heart is the fact that you don't have to carry it in. And the only tool you need to build it is a snow saw or machete.

It provides a snug, warm, quiet haven out of the wind and cold with drinking water provided by floor and walls and with a built-in, automatically body-shaping mattress.

Igloos, once they become part of the winter program, shorten greatly the period of forced hibernation at home each year.

Spiral ramp of giant-sized igloo.

Since human bodies freeze and have the tendency under adverse conditions to divest themselves of fingers, toes, noses, and other ill-placed tender parts, it is crucial, as it is in caving and rock climbing, to prepare carefully for any extended outings.

Ample information is available about sleeping bags and clothing, skis, snowshoes and other gear, so we will not attempt any discussion of them here.

Igloos, though, have not been promoted half enough, and can mean the difference between survival and comfort. In an emergency, even highway travelers could find it useful to know how to make one. Don't count on being able to build one straight from instructions in a book, though, your first time out and miles from civilization. Practice in the backyard, a local park, or some other handy site close to a safe retreat. The first few will take more time to construct than you thought, too.

Purists will say you've got to have this or that type of snow. And the wind-packed stuff, with no ice crust, that you can walk on and cut as if it were styrofoam, really is the best working material. But in an emergency, anything except unpackable powder or unhackable solid ice will work. Even scooping together slushy afternoon snow into a stomped-on pile a foot thick works. Rolled balls hacked down or stacked up and carved out will work, if the general principles involved are known.

Igloo building succeeds best if you have put some forethought into the site location, direction of door, and finished size. Goof anywhere else, even let the thing fall down and have to put it back up; these three elements are the critical ones.

SITE: Cold air flows downhill and collects in low pockets. So build your structure on a slope or ridge where temperature can be several important degrees higher. Never dig down into the floor of the igloo ... leave it as is or build it higher. Naturally, the site you choose should include a large enough area of packed snow — a 30-foot-square patch is ample, although half that might do.

DOOR: Since most bad weather comes from the west in the northeastern region, it's best to place your door facing the dawn. In fact, it's nice to see if you can get the door (and wind tunnel) aimed right at the sunrise. Make the door low, small, and *last*. Build the whole igloo first, then cut your door, after a nice heated argument about where the cold winds will come from and where the sun will rise. (In case things don't work out the door can always be closed up and a new one cut.)

SIZE: A five-foot, two-man igloo takes, with practice, two hours or less to build. We spent two days on a mansion 10 feet in diameter. Decide on the *smallest* comfortable size, or if pressured, on the smallest *possible* size ... never let yourself get tricked into a palace complex when a shack is needed for safety. Real emergency shelters can be as small as four feet in diameter, three feet high. Not roomy, but two people can survive. The smaller the igloo, the more body heat there will

WINTER IGLOO

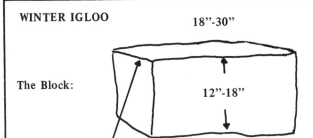

18"-30"

The Block:

12"-18"

8" or 10" MINIMUM

12" Better

Cutting Block

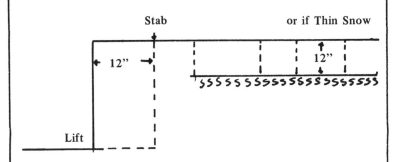

Stab   or if Thin Snow

12"   12"

Lift

Always cut to pry out under shorter dimension. They'll break the long way. Cut all sides, including underneath before lifting.

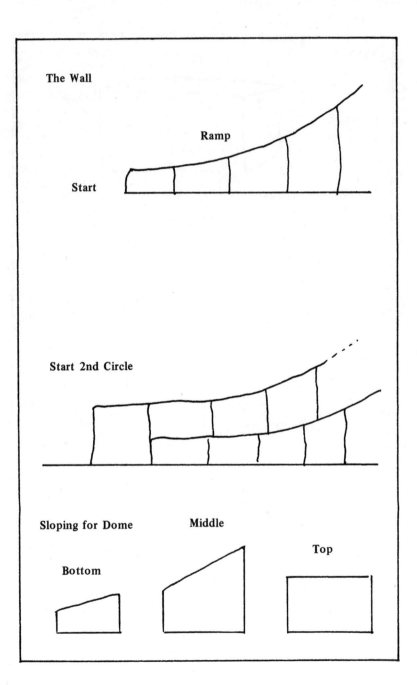

The Wall

Ramp

Start

Start 2nd Circle

Sloping for Dome   Middle

Bottom

Top

be to raise the interior temperature. A six-foot diameter house is very comfortable.

After you've decided on interior size, stand at the center point of your site, reach out with the machete or snow saw (or ski if you're building a palace) and turn, making a neat circle in the snow. Then step back and think over the site, size, and door location again. It pays to be sure before getting to the block cutting.

If everything looks good it's time to warm up with a little teamwork snow masonry. (One layer can keep up with two cutters.)

The cutter has to provide blocks at least eight to 10 inches wide and as long and high as possible for reasonable handling. Tough guys may like to use 40-pound hunks, if they'll hang together, but 20 to 30 pounds is more reasonable and still nice warming work. With any kind of material or size of block, the thickness is critical. They must be wide enough to give solid support to the next higher layer. Foot-thick walls will be more stable and last longer than seven-inch ones which might not hold long enough for you to complete the wall. (Anything that does hold until the wall is complete is fine, however . . . the igloo gains its strength *after* it is completed.)

The block cutter will mess up the first few but they will be adequate for the first row of wall. Since that first row is a ramp, increasing in height from snow level to full block halfway around the perimeter of the wall, there is no waste.

The layer, beginning at the low point of the wall circle, will gradually become a sloping ramp, as you smooth the top of the blocks down to form a slow upgrade. Taper the tops just *slightly* to the inside. If this first (or second) row of blocks is trimmed with the tops sloping outward, there's a good chance of a collapse after four or five rows.

By the time the first row is laid the cutter should be turning out good blocks and the layer will have his slash technique down pat. If blocks get broken, they should be laid aside for building the entry way and a sun shield later on.

The second row should be made of full blocks laid, according to simple cinder block laying principles, with the block on the top row placed over and halfway between two blocks on the row underneath. The rest of the igloo should be put up as a continuous spiral of blocks, with the tops gradually being sloped inward to produce a dome shape.

Your first igloo will probably be a cone instead of geodesic dome, but that's no problem; it'll work just as well. We've found, as a guideline, that sighting the slope of the block tops in to the center of the circle for the first two or three rows and then sighting the higher rows for the base of the opposite side helps a little to get a dome shape. Only practice will result in the smooth dome shape found in Eskimo pictures.

Although the top of the igloo will seem to hang in mid-air it *will* hang, even with the edges facing almost straight down. To help that

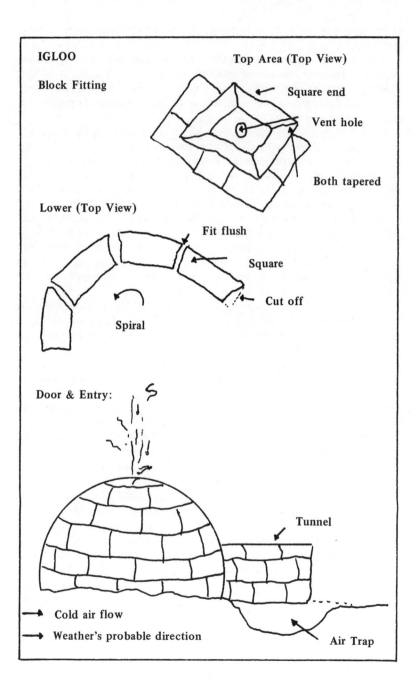

IGLOO   Top Area (Top View)

Block Fitting
                                                                    Square end

                                                                    Vent hole

                                                                    Both tapered

Lower (Top View)
                                             Fit flush

                                             Square

                                                 Cut off

                        Spiral

Door & Entry:

                                                                    Tunnel

→ Cold air flow
→ Weather's probable direction
                                                                    Air Trap

don't cut the end off the block, leave the square end there and fit the next block into it. Finish with a big fat block that you can cut a smoke hole plug in and then cut a door hole so the layer can get out to help plug holes and coat everything with loose snow.

Points about laying block: Trim the ends so they butt together well. Set them, don't slide them, with a firm thump. This will help bind the snow crystals together and keep the walls stable during construction. Fit the bottom of each new block flush against the top of the prior row by trimming off the top of the bottom block. The better the job of laying, the fewer cracks there are that will have to be plugged and the stronger the structure will be when it "cures."

Once you've got the layer cut loose through the door hole, build your air trap and entry tunnel.

The air trap is simply a dip into the snow outside the wall with a low tunnel built over it. We've no idea what the rules might be for the depth of the air trap ... a foot to 18 inches works ... but the wind tunnel had better be *high* enough to stand frequent travel in and out without filling collars with cold or knocking the thing down. Keep it to the minimum usable size and if there is some tendency for cold to enter just pile some loose snow across it between the air trap and living space.

An igloo gains strength after it's completed and put into use ... the snow bonds together from its own weight and from the heat let loose inside. Some people have made a big point about burning newspaper inside to put a coat of ice on the walls ... which is fine if you like a dirty snow house. We've always found we were hungry enough after building one to cook a little chow, and the heat from your backpacker's stove does a fine job of turning the inner walls into a solid icy structure without mess.

Cooking *must* be done with the vent hole opened, even in the most severe cold. Otherwise, the interior may heat to melting point, and nobody likes a roof that drips. More important, water is the big enemy of down clothing and bags. Wet, they're useless as protection against cold.

Cooking is very simple ... if you have a reliable fuel stove, a snow shoe or length of wood to set it on, and your usual utensils. Note, though, that anything put down may get buried. Our best results have been achieved by sticking spoons in the wall, hanging cups, pots, and other gear from them. (They also make first class candle holders.) By using the wall space you find that there is a surprising amount of room in a very small building. Things are so handy that you can lie back in the old sleeping bag, fix supper, argue a bit, and rack out without having to stir the old bones at all.

In the wilderness now, you have a home, complete with combination bedroom and kitchen, warm enough to live in without gloves or parka, a home which didn't have to be carried in on your back and which will disappear after you've gone. A single candle or carbide lamp gives plenty of light with aid from reflection from the white walls; the structure keeps wind out entirely, and provides some of the most comfortable winter sleeping imaginable. Still, there is one sneaky hangup. Heat. Too much of it.

If you go prepared for 100 degrees below zero, and you probably should, then a rude shock may be in store for you come morning when you crawl out of the sack soaked with sweat. Those snow walls retain heat, as well as keeping out the wind and cold. There is no need to shiver, but if you can stand to sleep just short of being chilly you'll avoid one of the more unpleasant problems that results from overheating in an igloo. Down clothing and bags, as we mentioned earlier, dry *very* slowly, if at all.

After you've built a couple of test igloos and feel you have the knack for hacking blocks and shaping a nice dome, you're ready for a few more pointers.

Protect your knees during the construction with the sort of black rubber kneepads used by house roofers. The person who is cutting snow blocks, in particular, tends to kneel a lot.

His knobby bones will press into the snow and get soaked; then while carrying the block to the wall, they'll freeze. The result can be a very painful puffy set of joints, and could result in severe frostbite. Pads can also be made from scrap nylon cloth and ensolite.

For igloos expected to endure long-term use, build a sun wall or second layer of wall on the south and west sides. Then pile all the loose snow and blocks you can find up on the top and sides. Sun will gradually erode the walls regardless of the air temperature. And the extra snow will both prolong the life of and strengthen your winter house.

Fanatics can try putting in an ice window in the igloo . . . but, you're likely to discover a principle that operates in any house window. The opening allows the cold to cut through and flow down the wall inside.

Snow is translucent enough to provide plenty of light during the day, and a single candle lights the place well at night. So there's really no need for a window.

A word of warning . . . snow caves are *not* igloos; they do not have the same principles of heat retention and ventilation. As a shelter during construction of an igloo they may have some use, and as a real emergency shelter, they can be dug quickly for *short* stays. If you do have to use a snow cave, try to follow the principles of an igloo . . . i.e. crawling *up* into the cave, with a vent *kept open*. Surprisingly, it is not that much easier to dig out a snow cave, unless it's mighty small. In high winds it will provide some relief from wind chill, but so will an igloo once the wall is up a short way.

Besides, with an igloo you can even take the fireside book and chess set along . . . Weather being what it is, that might not be a bad idea.

14

Make Your Own

.

Sick of what passes for quality and low price when you browse around the old camping store or catalogue? Have a lot of fun when your super pack *(super cheap)* leaves you 10 miles out with one strap gone and the bottom half missing? Enjoy the ripping seams, after getting ripped off at one of those impossible-to-avoid drooling sessions at a sale?

What's worse than the quality and price of so much of the "great" gotta-have-it stuff laid out to tantalize the backpacker's eye is the simple fact that we aren't likely to need it short of atomic war or landing of the Alpha Centaurians.

Make-it-yourself-itis is a beneficial disease. First, you'll never have the time to make all the great stuff you "might" need, so you'll tend to concentrate on the most important things. Then you'll get hooked by the satisfaction of making something yourself and seeing it age on the trail. "Makeitis" disease protects people from the sales, flashy ads, and "great grimmickry" of the annual catalogues. And it develops self-confidence and an ability to cope that often means more out in the woods than any single item of gear ever will.

Making things requires first that the *need* be well defined. Having once spent weeks on a beaded belt and then coming back from a trip suffering from poorly designed pack straps that would have saddle-galled a mule, we began to understand the importance of setting priorities. Feathered hats, fringed pack covers, and embroidered canteen pouches are fine ... nice things to do once you're out in the woods and feel a need to tinker while sitting around the fire telling lies. Such adornment, done in the woods, looks and is authentic. Made or purchased at home ... it usually looks corny.

What you *need* has to be selected, and then really looked at for what you want it to *do*, or *not do*. If an item may or will cause pain, wear, or unneeded weight, stay at the drawing table till the problems are solved, and then, convinced you have a good idea, try imagining every type of strain, field stress, function, and even places, that it will have to serve.

We have included things in this chapter that are not absolutely first priority, but everything we mention is useful. A brief word of warning:

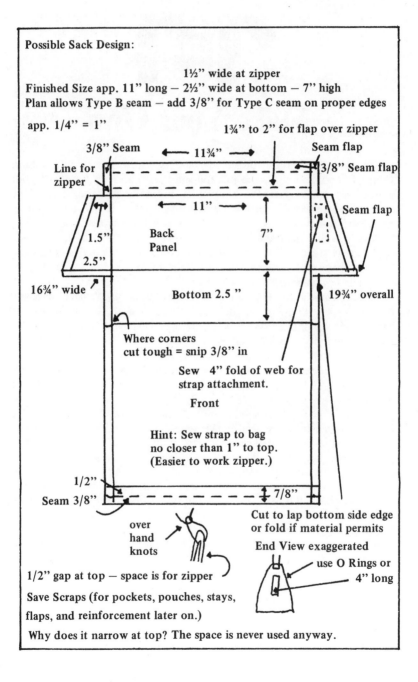

Possible Sack Design:

1½" wide at zipper
Finished Size app. 11" long — 2½" wide at bottom — 7" high
Plan allows Type B seam — add 3/8" for Type C seam on proper edges

app. 1/4" = 1"

1¾" to 2" for flap over zipper

3/8" Seam   ◄— 11¾" —►   Seam flap

Line for zipper   3/8" Seam flap

◄— 11" —►   Seam flap

1.5"   **Back Panel**   7"

2.5"

16¾" wide   **Bottom 2.5 "**   19¾" overall

Where corners cut tough = snip 3/8" in

Sew 4" fold of web for strap attachment.

Front

Hint: Sew strap to bag no closer than 1" to top. (Easier to work zipper.)

1/2"
Seam 3/8"   7/8"

over hand knots

Cut to lap bottom side edge or fold if material permits

End View exaggerated

use O Rings or 4" long

1/2" gap at top — space is for zipper

Save Scraps (for pockets, pouches, stays, flaps, and reinforcement later on.)

Why does it narrow at top? The space is never used anyway.

don't choose a tent or sleeping bag as your first item for do-it-yourself experimentation. You may waste a lot of materials and work hours. Few people have the tools and know-how for high quality tents and bags, though if you do, for heaven's sake take a shot at it. In theory there is nothing a backpacker needs that he can't make or improvise, and nothing to equal the satisfaction the packer gets out of going self-made.

To get started making things, collect all your junk, trash, and defunct goodies of every conceivable description. He who has the largest heaps will find the most nuggets of gold.

Among the high priority junk to collect as a matter of habit are plastic bottles, wire, aluminum tubing, defunct pots and pans, anything nylon, anything of heavy cloth, old socks, old belts, scraps of leather, nylon cord, hunks of foam, and big cardboard boxes (to keep it all in and to use in making patterns.)

Some general tips ... an old pressure cooker makes a fine tubing bender ... a hand sewing awl saves buying a new sewing machine ... soft aluminum, copper, or heavy brass wire makes fine rivets, and wood dowels of various sizes end up consumed in a host of projects. An electric drill can double as a lathe, while nails can make D-rings, belt buckles, and assorted odd attachments (later in the chapter you'll see how to case harden soft nails and metal.) Stock up on nylon thread (waxed), a good glue (such as Pliobond 20), one-inch and ½-inch nylon webbing (tubular), heavy "pack weight" nylon cloth, and the lighter polyurethane coated nylon used commonly in stuff bags.

Materials are available from many camping stores ... Recreational Equipment, Inc. in Seattle being one of the best known. But others locally may have your goodies ... price them, shop, and plan ahead. Especially plan to keep materials on hand for those quick jobs that always crop up the day before you leave on a trip. (We once made two rock-climbing rucksacks the day we left for a big trip ... saved $40 and they worked better than the models available.)

When beginning a project, after being sure of the need, function, and durability required, try to get the pattern or design laid out and at least placed or glued together all in one session. Every product becomes a matter of plan versus compromise. A basic design that minimizes seams, joints, and parts, will save huge hunks of time and effort during sewing, joining, and assembly. Also, the fewer things left in the design that can fail the better.

Seams can be glued 20 times ... but there's a limit to the amount of sewing a person can stand. Cloth can be drawn on till it changes color ... it gets cut once. A dowel or plastic strip will bend to the shape of a metal tube ... the tube breaks after a few bends. A strip of plastic will often serve instead of metal until the final design is assured.

Don't take the designs in this chapter as refined gems. Poke at them, see if you can balance out a better, simpler, more service oriented scheme. *Never* take a factory kit, pattern or design and try doing it by "a into b, ah, c to ..." Understanding *why* a thing is such and such a size, or shape is how it gets to be a friend on the trail ... not just another blight, like bugs, rain, and blisters.

POSSIBLES SACK

This is a good starting project. It familiarizes a person with the principles of seams, straps, getting the right sizes, and seeing how the thing will work when put into use. And it's more than likely a badly needed item for most backpackers.

First, why make a shoulder bag? Frontiersmen called them "possibles sacks" because they popped in everything possible from bullets to scalps.) Ever lose your wallet, or have it wear a hole in you hip pocket? Get annoyed by the rash caused by loose change or freshly fueled lighters? Need string when there ain't none to be had? Matches sweaty? No snack on that "little" stroll three miles from camp? Compass in the bottom of the pack? No toilet paper handy in a hurry? Spare roll of film? Jackknife, pencil, bug dope, and adhesive bandages always in the bottom of the pack or in one of those pack side pouches ... somewhere? OK, that's the need and service connected with a possibles sack.

How about design? Small enough to stay out of the way, easy to get into, big enough for all miscellaneous gear, durable since it gets a lot of rub and scrape, including a good strap with width designed not to cause a problem even when worn under a main pack strap. Color light or bright enough to help you find the thing in the dark, not so garish it's embarrassing to wear. No sharp edges, maybe no metal so you can toss it in the washing machine after it collects a few melted chocolate bar remains and doses of insect repellent.

Can you think of anything else that might influence design? If so, jot your ideas down right now on the design page and see what happens.

NEEDED: Heavy Pack Weight Nylon Cloth, approximately 20 inches x 17 inches, sewing awl or heroic sewing machine, approximately 45 inches of one-inch flat or tubular web, and a heavy, easy-sliding zipper. (Old Army field jackets have fine zippers for such projects.) And some good scissors, a razor blade (set in a short bit of wood dowel for a handle), and your trusty bottle of glue.

Cut a big cardboard box, both for a surface to work on that you won't have to clean the glue off, and to make a pattern from once the design is cut. After using the bag you can then change the cardboard pattern rather than working out all the lines on fabric again.

From the drawing you can see how simple the bag is. But note that the side panels overlap the front panels. It's annoying to get down to sewing a seam and find no material there to make a seam with.

For seams ... there are several simple types, one that might last forever (and might take forever), many that will do. Choose your type

of seam *before* cutting anything, and pencil in the type right on the
fabric by the seam line. Here's how seams may change your fabric cuts:

Seam "A" is quick and easy — no glue, and thin enough for even
modern sewing machines to survive. The edges are messy, though, and
the seam cannot be double-stitched effectively. This is the weakest type
of seam. B type works for quick jobs, and is quite strong. Just glue
down a 3/8-inch fold to one edge, and sew a 3/8ths-inch lap from the
other edge flat. C is the super seam. Fabric ends are neat, the product
tough. But it requires gluing a 3/8-inch lap of ends *first*, then folding
the tucks. With practice this can be done without gluing the tucks, and
can be done with 3/8-inch lap width. But for your first try, glue everything and use ½-inch lap (or even more.) Once you try it, you'll see why
D, the easiest seam, is included. With D you don't have to get ulcers
figuring out which way what end folds where. Seams get ratty with
wear, though, so take a little extra effort for a better seam and stay
happy.

One more note on seams. Try to place the external edge or fold
down. A bag with seams up will work fine ... and water running down
against the seam will tend to soak in a lot better, even though the
Pliobond helps waterproof all seams.

Always try to have removable straps on bags and packs. They are
easier to adjust, renew, or use for other things if need be. Leave a few
extra inches on the strap until you've hiked several days with it, then
pare it down to the most comfortable choice of length.

TENT POLE SCABBARD

Now that you've got your scraps from the possibles sack, how about
a tent pole scabbard? The lack of those on most ready made tents has
become a pet peeve of mine after seeing too many good packs and tents
chewed from pole ends.

Make a tube with a drawstring top long enough and big enough to
hold your poles. But first, head to the junk boxes and find a couple of
deodorant can tops or other plastic can tops that will contain the poles
in a fairly close fit. Then cut a circle with a 3/8-inch border bigger than
the cap and sew it into the bottom of your scabbard fabric. You'll find
this quickly shows you what width to cut the fabric after overlap. Then
cut your tube fabric out and do the long seam. Chuck in the tent poles,
pop your second cap on top, and pull the draw string. You'll have all
ends protected and a rattle proof package for those miserable hole cutters.

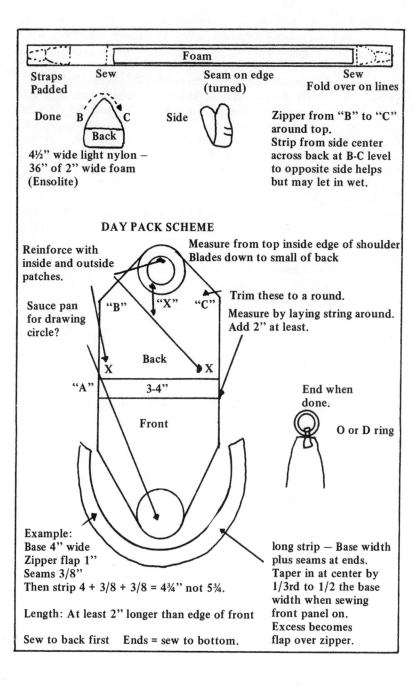

Foam

Straps
Padded | Sew | Seam on edge
(turned) | Sew
Fold over on lines

Done B   C   Side   Zipper from "B" to "C"
         Back   around top.
                              Strip from side center
4½" wide light nylon –   across back at B-C level
36" of 2" wide foam   to opposite side helps
(Ensolite)   but may let in wet.

DAY PACK SCHEME

Reinforce with   Measure from top inside edge of shoulder
inside and outside   Blades down to small of back
patches.
                        Trim these to a round.
Sauce pan   "B"   "X"   "C"
for drawing   Measure by laying string around.
circle?   Add 2" at least.

              Back
        X   X
"A"   3-4"   End when
                            done:
        Front
                                    O or D ring

Example:
Base 4" wide
Zipper flap 1"   long strip – Base width
Seams 3/8"   plus seams at ends.
Then strip 4 + 3/8 + 3/8 = 4¾" not 5¾.   Taper in at center by
                             1/3rd to 1/2 the base
Length: At least 2" longer than edge of front   width when sewing
                             front panel on.
                             Excess becomes
Sew to back first   Ends = sew to bottom.   flap over zipper.

Run a coat hanger through an extra wide seam to install the heavy nylon cord in your drawstring bag.

DAY PACK

Got some practice now and ready for trouble? Good. A day pack is one of the expensive so-so quality items on the market today. Yet it isn't too tough to make and well worth it.

Requirements: It must hold "day" junk, ride easy, get on and off and open up easily, should fold up and stuff away in a small space. Pick a heavy zipper (to heck with weight, use a monster) and position it so it will not interfere with shoulder slings for camera, possibles sack, etc.

Straps should be usable on your main pack also. Anything else?

Materials: Lots of heavy nylon cloth, sauce pan, soft pencil, sewing awl (no chance on sewing machine here, except for long seams), glue, cardboard (be sure to get a flat pattern of this project), 2-inch strip of foam (possibly narrow down your ensolite sleeping pad?) from 30 to 36 inches long, four rings (heavy "0" or "D"s, 1-inch wide that go on pack bottom) and one ½-inch x two-inch dowel.

Some odd materials here, but have patience.

Begin by measuring from between the top of your shoulder blades to the small of your back, subtract an inch or two (this is your pack height for trial test), then measure the width of the small of your back (elbows should not brush ends of the pack when done) for pack width. Add your seam widths, decide on thickness of the bottom (three or four inches is usual) and add it up, one continuous piece from top front panel to top rear panel. Go in from the edge of your nylon cloth width plus seams and draw the basic rectangle of the pack. Now get the sauce pan and put the edge against the center point of the width and draw a circle at top and bottom. (I used an 8-inch pie plate for my own packs.)

Next: come up to mid point of the long direction on your cloth ("A" on diagram) which is the center of the bottom and draw in your bottom lines. Come up from the edge of the bottom about 1/3rd of the height of the front and back panels "B". Draw a line from "B" to the edge of your circle. Now round off the corners at points "B" until they look fairly even. Then cut away.

The sides of the pack (and rounded top) can be made from a single strip as wide as the base, plus width of the seams. A zipper flap, if you want one, can be formed by sewing the inside edge of the strip. This tapers the thickness of the pack from bottom to top, and automatically leaves a protective weather flap over the zipper. (One inch is usually enough, more makes zippering more difficult.)

Cut your side strip at least two inches longer than the edge of the front panel. (Excess ends get sewn to the bottom as wear pads anyway.) Lay it flat and have fun trying to draw a curved line free hand style to guide you in sewing the zipper flap edge. The best bet is to bend a

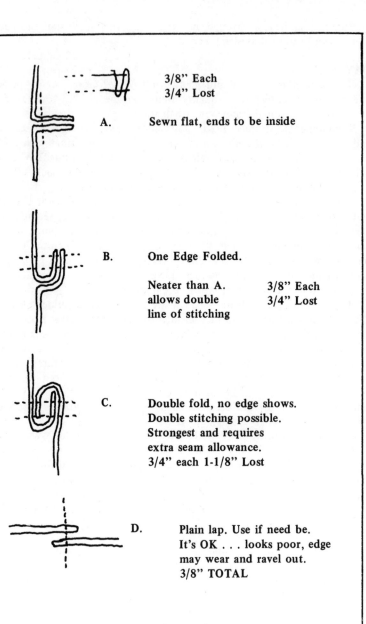

3/8" Each
3/4" Lost

A.   Sewn flat, ends to be inside

B.   One Edge Folded.

          Neater than A.   3/8" Each
          allows double   3/4" Lost
          line of stitching

C.   Double fold, no edge shows.
          Double stitching possible.
          Strongest and requires
          extra seam allowance.
          3/4" each 1-1/8" Lost

D.   Plain lap. Use if need be.
          It's OK . . . looks poor, edge
          may wear and ravel out.
          3/8" TOTAL

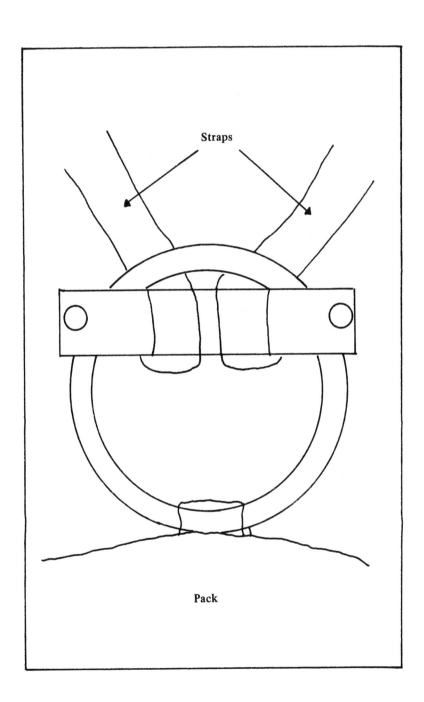

Straps

Pack

longish dowel to a right looking curve and have somebody else trace the line.

To reinforce the strap attachment points, cut circles or squares from scrap and sew one inside and out to the proper location. (As shown on diagram; debatable. Any location seems debatable. Just try your own logic.)

Straps, even comfortable ones, are easy to make. Sew a tube to contain a 2-inch wide foam pad out of light nylon cloth, fold the ends over to a wedge shape. On the upper end, fold again to make a loop with a D ring in it, or see if our idea works.

For attaching the two straps to the top center of your pack, try inserting a two inch long dowel 3/8 or ½ inch thick, through the loops. On the pack, sew a loop through which the dowel will fit like a button. Drill a hole through each end (or through the center of the dowel and tie it down with nylon cord. Fanatics can make a similar arrangement on the bottom ends of the straps too. A double D ring type buckle makes it a lot easier to adjust length, and the folded ends won't slip easily during a hike. Never bother with a toothed buckle, or most square flat friction buckles.

(Note on dowel attachment: round off the ends well or they may wear against your pack.)

STUFF SACKS AND DOUBLE PACKS

Another of our pet peeves is the racket some people make out of selling stuff sacks made out of remnants of material. You can do just as well at home, and get more utility from the product.

What do stuff sacks do? They compress bulky down items to minimum bulk. They also will hold anything, if reasonably soft, or packed without the corners jamming out. If they are made slightly less long than the back is wide, and are big enough in diameter to hold sleeping bags, if they have loops sewn at each corner, (i.e. four per end in a square,) with one at opposite sides in the middle then they can be lashed together in an impromptu pack, strapped outside a frame pack much more easily, and even hung up out of the way in camp or at home.

Two stuffers units drawstrings shouldn't take more than an hour to make. Get out the saucepan again, along with a bunch of waterproofed middle weight nylon cloth.

For groups who divide up loads, two or three stuff sacks and a bundle of tent pole scabbards are easy to lash together and put straps on if the day pack straps are dismountable.

TARP TENT (or Awning at home)

Ever question the wisdom of toting a 10-pound tent over a long single night hike, or worse yet, not bother taking it and ending up needing it on a day trip that didn't quite go as planned? A simple tarp can be quite comfortable for a night, even in a heavy rain, though the old tent is still recommended for lengthy stays.

Try getting six to seven yards of good polyurethane coated nylon (rip stop or plain) 48 to 55 inches wide. Cut it in half, lay the pieces side by side, sew a strong seam down the middle, well glued or sealed, then add strong corner loops of ½-inch flat nylon web. Reinforce the center and put a good loop there, more at the middle points of the side, middle points between edges and top center. You end up using a lot of loops; but the product requires no poles, can be set up in a score of ways (even tied to the pack and held down with rocks if need be,) and after a few experiments in the back yard, can prove to be a quick serviceable shelter that could turn out to be preferable to a tent many many times during the year.

Pre-tie long cords to each loop. They're handy to "borrow" for scores of other things and you never need all the cord to set up. A good tie system, to make it faster and easier, is:

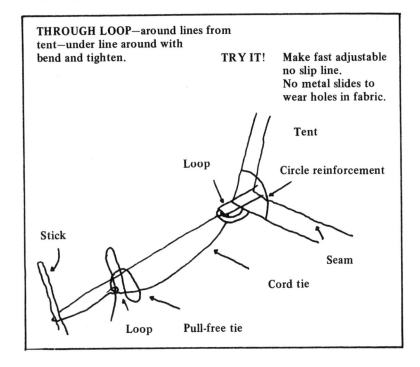

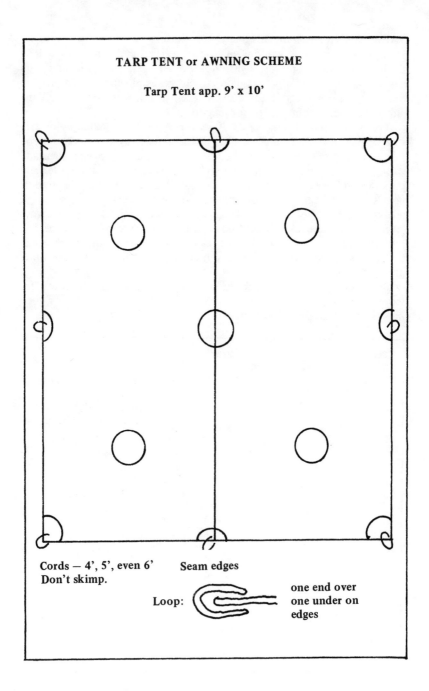

TARP TENT or AWNING SCHEME

Tarp Tent app. 9' x 10'

Cords — 4', 5', even 6'   Seam edges
Don't skimp.

Loop: one end over
                           one under on
                           edges

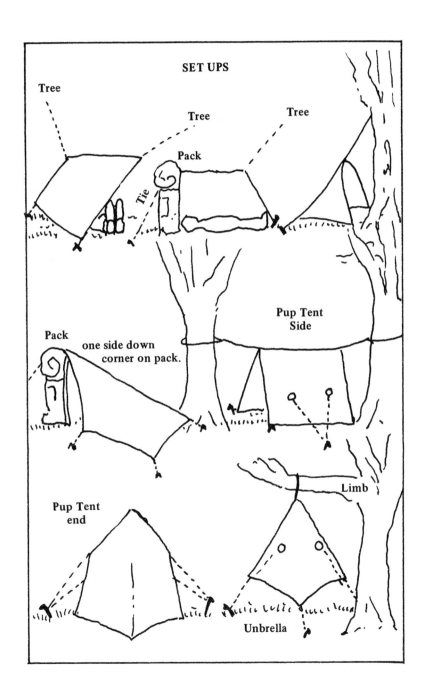

SET UPS

Tree

Tree

Tree

Pack

Tie

Pup Tent
Side

Pack

one side down
corner on pack.

Limb

Pup Tent
end

Unbrella

SUMMER SLEEPING BAG

It's probably dumb to add this to a make-it-yourself list, but in going over things people can, but usually don't, make we half-decided that a lightweight summer sleeping bag was one of the things we'd seen the least of.

Nearly every bag on the market is designed to keep a person warm ... sensible? Yet how about August, 80-degree muggy nights full of bugs? The choice is involuntary blood donation or a very low grade of sweat-soaked doze.

A bed sheet isn't quite enough, unless it's a really hot night, and the next might not be. Still, something around that weight would be useful. My first choice has been a pair of U.S. Army poncho liners. One is fine down to 60 degrees or less, two are good to about 45 degrees, and if it's a sweltering night, just pull it loosely over the top and snicker at the frustrated wing critters. Unfortunately I've no idea where to get the liners now. If you've an Army Surplus store around, check it out. They might prove expensive, but they are light, packable, warm enough for almost all summer camping, and stay warm even when soaked. (They dry very quickly.)

As a second choice, back to the bed sheet. Sew up a body size tube of sheet (it's heavy, may as well not carry extra), then get a length of light nylon and sew a tube of that. This proves useful for 55 to 60 degrees and up, depending on individual tastes in sleeping heat. It saves expensive bags for weather when they are needed, reduces pack weight, and lets a person adapt a little better to higher summer temperatures.

PACK FRAME

Of all the beasts that plague backpackers, none is so intimate and perfidious as the pack itself. Manufacturers have been struggling to find a really great design for years, and packers are still arguing back and forth about wicker or frame, hip extension or plain waistband.

Most of the arguments are great. But changing your mind between seasons gets expensive. Half for the fun, and half in hope of maybe coming up with something reasonably kind to the body, why not try making a pack frame? If nothing else, the experience will make the next selection from store stock a lot more critical.

As always, begin by defining your own particular needs, add your gripes against packs in general and try to figure out just what size and arrangement you want to end up with. The frame structure and system for putting it together shown here may not be what you want ... we're just trying to give some basic ideas and suggestions. Change them if you like.

Find a supplier of 3/4-inch aluminum tubing, 3/8-inch tube or ¼-inch aluminum rod, gather some coat hangers or heavy aluminum wire, find

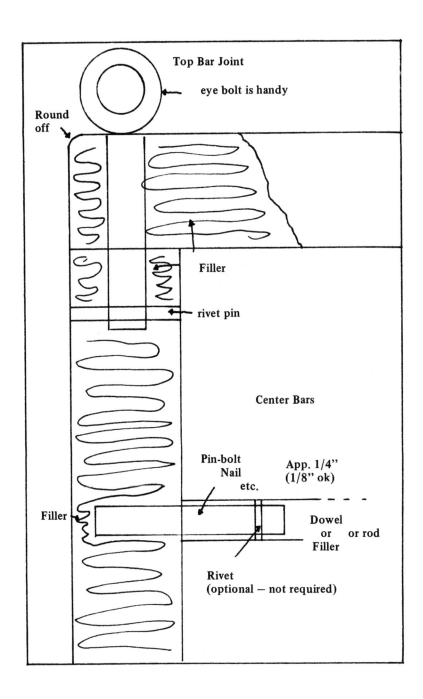

Top Bar Joint

eye bolt is handy

Round off

Filler

rivet pin

Center Bars

Pin-bolt
Nail
etc.

App. 1/4"
(1/8" ok)

Filler

Dowel
or   or rod
Filler

Rivet
(optional — not required)

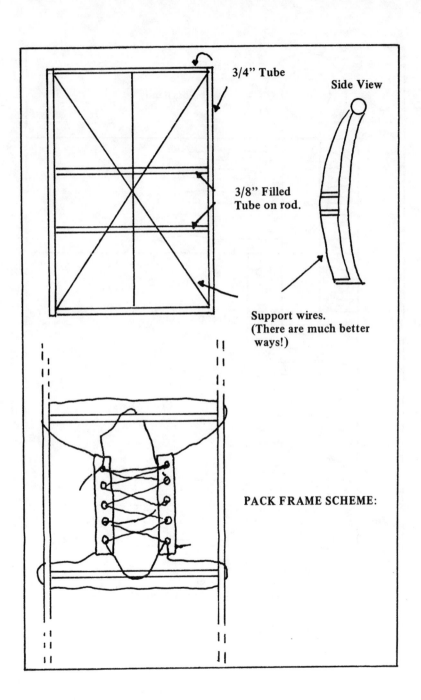

3/4" Tube

Side View

3/8" Filled
Tube on rod.

Support wires.
(There are much better
ways!)

PACK FRAME SCHEME:

some scraps of all that dowel we've been talking about, and get set with the old hack saw blade.

Height of the frame is not critical . . . attaching the straps is. So start with a pair of 3/4-inch tubes long enough to be at least as long as the largest pack you might want to end up with. Then try a few friends' packs until you know just where the vertical frame tubes go up the back. Then take your tubes, put the ends on a couple of boards or bricks on the floor and sit on them, using hands and backside to spread the weight over the middle third of the length. (If you've got a pipe bender this might be simpler.)

Gradually increase the height of the books, bricks or whatever until you've bent the tubes to a shape that fits the back where and as it seems fit.

Next step is to determine what width feels best. Try out an assortment of packs or adjust from your old one, and cut two slender rods or tubes and one thick one about three inches longer than the pack width will be. (You may want to strengthen these tubes with a flexible dowel inserted through them.)

If you happen to have an old pressure cooker around, put your feet in it and carefully curve your rods by pulling them up around the side of the cooker. (Clean socks might avoid certain comments during this operation.) Test the heavy tube by fitting to the proper hip area until it fits. The two slender rods need be only slightly more curved, and won't be against the back anyway.

Now measure from tip to tip on the short tubes and cut them to the width you want your pack to be.

Lay your vertical tubes on a sidewalk or flat rough surface and scrape them on one side (mark edge for drilling holes.) After computing where you want your cross bars there are several ways of putting them in place. One is to drill out a hole that fits the small tubes (requires making those tubes longer) and putting a thin pin through the vertical support to hold the cross members. This weakens the frame, but it will work. Just don't expect durability with 100-pound loads.

Another method, much harder to put together but better, is to drill a hole in the end of your rods and find a nail or anything metal that's strong and fits the hole or end of your tubing. Drill the vertical supports to size and stuff in some White Knife Auto Body Filler. (There are plenty of fast-hardening fillers available at an auto store.) *Quickly* put your nail or connecting rod into the hole and filler about halfway through the big tube. If the connector is rough it won't pull out after the filler hardens. Under normal conditions, there will never be any pull on the connection anyway.

For the heavy tube at the bottom of the frame, use one of 3/8-inch width instead of 3/4-inch to nail and follow the same procedure outlined above.

With the cross members in place and curves arranged properly, drill *down* through each end, if not through the connector inside the tube then at least through the edge of it. Use a very fine drill that will permit hammer mashing a bit of coat hanger wire through the hole until it's flush with the tubing.

For a top bar on the frame there is a tough choice. Best would be to bend your vertical supports from one tube, leaving the top bar neatly curved and in place. (It's possible to ruin a lot of tubing trying it, though.) As an alternative plug the top ends of your vertical support with auto body filler. Drill your top cross bar for a slender tube or heavy nail and drive a short length through. Drill the filler to fit your cross bar studs, and if desired, pin it in place with coat hanger "rivets."

If solidly done the frame is now ready for straps, bag, waistband, and use.

Using heavy cloth, lace a back support between the verticals so that the two middle cross bars will hold it in place and add another band across the bottom of the pack, using the bottom bar and lower center bar to hold that.

Straps made so they can be removed, connect to the bottom bar and upper center bar.

If the counter forces of the structure do not permit attaching the straps to that slender upper bar, then try adding a wire brace between top and bottom bars, wrapping round the middle bars enroute.

Some ingenuity will overcome the many minor frustrations of the job, and will help in designing a bag to put on the frame. (Hint: My first frame pack bag could have carried the Lewis and Clark provisions.)

Seasoned backpackers may sneer at this whole idea ... too heavy, probably not all that strong, hard to make fit, lot of time to waste making it ... and they are probably quite right. But such a frame will be *yours*, maybe better than what the store offers. And, counting nylon for the bag, straps, etc., your frame pack should cost in the realm of $15 − less if you're a good scrounge. As for the time required to make it, if you've a good drill, pressure cooker, and clean socks, it can be done on a winter's day.

So far the "makings" have been of the strictly utilitarian type, but very near to all backpackers' dusty hearts are the little camp luxuries, fiddle stuff, and gadgets. Some useful, some just nice, some dubious ideas are tossed in here.

CAMP KNIFE

That pig sticker hip knife ever prove less than handy and need sharpening beyond the edge that's easy to keep doing rough camp chores? A handy little gadget that takes maybe a half hour to produce is the

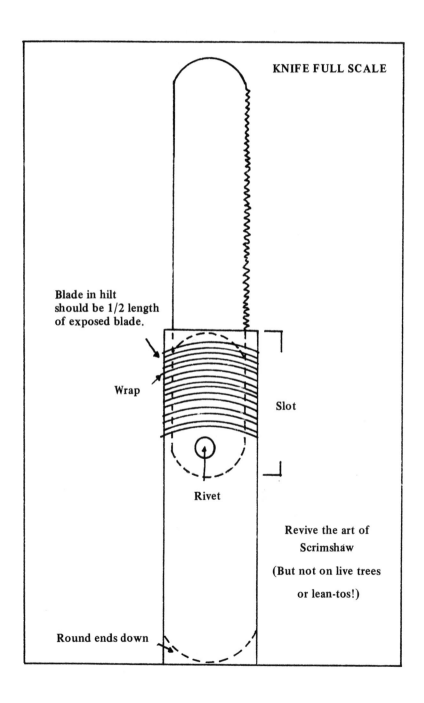

KNIFE FULL SCALE

Blade in hilt
should be 1/2 length
of exposed blade.

Wrap

Slot

Rivet

Round ends down

Revive the art of
Scrimshaw
(But not on live trees
or lean-tos!)

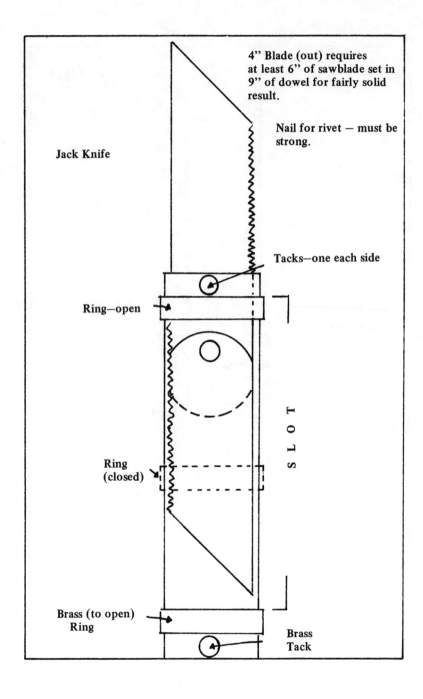

4" Blade (out) requires
at least 6" of sawblade set in
9" of dowel for fairly solid
result.

Nail for rivet — must be
strong.

Jack Knife

Tacks—one each side

Ring—open

Ring
(closed)

S L O T

Brass (to open)
Ring

Brass
Tack

hacksaw blade whittle-eat-saw-and-trim knife. Get an old hacksaw blade and some heavy wire that fits the hole in each end, add a length of 1/2 or 5/8-inch dowel and some copper wire or rawhide and you can make a very serviceable, fine edge, knife. (Find a length of ½-inch brass tube and you can make a beautiful jackknife.)

For a knife, merely break off between four and six inches of blade from a hacksaw. Drill a proper size hole two or three inches from the end of a hand-size length of dowel and cut a slot down to the hole for the blade. (It helps if the slot isn't quite straight.) Shove the blade in and hammer your wire down through the holes until it's flush with the dowel. Then wrap the split section of handle with wire or rawhide. Hone down the un-toothed edge of blade, and you've got a saw, butter knife, whittler's tool, and fine little thread cutter for ripping out seams.

Note that one end of the blade makes a knife with the saw teeth pointed forward, the other end back. Best is a knife with the teeth pointed toward the hilt ... it cuts a lot easier. Edge the tip for a chisel if you want one.

To make a jackknife, use a longer dowel slotted far enough past the rivet hole to accept the blade when folded back. Instead of wrapping the hilt with wire, find a length of brass (nice shiny stuff that won't rust in a wet pack) that fits fairly tight over your dowel. Now take some brass carpet tacks and with the ring on your knife put one in each side of each end. The brass ring will slide forward to lock the blade open, then back to lock it closed.

CAMP SLIPPERS

One of the many blessings oft done without is the chance to get out of boots after a hard day's hike. Feet need the air, change of pressure and wear. Getting them out of the business boots after arriving at camp can keep feet healthier and happier.

An easy slipper to make is from heavy old socks. Put two together, one inside another, and stand on a piece of ensolite. Trace the foot, cut out the ensolite, and glue it to the bottom of the socks. From pack nylon or leather, trace another foot pattern, angling the marker this time in order to get a pattern about one inch to 1½ inches bigger all round. Glue the sole to the ensolite.

At various points around the sole, slits will have to be made to allow folding upward over the foam to the sock. Experiment folding and cutting where the material tries to crease. Once the slitting is done stitch up the sole flat, adding a band over the arch and behind the heel for strength and shape.

(Known as socks with soul.)

We've used various types even when winter camping in an igloo. They work. But practice. Make one out of junk first, and you'll learn enough to find your first pair turn out quite well. To be fancy and assure durability, add a binding strip around the top of the sole and sew a nylon cover to the top of the foot and around the ankle. Lot of trouble, you say ... check the price and durability of similar products out on the store shelves.

BELTS

Dumb thing to make, but it can improve life for skinny people whose hip bones love to stick out where they can get galled by a leather belt or pack waistband.

Make a nylon tube and foam core as described for a pack strap. Two D rings or something similar for a buckle, and the hips are far less threatened then before. (Makes a spare pack strap too.)

It may be wise to stitch down the middle of the belt and zig zag across, too, to prevent the foam from rolling up under use. A little extra effort and the stitching can become a fancy pattern in various colors ... with beads, fringe, six or seven pouches, a scalping knife and sword scabbard.

A wide, fat version can be attached to almost any pack except to the day pack we've described. The day pack works much better if allowed to hunch down and swing as it wants. The design keeps it out of the way and a band would be too high and constrictive. For frame packs, improve their personality with this waistband, and it takes only an hour or so to make.

MAP CASES

Ratty sodden pulp never makes for an easy-reading map. But that's what we've got more often than not on long hikes. Next trip, try stealing some of the golf bag tubes from the family fairway fiend. Those nice long plastic tubes are perfect for a rolled map. Cut the bottom end off to within 2 inches of the map length, roll and go. Out on the trail, use your hacksaw camp knife to cut and make wooden plugs for each end of the pilfered tube. You can carve a map identification in the plugs. Make the bottom one permanent, the top fancy and easy to get in and out.

By the way, if the family golfer has black tubes in his bag it might be worth going out and buying a few tubes. Black ones have a way of disappearing after sitting around the fire plotting half the night. White ones are easy to locate; some are transparent enough to see black printing through.

I've intended to try using golfer tubes for tent pole and peg containers, but have never gotten around to it yet. It might be worth trying.

WHITTLIN' STUFF

Sitting around camp doing nothing? Got a day of massive drips sloshing down the mountains? Blisters past the point of further maltreatment? Then it's a great time to revive the arts of scrimshaw and whittlin'.

If you've made a hacksaw knife, and maybe put together a sheath that will carry a bit of sharpening stone with it, then there's a lot to do on those blah camp days.

Ever try a wood fork? Spoon? Having that saw edge and chisel point on your camp knife makes them easy. Carve a button or ten, and maybe a real fancy map case plug. Or sculpt a blistered toe.

The hacksaw teeth are fine for coaxing an inscription into a beach pebble for a gift, and I've even seen a stone belt buckle. Find an old dead limb that's soft in the middle, hard outside, and with luck it's possible to produce a real scary sounding horn styled after the old cowhorn type. A split hardwood "reed" or a knowledge of trumpeting can, assuming much whittlin' and disastrous practice, result in the most unearthly calamity of sound ever heard in them hills.

A bit of old metal, a big washer, or one of those old soft iron plates used on railroad ties, and your hacksaw, can combine to make memorials of your trip, a gift for the mate, a present for the folks, or a dangle of your own. It eats up waste time quickly. Try scrimshawing a design in a bit of soft metal sometime. Then wrap it in a bit of leather, wrap that in tinfoil or an old tin can and toss in it a hot fire. Let it heat 30 minutes to an hour, or until supper stuff is picked up. Take it out and let it cool *without* unwrapping it. If you polished it well before firing it the metal should be well hardened, possibly with the delicate coloration of tempered steel, depending on the formula of the metal you started with. (If you have the right metal it will harden enough so that the hacksaw teeth won't faze it, it'll dull a file, and make a fine striker for a flint and steel firestarting set. It will also become brittle if left in the fire too long.)

Speaking from pleasant past experience, it's sometimes fun to just waste a day, nice or no. Make a sailboat and let her do the day's exploring. Recently the rage has been to try to make a model hang glider and see how far it would fly from the local boulder. Make-itis adds a dimension to waste camp time ... and it can waste a heck of a lot of time. But if the idea of making things for yourself, things that work for you, simplify life, provide comfort, and are just plain fun appeals to you, go ahead. The secret is junk, time, and a devious imagination.

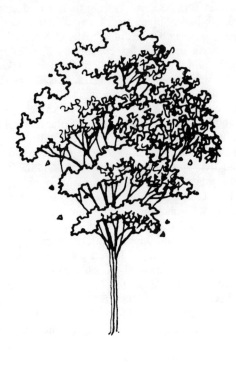

15

The Backpacker's Camera

A good thing for photographers to remember on backpacking trips is just to keep it simple. Plan your photography gear for the maximum efficiency from each item. And don't forget that if the camera is in the bottom of the pack it is protected, but you'll miss many chances for good shots on the trail. Equipment should be simple, easy to use, and most important, easy to get at while walking.

Habit will make having a shoulder slung camera a comfortable part of hiking. A strap that slips easily will make a big difference since the camera can be pulled to action even with a pack on. The idea is to always have your camera on your shoulder, loaded, ready, and preferably preset for the light conditions through periodic checks and changes. Think like a mountain man did back in the days of hostile Indians. He never left his weapon out of reach.

And don't tell yourself that your equipment isn't good enough. Any decent 35mm camera, even an Instamatic, can be used to take good pictures if you think about what you are doing.

Photography in the woods acts like a wine. It mellows a trip, and deepens it. The pace slows a little, but things are seen more fully, and more things are seen. Deliberately or not, the camera-toting hiker will form habits of looking more often and more closely, and after a few trips you'll end up going out of your way to look at things. With this looking comes understanding, and out of that, a deeper appreciation and respect for the wild.

A trip may last a few days, but the photographs remain even if the wilderness where they were taken is destroyed. Having these pictures is a kind of preservation of what the area was and what it did to you.

Never bother to calculate the weight of a camera, film, lenses, flash, miscellaneous gear, etc. Never. It's depressing. Instead, plan your camera gear for maximum use.

Some hikers accept the slight decline in quality and take only a wide-range zoom telephoto lens. Zooming helps reduce the number of lenses, moving around, and fiddle time. And pictures tend to be stronger and closer to the subject. There are some subjects that you will want to fill the frame. A wide angle, with short focus, helps do that and it even has applications for scenics.

For closeups, a macro lens can be used; it can also double as a 50mm lens.

The important thing to remember is that your full set of equipment should be slung on your shoulder, never out of easy reach.

Having had the experience of climbing Mount Mansfield in Vermont with two containers of film and six of rock sample, only to find two rolls used before we got anywhere near the top, here is another bit of advice: Camera gear becomes highly frustrating dead weight once the film supply is used up.

Plan on taking more film than you think you'll need, but base your estimations on your own picture-taking habits. If you shoot five rolls of film at a party, for example, while someone else shoots one, you'll use more on the trail, too. The more a hiker totes his camera, the more he tends to shoot. But eventually, a balance develops between energy, hours, and the eye. Once you have this experience, planning becomes easier.

Don't worry in advance about finding things to shoot. Good hiking photography is, at least in part, a matter of taking a good picture, properly exposed, in focus, and with a dose of thought behind framing, subject selection, angle, and special effects. It can be of any of the many fine things you will find out in the woods. The first key to good pictures is to see and understand your subject. Whether you're comparing a blade of grass to a mountain cliff or photographing an autumn mushroom, spring bud, hunk of winter ice, or a blister on your toe, this understanding will show through.

It wouldn't hurt to pick up a few copies of *National Geographic*, the Sierra Club Books, or other books with good scenic photography, just to get ideas of what to look for. You can pick up many thoughts on how to look at potential pictures so that shots will begin to leap at you and beg you to take them. Then, if your pictures don't look like *National Geographic's*, you can figure out why.

You might want to make a polarizer part of your equipment. To find out its effect on lighting situations, don't just read about them, shoot with one. Shoot at night, into the sun, anything to help you understand the effect on your pictures. Always try to make each picture work but don't let that keep you from experimenting. Few people always take good pictures, so always try to improve but don't hold back.

And a little note on film: Both black and white and color films have their merits. Some people find color slides cheaper, easier to handle, or more enjoyable, but if you're into black and white and feel you can be more creative by using it, do so.

But keep taking pictures. Around camp try a fire shot, or a picture of the gear and how it's being used. During the day, shoot the light coming off a leaf or a pond, or even the miserable mosquito as he puffs up with your and your companion's blood. Shoot for the possible, that is, don't fiddle with light meters and flash fill to the extent of losing the picture. If you meet a bear on the trail in early morning, your camera should be preset to the light. If not, there is no hope of fiddling around. You can just ease your camera up, take a guess at focus and exposure, and shoot. After the first shot, you can change your settings and, if the bear is still around, click again. The idea is to get what you can first and then try for better. But you're best off being ready when you first meet the bear.

In camp you can experiment. If you don't know what the exposure is for firelight, try adding a flash or two during a time exposure. Keep a note of what you've done so you can evaluate your results. But don't try to avoid wasting film when this kind of experimentation isn't feasible. It may seem that film costs a lot when you're at home gearing up. But compared with the overall cost of a trip, and the time and effort put into it, the film you use will be a bargain.

Once you get home, it may hurt, but be impersonal in culling out the weedy pictures. Although it might be hard to apply your knowledge of what a good shot looks like to pictures that are near and dear, it's a healthy process that leads to improvement on the next trip.

And don't worry. You will improve. Just think about what you're doing, remember what you've learned, and set your standards high. The wilderness deserves it!

Some Tips for Backpacking With a Camera

Get used to wearing a camera before going out. Even to the point of wearing it around the house.

Be sure your camera slips easily on your shoulder. It should be hung just high enough to avoid bumping your hip bone, saving wear and tear on your hip as well as the lens mount and back plate of the camera.

Don't confuse yourself by having more kinds of film than you can use · productively. The latitude you gain may be more than counterbalanced by the fact that you are not familiar with or used to using a particular film, and you do not know how it will react under various conditions.

Shoot low morning and evening shots with a tripod or other means of keeping the camera still. A rock, the ground, a rotten stump; even hanging the camera from a tree or stuffing a forked branch in the ground, is useful. If you use a walking stick, there are a number of C-clamp tripod heads available that can be attached to it. Often, however, they don't work as well as some of the more natural surrounding objects.

For flash, use a rechargeable unit with interchangeable batteries. At night, try a time exposure of background and refocus for a flash filled foreground subject. Try using it to fill in shadows during the day, to put some life into closeups.

Film: Once used, keep in in its can, bag it, and keep the bag in a home. Losing film once it's shot is definitely something to be avoided.

Travel: Keep your camera and film out of the sun both in the car and on the trail. In the car, it's also a bad idea to keep them in the trunk.

To avoid letting vibrations get at the screws in your camera guts, a pillow or foam padded box is a good storage idea.

Pack your supplies so they're easy to get at. This includes taking the film can out of the box at home and not even bringing that extra cardboard into the wilderness.

Know your film and take the instruction sheet from the film box with you. Even though you know it by heart, there will be a day when it will answer a question that will save a fine shot. Memorize the camera settings for basic lighting for your film speed: dawn, early morning, full day, gray day, evening, sunset, and moonlight time exposure. If you can't memorize them, write them on a little card taped to your camera ... It helps to do the same with flash unit distances.

Lastly, in the interests of companionship, don't put your fellow hikers through posing gyrations unless they want to do it. Part of being a good photographer is that you do the work, not everyone else.

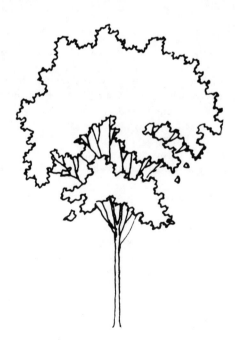

16

The U.S. National Trails System

The system was established under Public Law 90-543, October 2, 1968, "to provide for the ever-increasing outdoor recreational needs of an expanding population and in order to promote public access to, travel within, and enjoyment and appreciation of, the open-air outdoor areas of the Nation . . ."

The saga of the trail is as old as the history of our country — trails played a basic part in the lives of the early settlers as they traveled from place to place and sought game, and they became the superhighways of the American pioneer.

Trails still play an important role in that they provide a recreational outlet for the increasingly urban American population. The Bureau of Outdoor Recreation cites a 1972 survey indicating that biking, walking for pleasure, and hiking and horseback riding accounted for over 20 percent of total summer recreation. Since then, there has been a real upswing in the number of people hitting the trails rather than the concrete highway.

National Recreation Trails are designed to be accessible to urban areas, to satisfy a variety of outdoor recreational enthusiasts — horse, hiking, bicycle, or motorcycle trails — and in some cases to serve multiple uses. Unlike the Scenic Trails, their paths may cross utility rights-of-way, abandoned railroad rights-of-way, and areas around reservoirs and levees.

An interesting aspect of the Recreational Trails is that, while their primary objective is recreation for the urban American, other uses such as power lines, sheep driveways, and logging roads may be considered compatible and thus share the same path.

A user fee may be charged for the use of the Recreational Trails.

In the Northeast, the only Recreational Trail listed as of January 1975 is the Harriman Long Path in Harriman State Park, New York. The trail is a 16-mile foot path managed by the Palisades Interstate Park Commission. The trail is near the Hudson River about 20 miles north-

199

west of New York City and winds along wooded ridge tops and crosses a portion of the Appalachian National Scenic Trail.

Application for designation as a National Recreation Trail may be submitted to the Bureau of Outdoor Recreation by the governmental unit or private organization which owns the land.

National Scenic Trails bypass highways, power lines, commercial and industrial developments, and other scenic detractions and are extended, usually running several hundred miles. They should be continuous for their entire length. These trails are designed for hiking and other compatible uses and the National Trails System Act prohibits the use of motorized equipment.

Routes are chosen to provide for maximum outdoor recreation potential, maintaining the accuracy of historical routes, while at the same time providing for the enjoyment of scenic and natural qualities of the trail route.

Running from Mount Katahdin, Maine to Springer Mountain Georgia, the 2,000-mile-long Appalachian Trail is the only National Scenic Trail in the Northeast. At present there is only one other Scenic Trail, the Pacific Crest, extending from the Mexican-California Border along the ranges of the west coast states to the Canadian-Washington border. With the aid of access trails, a hiker may join with the Appalachian Trail in Maine, New Hampshire, Vermont, Massachusetts, Connecticut, or New York, for as extensive a trek as desired.

There is no fee for the use of the National Scenic Trails.

Public Law 90-543 also provided for the establishment of connecting or side trails to provide points of public access to the national recreational or scenic trails. The NTS Act encourages states to consider in their state-wide outdoor recreation plans the need to establish recreation trails on lands owned or administered by the state. The Secretary of the Interior is directed to encourage states, political subdivisions, and private interests including non-profit organizations to establish such trails.